D1365265

Science-Based Innovation

Science-Based Innovation

From Modest Witnessing to Pipeline Thinking

Alexander Styhre
Chalmers University of Technology, Sweden

First published 2008 by
PALGRAVE MACMILLAN
Houndmills, Basingstoke, Hampshire RG21 6XS and
175 Fifth Avenue, New York, N.Y. 10010
Companies and representatives throughout the world

PALGRAVE MACMILLAN is the global academic imprint of the Palgrave
Macmillan division of St. Martin's Press, LLC and of Palgrave Macmillan Ltd.
Macmillan® is a registered trademark in the United States, United Kingdom
and other countries. Palgrave is a registered trademark in the European
Union and other countries.

ISBN-13: 978–0–230–01354–4   hardback
ISBN-10: 0–230–01354–6   hardback

This book is printed on paper suitable for recycling and made from fully
managed and sustained forest sources. Logging, pulping and manufacturing
processes are expected to conform to the environmental regulations of the
country of origin.

A catalogue record for this book is available from the British Library.

Library of Congress Cataloging-in-Publication Data

Styhre, Alexander.
   Science-based innovation : from modest witnessing to pipeline
   thinking / Alexander Styhre.
      p. cm.
   Includes bibliographical references and index.
   ISBN 0–230–01354–6 (alk. paper)
      1. Creative ability in science—Management. 2. Management science.
   I. Title.

   Q172.5.C74S89 2008
   658.4'04–dc22   2007052982

10   9   8   7   6   5   4   3   2   1
17   16   15   14   13   12   11   10   09   08

Printed and bound in Great Britain by
CPI Antony Rowe, Chippenham and Eastbourne

"Le savant a une patrie, la science n'en a pas"
Louis Pasteur

Contents

List of Tables and Figure viii

Preface ix

Chapter 1 Introduction: Science Under the Auspices of 1
Management Objectives

Part I Theoretical Perspectives on Science-Based Innovation 21

Chapter 2 Knowledge Work and Innovation 23

Chapter 3 What Do Scientists Do?: Components of Scientific 53
Work

Chapter 4 From the Laboratory to the Pipeline: New Drug 94
Development in the Pharmaceutical Industry

Part II Science-Based Innovation in Practice 129

Chapter 5 Innovation Work as Play and Systematic 131
Risk-Taking

Chapter 6 Leadership and Emotional Management in 159
Science-Based Innovation Work

Chapter 7 Management Control in Science-Based Innovation 192
Work

Part III Reflections 215

Chapter 8 Thinking of Science-Based Innovation 217

Appendix: Glossary 234

Notes 239

Bibliography 241

Index 267

List of Tables and Figure

Tables

2.1 Knowledge types and names   24
2.2 Distinctions between data, information, knowledge   26
     and wisdom
2.3 Two types of knowledge   29
2.4 Alternative perspectives on knowledge in organizations   29
2.5 Schools of innovative research   41
2.6 The main feature of the three perspectives   42
6.1 Trends in leadership theory and research   168
6.2 Themes in new leadership literature   175

Figure

4.1 The drug discovery research process   110

Preface

This book is an outcome from a research project aimed at examining the innovative capacities of large bureaucratic organizations in Swedish industry. Some of the research findings were reported in *The Innovative Bureaucracy* (2007) but that work was for me primarily a groundwork in the field of organization theory—an engagement with the concept of bureaucracy and its manifold (often derogatory) uses and meanings in the literature. This book is complementing *The Innovative Bureaucracy* in terms of making the intersection between innovation management and scientific work the principal theoretical framework guiding the analysis and in terms of further exploring the empirical material generated. It is however noteworthy here that some quotes—12, to report an exact figure—from the interviews, here presented in Chapters 6 and 7, appear in the *The Innovative Bureaucracy*. I have been fortunate to have been given the opportunity to conduct a series of research projects in the pharmaceutical industry since the end of the 1990s but the papers and books chapters being written on basis of these research projects never became, I thought, more than snapshots and disjointed passages from the overall research. I thought that it might be the time to delve more thoroughly into the domain of what is here called "science-based innovation". The present book is therefore an attempt at integrating a number of complementing themes of research that I have been working on since the end of the 1990s: Knowledge, science, new drug development, leadership, management control, and innovation. The text is strongly indebted to the science and technology studies (STS) literature and historical studies of scientific work and procedures. For me these texts are of central importance for the domain of research commonly referred to as knowledge management. Prior to any articulation of a coherent, integrated, and officially announced knowledge management program—the publishing of a special issue in *Strategic Management Journal* on knowledge management edited by J.-C. Spender and Robert Grant in 1996 is arguably a central point of reference here—STS scholars had for years been engaged in identifying and formulating procedures and vocabularies for knowledge-intensive scientific work. This book is an attempt at bringing this most intriguing literature examining laboratory work and other scientific milieus and the loosely tied network of texts addressing knowledge management and innovation work. The book is separated into two parts, one more theoretical in terms of primarily reviewing relevant literature and one more empirical in terms of drawing on organizational activities and concerns. However, as always, the line of demarcation between the theoretical and the empirical is a porous and fragile one; instead of being separated by an epistemological iron curtain, the two types of scientific resources are folded into one another in various ways. The key point here is that this book is making claims of being, in addition to the theoretical overviews and discussion, an empirical account of science-based innovation—it is a work that aims at addressing ongoing and practical concerns in companies and industries engaging in science-based innovation. Still, it is not a "normative" book in terms of taking on the burden of articulating a number of recommendations for practitioners managing or conducting science-based innovation work. If there is a normative message in the book (which there may or may not be; at the point of writing this preface I do not know for sure), it is articulated in terms of recognizing the complexity and institutional variety of any scientific undertaking. That is, to reduce the management of science-based innovation work to a set of "dos and don'ts" is not to fully take into account the contingent, situational and contextual nature of knowledge mobilized in this work. Thus, rather than delineating science-based innovation as a number of fixed and interrelated procedures and operations, it needs to be examined in terms of a complex social practice operating under the influence of ambiguity, non-linearity and emergence. If nothing else, such a position may be what pays homage to the STS literature and its insistence on understanding the object of study. However, this does not mean that I am opposed to managerial work or managerial thinking per se—quite the contrary—but too much knowledge management and innovation management literature is reducing and eliminating complexity rather than recognizing it. That is to say, from my point of view, management studies can operate in two directions: by simplifying or by multiplying. I believe Robert Chia has articulated this idea eloquently at a number of times, for instance in his paper on business school teaching (Chia, 1996a). Hopefully, given these reservations and choices, the book still is capable of providing some insights into the theory of and/or day-to-day work pursuing science-based innovation.

* * *

I am, as usual, thankful for the help and support I have received from a number of friends, colleagues including Mats Sundgren, Sofia Börjesson, and Jan Wickenberg. Mats Sundgren has with great patience and precision carefully sorted out and corrected a range of details in the text and explained the intricate practices in new drug development work. I am thoroughly indebted to Mats for this effort. Without his help the text would look very different. Mats also participated in the interviewing work in AstraZeneca and played a very important role when posing the more technically detailed questions to the interlocutors that an "outsider" would not be capable of articulating. Sofia Börjesson collaborated with me in the research project and Mats Sundgren and Jan Wickenberg made an important work to help organizing interviews. I am also grateful to all the AstraZeneca co-workers for dedicating some of their precious time to my research and agreeing to be interviewed. I would also like to thank all the anonymous reviewers and occasional editorial comments on my papers for pointing out a range of sources for improvement in my work. Without such collaborative work much scientific pursuits would end up in a less theoretically interesting and practically useful form. Finally, I would like to thank my family for helping me standing firmly on the ground and not drifting away into endless theoretical speculations and concerns.

The study presented in this book was financially supported by The Bank of Sweden's Tercentenary Fund.

1
Introduction: Science Under the Auspices of Management Objectives

Introduction

In the report *Science 2020*, issued by Microsoft Research in 2006 and based on the collaboration between representatives of a range of scientific disciplines, the concept of *science-based innovation* is playing a central role. In the introduction of the report, it is stated: "A scientific revolution is just beginning. It has the potential to crease an era of *science-based* innovation that could completely eclipse the last half century of *technology-based* innovation, and with it, a new wave of global social technological and economic growth" (Science 2020: 10).[1] In the concluding section of the report, the tone is less dramatic but the emphasis on science-based innovation is still central to the arguments advanced: "In a way that we have never seen before, science really will be absolutely vital to societies, economics, and our future on this planet towards 2020; and science-based innovation is likely to be at least equal technology-based innovation in its contribution to economic prosperity" (Science 2020: 72). In its June 14th issue, 2007, The Economist declared that "what physics was to the 20th century, biology will be to the 21st". The intersection between science and biology is arguably one of the most interesting domains for innovation research, characterized by quick scientific and technological changes and new competitive landscapes. Science-based innovation emerges in many forms but what we are concerned with here are the domain of new drug development, an intersecting point were developments in molecular biology, medicinal chemistry, computational biology, systems biology, bioinformatics, and so forth meet and integrate (Drews, 2000). More specifically, in new drug development, new scientific fields and specific practices such as genomics, pharmacogenomics, proteomics, combinatorial chemistry, medical imaging, medical informatics, and clinical trial simulation are examples made possible by technologies such as cell-based assays, computer drug design, high-throughput screening, magnetic, integrated DNA Technologies, resonance tomography, micro endoscopy, have fundamentally altered the way new drug-development is pursued. Like perhaps no other industry, the pharmaceutical industry serves as the nexus between advanced science and more practical, managerial and financial concerns. In other words, the pharmaceutical industry may be argued to pave the way for what the *Science 2020* report calls science-based innovation.

This book seeks to explore how science-based innovation is organized and managed in a large pharmaceutical company.[2] The analysis emphasizes what Lyotard (1984) calls the performativity of science, its ability to provide goods and services that are possible to sell in the market. The development of modern science demonstrates a long and winding trajectory characterized by setbacks, quantum leaps, and disruptive changes, but also an accumulation of scientific know-how. Science is one of the most complex human activities and one must recognize the overdetermination of science; its emergence springs from many sources. Still, scientific endeavours have only recently become subject to managerial objectives and concerns, at least in the modern sense of management as activities aimed at coordinating complex undertakings to maximize effectiveness. In addition, the growth in science-based innovation work is rarely accounted for in the management literature but, on the contrary, there has been much debate on what has been portrayed as a "service economy" or the "Wal-Martism" succeeding the Fordist regime of production (Fishman, 2006). One of the principal challenges for the industry based on science-based innovation is the time-span between investment and the cash flow generated by the investment (Ramirez and Tylecote, 2004: 109–110). Nightingale (1998: 690) even argues that innovation and science are complicated to combine because they start from very different positions: "[T]heories that treat the output of science as 'information that can be directly applied to technical change' are problematic because science answers the wrong question. The stylised innovation process starts with an intended end result and then tries to find the unknown starting conditions that will produce it. But, science can only go in the opposite direction, from known starting conditions to unknown end results". In addition, it is becoming increasingly complicated for outsiders such as financial analysts to monitor and predict the outcome from advanced scientific work. Ramirez and Tylecote (2004: 109–111) argue: "Technologies like genomics, high-throughput screening and bio-informatics have become buzzwords. Analysts will ask companies if they have invested in them and so long as this is the case they will be satisfied. The lack of scientific background among industry analysts is part of the problem, however. Even when this exists the present rapid pace of change of science means that it is not always easy to understand or appreciate their implications fully". As a consequence, there is a continuous trade-off between short and medium term in scientific work, a negotiation between shareholders' interest and the scientific objectives. The Head of Corporate Finance in AstraZeneca outlines the problem:

> If we go out to the market and say 'we've got these enormous opportunities to drive growth in 2003 but in order get there we are going to take a hit in our earnings growth in 2001 and 2002' then it's like a profit warning for those two years and so the decision is 'sell' … The main problem is the mismatch between what is perceived to be most value adding to shareholders in the short-term versus the long term. (Head of Corporate Finance, AstraZeneca, cited in Ramirez and Tylecote, 2004: 109–114)

One of the consequences is that there is little room left for more "experimental" activities. The Head of Corporate Finance in AstraZeneca continues:

> The room for blue sky stuff today is very limited; the question is whether this is good or bad? There is nothing wrong with an environment that says that the very academic approach is inappropriate for industry. But equally it would be wrong to say you should do none of it. I and some others think that the current environment is tending towards a situation where there is an inhibition of our ability to put resources into things that are high risk, high return long-term developments because the pressure are really to get results earlier". (Head of Corporate Finance, AstraZeneca, cited in Ramirez and Tylecote, 2004: 109–115–116)

In addition to the incongruence between the quarter capitalism and scientific endeavours, some authors argue that science per se has gradually lost its social capital in the eyes of politicians and decision-makers. Ezrahi (2005: 273) argues:

> Science is no longer the resource it once was, with which policies and public choice could be legitimized as impersonal, objective, and technical. It is no longer important as it once was as a component of

modern state authority. Consequently, scientists are much less in demand by politicians who seek to legitimate their positions and actions before an informed and skeptical public, and therefore politicians have on their own part diminished incentives to buy the cooperation of scientists by large allocations of public money to, and by public (political) endorsement or, basic research and the general goal of the advancement and the diffusion of knowledge. (Ezrahi, 2005: 273)

It may be that science is no longer saved from criticism and demands for output and effectiveness, but the growth in various sorts of knowledge-intensive work is significant. Barley and Kunda (2006) report labour statistics showing that professional and technical staff has in fact doubled since the 1950s. This group is today the largest sector representing 18 percent of the workforce. Various science-based industries then constitute a major sector of the economy. Thus, one may argue, as Owen-Smith (2001: 428) does, that "laboratory ethnographies ... are the shop-floor studies of the post-industrial era". Moreover, the pharmaceutical industry is today influencing the everyday life of individuals and therefore it deserves to be examined in greater detail. Busfield (2006) argues that the pharmaceutical industry is more concerned with the financial performance than being considered with the patients' interests.[3] For instance, pharmaceutical companies provide handy individual solutions to health care problems that often have social and structural origins. They also have the ideological, economic and political power to market and promote their products as legitimate solutions to such social problems. Clarke *et al.* (2003) here speak of *biomedicalization* as the tendency to emphasize individual health and well-being as a responsibility of the individual and what is achieved through a combination of the use of technoscientific biomedicine and various social practices such as training, dieting, self-monitoring, and so forth (see also Rabinow's, 1992, discussion the concept of *biosociality*). The concept of medicalization was coined in the early 1970s to theorize the extension of medical jurisdiction, authority, and practices into increasingly broader areas of people's lives, especially particular social problems deemed morally problematic (e.g., alcoholism, abortion, and drug abuse). Biomedicalization is an extension and intensification of this ambition to regulate and control individual health grounded in new scientific procedures, technologies, and machinery, but also in new ideologies and beliefs. Clarke *et al.* (2003) write:

Biomedicalization is characterized by its greater organizational and institutional reach through the meso-level innovations made possible by computer and information sciences in clinical and scientific settings, including computer-based research and record-keeping. The scope of biomedicalization processes is thus much broader, and includes conceptual and clinical expansions through the commodification of health, the elaborations of risk and surveillance, and innovative clinical applications of drugs, diagnostic tests, and treatment procedures. (Clarke *et al.*, 2003: 165)

The contemporary obsession with health may then be regarded as an indication of a biomedical hegemony imposing an image of individual health not as an effect of luck or coincidence but as the outcome from an ongoing and continuous "self-transformation" (Clarke *et al.*, 2003: 172). "The body is no longer viewed as relatively static, immutable, and the focus of control, but instead as flexible, capable of being reconfigured and transformed", Clarke *et al.* (2003: 181) conclude. The massive growth of the pharmaceutical industry is an indication of such "projects of the self". Among other things, in the biomedicalization paradigm sketched by Clarke *et al.* (2003), pharmaceutical industry is increasingly influencing the production of technoscientific facts. Today, university research institutes and research facilities are in many cases sponsored by the pharmaceutical industry. A study reports that industry-sponsored research is 3.6 times more likely to produce results favourable to the sponsoring company than "autonomous" laboratories (Clarke *et al.*, 2003: 169). What is at stake here is not only the credibility of individual research institutions and certain scientists but the concept of truth itself. Therefore, taken together, the production of science-based innovation is a series of interrelated procedures that deserves to be examined in greater details within the knowledge management and innovation management literature.

Knowledge-intensive work

In the management discourse, the concept of knowledge and a number of variants of this concept (e.g., intellectual capital, know-how, capabilities, etc.) have become of central interest for understanding how firms and organization constitute sustainable competitive advantage. If we think of a firm, as Edith Penrose (1959) did in a classic study, as bundle of resources, then the intangible resources that we commonly refer to with the amorphous concept of knowledge become of central importance in a society increasingly preoccupied with abstract, intangible and intricate matters, demanding a great deal of expertise and specialist competence. In the management discourse, the notion of *knowledge intensive firms* (KIFs) has been suggested to capture this specific type of firm relying on know-how as its central resource. "The category of knowledge-intensive companies", Alvesson (2001: 863) says, "refers to firms where most work is said to be of an intellectual nature and where well-educated, qualified employees form the major part of the work force". Elsewhere, he exemplifies: "Typical examples of companies in this category are law and accounting firms, management, engineering and computer consultancy companies, advertising companies, R&D units, and high tech companies" (Alvesson, 2000: 1101). What is characteristic of these KIFs is that they treat knowledge as a tool or instrumental resource aimed at providing some utility or serving some function: "Knowledge—at least in the context of the business world and of management studies—is normally treated as a functional resource, representing a 'truth' or at least something instrumentally useful on a subject matter and/or a set of principles or techniques for dealing with material or social phenomena" (Alvesson, 2001: 865). However, KIFs may be a useful label to group a number of firms increasingly dependent upon their ability to develop, exploit and share particular knowledge bases, but it remains too an elusive a category to fully serve its function. For instance, the difference between "knowledge in general" and scientific competence is not a hairsplitting one but is one decisive difference between on the one hand a set of specific skills and expertise and on the other hand a highly professional domain regulated and monitored by a series of institutions and stakeholders. In general, the knowledge management discourse is poorly equipped for understanding and examining how science-based innovation is organized and managed. Since science operates along its own idiosyncratic and paradigmatic routes, guided by institutions and practices, one must not think that a KIF and a science-based corporation are synonyms. A KIF is a general example of a knowledge-intensive organization while the science-based corporation is a specific case. Oliver and Montgomery (2000: 35) speak of the science-based corporation as a "hybrid form": "In this new organizational form, advanced knowledge generated by scientific professionals is used in the creation of new products, such as in the biotechnology or computer industries. Thus, we suggest that the knowledge firm can be viewed as a hybrid of an established knowledge-creating organization—the research university—and an established production-oriented, market-driven enterprise—the large corporation". Science-based innovation, for instance in the case of biotechnology or computer industries, is therefore a social practice that is anchored in routines and institutions that are located outside of the particular firm; while know-how *in general* may be local and situational, science-based innovation work is always already established qua legitimate social practice prior to its organizational inclusion. Science-based innovation is therefore not what is separated from the context or environment but is continually collapsing the difference between inside and outside, the local and the global.

The argument put forth in this book is twofold: First, it is claimed that knowledge management and innovation management theory must become better equipped for understanding the specific case of science-based innovation work as a particular or even idiosyncratic form of knowledge-intensive work. Such a furnishing of knowledge management theory includes an increased emphasis on the so-called social studies of science research tradition including a variety of perspectives such as studies of science and technology (STS) and actor-network theory (ANT), a tradition of research that have dedicated substantial efforts to study scientific work *in situ* and *in actu*. Second, the book seeks to show that understanding science-based innovation implies to broadening the scope of analysis beyond instrumental and functionalists view of scientific work and knowledge-based work. Rather than assuming that science is a self-enclosed and inherently rational machinery, a box of tools and processes neatly organized into a functional unity, science-based innovation work must be regarded as a "field" in the sense Pierre Bourdieu (1990) inscribes into the term. That is, the field of scientific practice is characterized by alliances, negotiations, political struggles, controversy, passions and desires, short-terms gains and long-term strategies, quarrels over credibility and resources, in short the all-too-human qualities, debates and discussions that are present and observable in all domains of human lives. Therefore, it must not be assumed that science-based innovation work is devoid of emotionality, playfulness, and personal and organizational risk-taking; it cannot be assumed that researchers are operating without the burden of managerial control mechanisms that in cases are poorly embedded in scientific ideologies; one ought not to downgrade the influence of leadership in high performing scientific teams, to mention a few aspects of science-based innovation work that may be too little emphasized in the knowledge management literature. Taken together, science-based innovation needs to be examined in its full social, cultural, emotional and cognitive complexity. This book is an attempt to move in that direction.

Fluid epistemologies and social practice

In what may be called formal sociological theory, that is, theorists pre-occupied with formulating theories of society prior to any detailed empirical observations (see e.g., Parsons, 1951; Luhmann, 1995), there are a number of writers that have suggested that the contemporary age, the second modernity (Ulrich Beck) or the late modern (Anthony Giddens), hypermodern (John Armitage), supermodern (Marc Augé) or postmodern society, is an age characterized of transient social relations and fluid and fluxing institutions and coalitions (Bauman, 2000; Urry, 2000). For instance, Nigel Thrift (2005) speaks of contemporary capital-ism as a network organization unfolding as a "virtuality":

> I regard capitalism as a set of networks which, though they may link in many ways, form not a total system but rather a project that is permanently 'under construction'. Capitalism firms may be able to mobilize power and enroll allies but they are as uncertain about the future as we all are because the future unfolds as a virtuality—it is continually creating temporary actualizations out of new ques-tions—not a known quantity, or at least a distinct possibility. So capitalist firms may sit on the bridge of this world, able at their best to steer it in certain directions, but they still cannot know what is around the corner, whether it be an emerging energy crisis, a finan-cial downturn, a set of protests that threaten a brand's image, or something more mundane like a cashflow crisis. This essentially per-formative notion of capitalism, conceiving of it as a continually renewed set of responses to new drivers, means that I see capitalism, to repeat, as constantly mutating entity, made up of a field or net-works which are only ever partly in its control. No matter how many assets are enraged, it must constantly face the pressure of unexpected events. (Thrift, 2005: 3–4)

The epistemology advocated by Thrift (2005) and others emphasizes becoming over being and fluidity over stability; what is fixed is vanish-ing into thin air and institutions are de-territorialized and made durable through their circulation rather than through their location. We may speak of *routes* rather than *roots* (Clifford, 1997). A number of theorists and philosophers have sought to formulate theoretical frame-work capable of capturing such a transience and fluidity. Vattimo (1992) speaks of a tradition of "weak thought" after Nietzsche and in organization theory Tsoukas (2005: 5) speaks of an "open-world ontology": "An open-world ontology assumes that the world is always in a process of becoming of turning into something different. Flow, flux and change are the fundamental processes of the world. The future is open, unknowable in principle, and it always holds the possibility of surprise". Robert Cooper (2005) speaks of "relationality" as a theoretical construct addressing the distributed nature of entities such as objects:

> Objects reflect not so much themselves but the flux and flow of the connections and disconnections they become part of. Objects become the carriers and transmitters of human agency in space and time. They point to an aboriginal, pre-objective world in which categories and things cannot be found as discrete, bounded entities but which are continually subject to multiple changing circumstances in which they move as carriers and transmitters of human agency. Everything is relative to everything else. (Cooper, 2005: 1691)

In general, the ambition to understand what is fluid and fluxing erects new challenges for the social sciences. Since organization theory and management practice has over the years emphasized routines, rules, standard operation procedures, and other firms of fixed or semi-fixed social arrangements, a continuously reshaping and modifying organization becomes an oxymoron: organization is in fact what is stable and predictable. However, just as no human organization is completely stable, it is never wholly fluxing but is always stable at some points and connections. Organization theory offers a series of concepts capable of capturing the duality of stability and change, for instance, *rules, routines, scripts,* and *practices.* All these concepts rely on the ability of humans to intelligently mediate between specific situations and contexts and overarching organizational objectives and institutional demands. For instance, Feldman (2000) says routines are in fact more stretchable than one has previously recognized and in fact serve as "grammars of action" (Pentland and Rueter, 1994) and are what bridge the past and the future in organizations (Nelson and Winter, 1982). In a similar arguments, Tsoukas (2005: 75) says that "rules ... are far from perfect: the links between general categories and the particular instances they seek to relate to is always precarious". Elsewhere, Barley and Tolbert (1997: 98) speak of scripts as "[o]*bservable, recurrent activities and patterns of interactions characteristic of a particular setting.* Scripts encode the social logic of what Goffman (1983) called an 'interaction order'". Human agency and social practice are structured in accordance with routines, rules and scripts which in themselves are capable of being bended to respond to emergent situations. In fact, it is possible to define knowledge-based work as the agent's ability to respond to changes on basis of a series of organizational resources such as routines, rules, and scripts. Cooren (2004) speaks of organizational activities as being "discursively structured", that is, written texts and documents are not merely artifacts but are rather to be conceived as what actor-network theorists call *actants*, non-humans endowed with agency. Cooren (2004: 388) thus speaks of "textual agency": "The textual agency approach suggests that what constitutes an organization is a hybrid of human and nonhuman contributions. Signs, memos, and contracts display a form of agency by doing things that humans alone could do. Created by human beings, these texts participate in the channeling of behaviors, constitute and stabilize organizational pathways, and broadcast information/orders". Cooren (2004: 388) continues: "[t]extual agency, especially in its written form, enables delegation through *tele-action*, and *tele-communication*. By remaining, these textual agents fabricate relatively fixed spaces and times; they define objectives; they forbid specific behaviors; and they invite or enforce humans to follow specific organizational pathways".

Organizations are thus constituted not only by human action and material and symbolic resources but also by written documents and scripts which plays a central role in bridging agency and structures. Tsoukas (2005) examines narratives as one particular form of category serving as a scripts that can be continuously modified and retranslated (see Boje, 1991):

> Narratives are indeed an important category of organizational knowledge and discourse, and are constructed around memorable episodes derived from participating in practice. Unlike prepositional statements, narratives are contingently linked to individual action, thus facilitating individual adaptation to a large number of unforeseeable circumstances. Furthermore, narration facilitates social interaction, preserves a community's collective memory, enhances a group's sense of shared identity as participants in a practice, and serves as a repository of tacit organizational knowledge. (Tsoukas, 2005: 87)

In order to know, individually and collectively, we narrate our experiences (Orr, 1996). Narratives are thus simultaneously a *mode of knowing* and a *mode of communication* (Czarniawska, 1997: 17); we know when we account for our experiences but we also communicate our know-how in such accounts. Seen in this view, human action and agency is always communicative and embedded in the ability to share knowledge between individuals and in communities. In Robert Cooper's (2005: 1691) formulation: "Since everything in human experience is densely interconnected and intermeshed in the *event*, human agency is a dynamic mix of relationships that intrinsically resist the institutional differentiation of sociology and psychology, and instead cross and transgress all attempts to categorize and objectify our experience of reality".

If human agency is perceived as script and narrative-based activities, we are capable of affirming both a fluid and changing view of the world and the demands for semi-stable and predictable organizational routines and operations. Human agency thus serves as an intermediary role in between organizational realities and ontological and epistemological conditions in terms of accommodating both fluidity and change and social structures. However, the concept of human agency is a theoretical construct that we will not employ in the following analyses. Instead, the notion of *practice* or *social practice* will be favoured (Bourdieu, 1990, 1977; de Certeau, 1984). The philosopher Alasdair Macintyre (1981) has advocated practice as an analytical category where "practice" denotes the "coherent and complex form of socially established cooperative human activity" (Macintyre, 1981: 187). Macintyre's definition of practice is a normative one; practice is what is capable of fulfilling some legitimate and commonly agreed upon standard. The baker is not only baking bread detached from institutions and expectations but is actually seeking to accomplish an act that fulfils a variety of, say, aesthetic, nutritional, and organizational demands and expectations—that achieve "excellence". Practice is thus *regulated*. Macintyre (1981: 194) continues: "Practices must not be confused with institutions. Chess, physics and medicine are practices; chess clubs, laboratories, universities and hospitals are institutions". Practices are inextricably entangled with institutions; without institutions, practice would become a mere gesture without any meaning:

[N]o practices can survive for any length of time unsustained by institutions. Indeed to intimate is the relationship of practices to institutions—and consequently of the goods external to the goods internal to the practices in question—that institutions and practices characteristically form a single causal order in which the ideals and the creativity of the practice are always vulnerable to the acquisitiveness of the institution, in which the cooperative care for common goods of the practice is always vulnerable to the com-petitiveness of the institution. (Macintyre, 1981: 194)

For Macintyre, practice is always embedded in institutions. Other researchers emphasize the connection between practice and insti-tution. Schatzki (2002: xii) speaks of the "site of the social" as "[a] mesh of practices and orders: a contingently and differentially evolving configuration of organized activities and arrangements". The site of the social establishes certain "arrangements" constituted by practices and entities. Such arrangements are "labile phenomena", and are "only transitory fixations" (Schatzki, 2002: 24). The concept of practice—defined as "a set of doings and sayings". (Schatzki, 2002: 73)—is here central because it is what is capable of establishing meaning: "Meaning ... is carried by and established in social practices ... Meaning is not a matter of difference, abstract schema, or attributional relativity, but a reality laid down in the regimes of activity and intelligibility called 'practice'" (Schatzki, 2002: 58). Schatzki (2002: 101) clarifies his posi-tion: "Practices establish particular arrangements. These arrangements are defined packages of entities, relations, meanings, and positions, whose integrity derives from the organization of practices". In Schatzki's view, the social is a multiplicity composed of a number of arrangement constituted by entities, relations, and meanings, all guided by the con-cept of practice. Similar to Macintyre (1981), Schatzki (2002) emphasizes practices as what is a collective accomplishment, but in opposition to Macintyre he is emphasizing the transitory and fluid nature of any arrangement and subject-position. Schatzki points at the recursive nature of the agent and the arrangements:

> [I]t makes sense to say that an agent is both an arrangement and an effect thereof. An actor is its compositional network because anything is that which it is composed. An agent is also an effect of its com-positional arrangements because its capacity to act as a single entity depends on the co-operation of its components. (Schatzki, 2002: 209)

In a similar formulation, Chia and Holt (2006: 640) point at the entan-glement of practice and subject-position: "[P]ractices are *not* just what people do. Rather, practices are social sites in which events, entities and meaning help compose one another (Schatzki, 2005). Practices are identity-forming and strategy-setting activities".

A definition of practice emphasizing its institutional embedding is highly useful when examining science-based innovation qua social practice because scientific work is always strongly dependent upon routines and working hypotheses not locally developed but internationally enacted and agreed upon. All laboratory work is laboratory work along a series of routines, rules, scripts, and textual agencies that are claiming to be *universally* applicable rather than being merely local and contingent. Scientific work is, as Max Weber says, primarily and primordially work in accordance with specific *methodologies*: "Science can contribute ... [with] methods of thinking, the tools and the training for thought" (Weber, 1948: 150). "For Weber, science contributed methods of thinking, the tools and the training for disciplined thought. It contributes to gaining clarity; that is all", Paul Rabinow (2003: 99) remarks. Therefore, laboratory work is an eminent example of a social practice that is grounded in institutions. This strong emphasis on institutions does not suggest, however, that scientific laboratory work is devoid of creativity, contingencies, tricks of the trade, the scientist's sleight-of-hand, and a variety of other highly idiosyncratic and entrenched scientific skills. Studies of laboratory work suggest that work is largely a matter of dexterity and tactile and perceptual abilities (Lynch and Woolgar, 1988), that is, capabilities and skills that cannot be fully regulated, monitored, and prescribed by institutions, routines, rules, or scripts. Therefore, laboratory work—a central practice in science-based innovation—is a work that stabilizes underlying natural realities in the form of graphs, formulae, images, and diagrams through the use of a broad range of resources, be they material, textual, cognitive, or perceptual.

The social world is increasingly recognized as being fluid, fluxing and changing. In such environments, organizations (e.g., firms) must be capable of safeguarding stability and mutual adjustment to the environment. Routines, rules, and scripts are some resources mobilized when bridging human agents and organizational structures. Routines and scripts are represented in written documents and accounted for in narratives and stories but are never conclusive but must always be open for negotiation. Therefore, human agency and social practice evolve as a continuous development of a number of semi-structured activities grounded in institutions outside of the particular organization. In all scientific work, there is a continuous adaptation to new practices and theoretical developments in the community of researchers; no laboratory can operate as a closed system but must always be closely connected to other scientific activities. As a consequence, science-based innovation is a complex organizational activity bridging long and short-term objectives.

Scientific work as human practice

The notion of practice is commonly associated with the mundane matters of everyday life and the repetitive procedures that make up everyday life. Some sociologist and cultural anthropologists have even attempted at making what is mundane and "socially unmarked" (Brekhus, 2000) as their domain of research (e.g., de Certeau, 1984). However, the notion of *practice* is here used to denote any organized and structured human activity aimed at providing some good or service. Scientific work is a particular form of social practice, heavily governed by jointly agreed upon practices and standard operating procedures. Scientific work is a social practice accompanied by narratives of extraordinary accomplishments. Scientific procedures are one of the distinguishing marks of modernity and much human progress in terms of longevity and material standard can be credited to the sciences. However, thinking of science as anything else but a tightly interconnected net of practices, routines, mechanisms for control and discipline, materials, and so forth, would imply to portray scientific work as a rational machinery devoid of human ingenuity and politics. It would also be an image of science that neglects the historical development of scientific procedures and practices. At the early phases of modernity, scientific work was not the epitome of human rationality and progress it has become today; instead, science was scattered across a number of small communities, in many cases representing a radical endeavour in opposition to theological doctrines, and still clearly dependent on Aristotelian and scholastic doctrine. The early empiricists like Robert Boyle, influenced by the Scottish empiricists philosophers (e.g., David Hume), sought to establish scientific routines and procedures that should be shared in scientific communities. Boyle's contribution to science—besides the airpump he developed to conduct his pneumatic experiments with greater accuracy—was his emphasis on "modest witnessing" (Shapin and Schaffer, 1985; Shapin, 1994). Modest witnessing implied that credible and intelligent observers—"witnesses"—should testify and account for the experiments conducted. The observers should not jump to conclusions or make too hasty references to other experiments but should primarily provide a tempered and modest account of what could actually be observed. Boyle regarded the practice of modest witnessing as a warrant against subjectivity, but it also made scientific experiments a joint activity, engaging a number of credible gentlemen. During the course of scientific progress and continual refinement, the practice of modest witnessing has been transformed into a number of institutions in scientific communities, for instance the double-blind peer review system used by the scientific journals in various disciplines and domains of scientific activity. Another consequence of Boyle's approach was the emphasis on clear and intelligible accounts of the methodology employed in the study or the experiment. The virtue of the ability to replicate past studies, so central to positivist epistemologies, remains influential to date.

During the progress of science from some kind of underground or amateur activity in small and dedicated communities and societies to the role of being regarded the principal motor for social progress, scientific work has become a tightly knitted network of activities, routines, and standard operation procedures. Above all, scientific work has developed its own idiosyncrasies and traits, its own ideologies, and its own standards and methods for evaluating performance and scientific output. The university is the principal institution for scientific work. The connections between industry and science is of rather recent origin and has its roots in the nineteenth century where for instance advances in organic chemistry and the burgeoning German chemistry industry were mutually reinforcing one another (Bowker, 1995). The new synthetic chemistry resulted in important applications in the production of dyes, pharmaceuticals, and other products in the late nineteenth century. However, systematic industry research and development and what in this book will be called science-based innovation are primarily a product of the twentieth century. One of the concerns for all firms relying on its ability to manage and develop science-based innovation is how to bridge (long-term) scientific objectives and (short-term) demands for financial performance and other managerial objectives. Such seemingly opposing demands are, it is noteworthy, of rather recent origin. The period after World War II has been characterized by a continuous rationalization of activities and the deregulation of the financial markets in the Western world in the 1980s and 1990s led to a strong orientation towards the financial markets. The American type of corporate governance emphasizing shareholder value and financial performance at the expense of long-term commitment and perspectives has now become more or less the one and only model governing corporations. During previous regimes of corporate governance, scientific undertakings were regarded a long-term investment, promising to provide new scientific results that could be commodified and marketed after adequate development activities. Today, the patience with scientific work's demand for time and resources is, studies suggest, less explicit. Scientific activities and work are today not holding any privileged position vis-à-vis other organizational resources and capabilities. No scientific domain or discipline, to paraphrase Adorno (1974), "escapes the marketplace". That is, all scientific work must prove itself profitable and capable of generating new goods or services, in short, the sciences are made legitimate through their performativity, their ability to solve problems and provide new opportunities. Today, science-based innovation becomes yet another organizational resource or asset to be managed and organized.

Outline of the book

The subtitle of the book, *From modest witnessing to pipeline thinking*, is aimed at capturing the movement of scientific endeavours from being a matter of interest for communities of gentlemen, engaging in private experimentations for the sake of general interest and curiosity, to the position of science today, as being a production factor in global industries such as the pharmaceutical industry wherein the output is carefully monitored, measured, and controlled. Today, science is not only what is advocated by its spokesmen and spokeswomen as what is *potentially* capable of handling a long series of human challenges but is mobilized *in actu* in a wide range of organizations and companies. Hopefully, the book is capable of pointing at what Michel Foucault called "the history of the present" wherein science is not a production factor of a general kind but one developed from particular historical, cultural, economic and social conditions. Having said that, it is worth emphasizing that the book does not aim at formulating a comprehensive and integrated "theory" of science-based innovation because such an assemblage of practices, technologies, and tools is not packaged into neat and compartmentalized theories without a significant loss of complexity. The objective of the book is instead to point at the connections between knowledge management and innovation management literature and the literature addressing science and science-based innovation. Moreover, in the second part of the book, some practical concerns regarding risk-taking, leadership, and management control in science-based innovation are addressed on basis of an empirical study of a major multinational pharmaceutical company. If there is a moral or a message that deserves to be emphasized here, it is the *approach* to the study of science–based innovation that should be considered. Rather than assuming that science is a social and organizational resource easily tapped into one must recognize the historical, cultural, social, and economic constitution of science. In the final chapter, such an approach is discussed in terms of a thinking that is capable of "complexifying things" and to operate prior to a proper and integrated language, what Friedrich Hayek (1978) calls the thinking of the puzzler.

This book is structured into two parts: The first part, comprising Chapters 2, 3 and 4 constitute the theoretical framework of the book. Chapter 5, 6, and 7 are empirically based chapters reporting different aspects of science-based innovation that are only occasionally accounted for in the knowledge management literature. The final eighth chapter is a concluding and analytical part seeking to point at some findings and contributions from the study.

In Chapter 2, the knowledge management literature is reviewed and critically discussed. It is emphasized that much knowledge management theory remain too focused on establishing a taxonomy of knowledge(s) and that much contributions to the field are preoccupied with conceptual elaborations, for instance, the endless discussion on how to understand the qualities of tacit knowledge. In addition, the literature on the management of innovation will be reviewed. Similarly to the knowledge management discourse, the innovation management literature says little about science-based innovation.

In Chapter 3, the literature on social studies of scientific work is addressed and introduced. Rather than formulating some conclusive model of what scientific work is and how it is to be studied in context, the chapter seeks to show the plural understandings and views of science. Rather than assuming that science is once and for all fixed and immutable, this body of literature shows that there is a great deal of dynamics and capacities for change in scientific communities and groups.

In Chapter 4, the more conceptual and historical perspective provided in the preceding chapter is discussed in more practical terms in the field of new drug development work in the pharmaceutical industry, However, first, a sociological view of science is introduced and discussed in some detail. Of specific importance here is what Robert Merton called "the Mathew effect", the unequal distribution of authority and, *ipso facto*, attention and status in the field of science. Chapter 4 also includes a methodological section where the study is positioned in epistemological and methodological terms vis-à-vis other studies.

In Chapter 5, the first chapter of Part II of the book, science-based innovation is examined as a form of playing in terms of being both dependent upon clear and transparent rules while simultaneously expecting the researchers to move beyond such rules and what is taken for granted to provide anything new in their work. In addition, very much a consequence from the first assumption, science-based innovation must always include some degree of risk-taking, that is, the willingness to invest time, energy, financial resources, and personal and collective prestige to take some risks with the promise to advance science beyond its entrenched positions.

In Chapter 6, the importance of leadership and for recognizing the emotionality inherent to all scientific work are discussed. It is commonplace to think of science as what is conducted in isolation by individual talents and/or small autonomous groups of elite researchers. Such romantic views of science is poorly connected to existing scientific activities in large corporations where teams and individual researchers are located in hierarchies and networks of relations that are influencing the day-to-day work substantially. During such conditions, there is a great need for leadership practices that support rather than reduce the ability of the team or the individual to perform one's work effectively. In addition, the common sense view suggests that scientific work is always already conducted *sine ira et studio*, without any specific interests or emotional investments. As opposed to artistic activities, often regarded as domains where emotionality and creativity are the *sine qua non* for the performance, scientific work is often mistakenly conceived of as what is devoid of any strong emotional investments and commitments. Such a narrow view of scientific activities is discussed and criticized in this chapter.

In Chapter 7, the issue of management control is revisited. In much knowledge management literature, the "knowledge worker" is introduced as the first labourer that cannot be exploited because his or her skills and competencies are embodied, cerebral, perceptual and cognitive, that is, they are not possible to separate from the individual in terms of codification and other forms of extracting know-how from the individual. In addition, knowledge workers are often regarded as a form of workers that are operating in domains where ambiguities regarding skills, competencies, performance imply that the only way to manage and control a knowledge worker is through what may be called "soft means of control" (Legge, 1995), that is, through the individual's identification with the employing company, the individual subjectification process, or through other indirect or "weak" forms of control. As opposed to this view, portraying knowledge workers as what are only loosely coupled with their employer and essentially capable of moving around freely, the management control practices in the pharmaceutical company will be examined in detailed and it will be shown that "old school forms of managerial control" is not antiquated and abandoned even in the so-called knowledge society.

In the final chapter, Chapter 8, some conclusions and contributions to the literature on science-based innovation and the field of knowledge management theory will be discussed. The objective here is not to formulate a conclusive theory or an integrative perspective on knowledge management but to address epistemological concerns regarding the research on how knowledge is developed, used, and distribution in the intersection between science and commercial interests.

Summary and conclusion

In this introductory chapter, the notion of science-based innovation has been discussed qua social practice, that is, a day-to-day process of operating within a highly regulated field of expertise in accordance with predefined and jointly agreed upon rules and standard operating procedures. The field of knowledge management theory has to date dedicated only a limited amount of space and time to discuss how firms are capable of bridging scientific practice and managerial objectives. In this book, a number of aspects pertaining to scientific practice and knowledge intensive firms will be examined.

Part I

Theoretical Perspectives on Science-Based Innovation

2
Knowledge Work and Innovation

Introduction

Knowledge management has emerged as one of the most influential theoretical frameworks in the recent management literature. Prior to the 1990s, there was virtually nothing written about "knowledge management" (Spender and Grant, 1996) even though writers such as Machlup (1962) addressed the use of knowledge as a social and organizational production factor. Since the second half of the 1990s, there has been a substantial number of paper and books published on the topic; journals addressing knowledge management practices have been established, and new conferences and scientific associations and interests groups have been created—the notion of knowledge management has been instituted as a legitimate perspective on organizations. Even though the bulk of the "first wave" of knowledge management theory was published in the intersection between management and information technology (Scarbrough, Robertson and Swan, 2005), today the focus has shifted from information technology to a broader view of knowledge. It is however important to emphasize the tradition of the sociology of knowledge founded by Karl Mannheim in his *Ideology and Utopia* (1936) and later on further developed by Robert Merton (1957) as an important forerunner to the managerial engagement with knowledge. In the sociology of knowledge tradition, knowledge is what is socially constructed and is therefore not only of ontological and epistemological interest but is equally a sociological concern.

In this chapter, two domains of literature will be covered: The knowledge management literature and the literature on the management of innovation.

Managing knowledge

Central terms and definitions

To say the least, knowledge is a term that covers a wide range of perspectives and phenomena. A long time ago, prior to any knowledge management perspective. Robert Merton (1957: 467) wrote: "Even a cursory survey is enough to show that the terms 'knowledge' has been so broadly conceived as to refer to every type of idea and every mode of thought ranging from folk belief to positive science". To speak of knowledge is therefore always to speak of knowledge in the plural; knowledge is a multiplicity including a variety of know-how and interests. As a consequence, a number of writers have struggled to define knowledge in lexical terms, that is, to provide the concept with a neat and comprehensive formulation that includes the different perspectives. Gourlay (2006), distinguishing between know-how (procedural knowledge) and know-that (propositional knowledge), provides an overview of how some central terms in the knowledge management discourse are used in different social science disciplines and philosophy (see Table 2.1).

Daniel Bell (1973), who in the 1970s spoke of the emergence of "the post-industrial society", defines knowledge as "[a] set of organized statements of facts or ideas, presenting a reasoned judgment or an experimen-

Table 2.1 Knowledge types and names (Adapted from Gourlay, 2006: 1426)

Discipline	Knowledge-how	Knowledge-that
Philosophy	Knowledge-how; procedural knowledge; abilities	Knowledge-that; propositional knowledge
Philosophy (Polanyi)	Tacit knowledge	Explicit knowledge
Psychology	Implicit knowledge; tacit abilities; skills	Explicit knowledge; declarative knowledge
Artificial intelligence	Procedural knowledge	Declarative knowledge
Neuroscience	Covert knowledge	Overt knowledge
Management studies; education	Tacit knowledge	Explicit knowledge
IT studies	Knowledge as process	Knowledge as object
Knowledge management	Know-how	Know-what
Sociology of science	Tacit; encultured (forms of life)	Explicit/Symbolic

tal result, which is transmitted to others through some communication medium in some systematic form" (Bell, 1973: 175. The original in italics). Liebeskind (1996: 94) defines knowledge as "[i]nformation whose validity has been established through test of proof". More recently (Bierly, Kessler and Christensen, 2000: 600) offer the following definition: "We define knowledge as clear understanding of information and their associated patterns and learning about knowledge ... as the process of analysis and synthesis of information". These three definitions relies on a shared set of assumptions: (1) knowledge is derived from or constituted by information, (2) knowledge must be verified though empirical testing. Seen in this view, knowledge does not constitute a plane of its own but is conceived of as aggregated and verified data and information; the roots of knowledge are possible to find in its "elementary forms", that is, data and information. Several knowledge management theorists address the relationship between data, information and knowledge. Boisot (1998) writes:

Knowledge builds on information that is extracted from data. In practice the three terms are often confused. Data is discrimination between physical states—black, white, heavy, light, etc.—that may or may not convey information to an agent. Whether it does so or not depends on an agent's prior stock of knowledge ... whereas data can be characterized as a property of things, knowledge is a property of agents predisposing them to act in particular circumstances. Information is that subset of the data residing in things that activates an agent—it is filtered from the data by the agent's perceptual or conceptual apparatus ... Information, in effect, establishes a relationship between things and agents. Knowledge can be conceptualized as a set of probability distributions held by an agent and orienting his or her actions. (Boisot, 1998: 12)

Elsewhere, Sanchez (2001) engages in a similar analysis:

Data are representations of the events that people notice and bring to the attention of other people in the organization. Data consists of qualitative and quantitative descriptions of events. As descriptions, data are always incomplete representations—some aspects of an event are notices and recorded in some way, while other aspects either are not noticed or are not included in the representation of the event. How the event becomes represented in data depends on what aspects of an event an observer notices and thinks will have significance, personally or for the organization. Just as it has been noticed that 'all facts are theory laden', all data are *selective representations of events*, implicit in which are some presumptions about which events and which aspects of these events are likely to have significance in some context of interest. Thus the data entering an organization are greatly influenced by the interpretative frameworks ... that determine which events are noticed and how those events are represented by the organization. (Sanchez, 2001: 5)

Yet another passage addressing the relationship between data, information, and knowledge is provided by Newell *et al.* (2002):

Data, information, and knowledge are inextricably linked. Data provide a record of signs and observations collected from a variety of sources. These data are presented in a particular way in relation to a particular context of action and so becomes information. Information is thus data endowed with relevance and purpose (Drucker, 1980). Data and information are selectively collected and presented—they do not provide and objective account of the 'real world'. More importantly, data and information are meaningless to some without relevant knowledge. Knowledge provides the means by which these data and information can be interpreted. (Newell *et al.*, 2002: 102)

In addition, Bierly Kessler and Christensen (2000: 598) present a table including an additional level, that of "wisdom" advocated by Plato, as a fourth level of analysis (see Table 2.2).

Table 2.2 Distinctions between data, information, knowledge and wisdom (Adapted from Bierly, Kessler and Christensen, 2000: 598)

Level	Definition	Learning process	Outcome
Data	Raw facts	Accumulating truths	Memorization (databank)
Information	Meaningful, useful data	Giving them form and functionality	Comprehension (information bank)
Knowledge	Clear understanding of information	Analysis and synthesis	Understanding (knowledge bank)
Wisdom	Using knowledge to establish and achieve goals	Discerning judgments and taking appropriate action	Better living/success (wisdom bank)

What Boisot (1998), Sanchez (2001), Newell *et al.* (2002) fail to account for is that knowledge cannot be a simple aggregation of data and information—a string of data turned into information becoming valuable knowledge for the skilled and trained observer. Knowledge can never be self-identical or enclosed but is always what emerges in networks where data and information are continually related to practical undertakings and critical reviews. Knowledge is thus not data and information amassed but is what is discontinuously and disruptively *derived* from available data and information. The history of science shows that scientific breakthroughs are not of necessity the outcome from the continuous production of data turned into information but knowledge—scientific knowledge, that is—is what may emerge on basis of seemingly ephemeral and marginal inputs. This "under-determination" of data in theory construction is often referred to as the Duhem thesis after the French physician Pierre Duhem. Knowledge is thus like all intelligent human thinking not solely a matter of "input material" but operates as a process of synthesizing heterogeneous components. Reductionist thinking, assuming that knowledge is constituted solely on basis of data and information, dominates the orthodox knowledge management literature. When exploring constructs like data and information in greater detail it may be noticed that what appeared to be uncomplicated "entities" are in fact in themselves situated and contingent observations open for criticism. For instance, scientific data are in many cases the outcome from procedures of selection and categorization (Bowker and Star, 1999; Roth, 2005) or are inextricably entangled with the use of laboratory technologies setting the boundaries for what is proper data and what is not. Therefore, the entire series data-information-knowledge remains a model assuming a linearity that cannot fully capture the fluidity and the contingent and fluxing nature of intellectual resources. "Knowing means imposing regulating forms on chaos", Heidegger (1987: 77) says. Knowing is here what is, in pragmatic terms, capable of serving to structure and organize what is seemingly complicated; rather than being a "final word" on a matter, knowledge is contingent, provisional, and practically oriented. Rather than seeking to define knowledge in lexical terms, one may benefit from allowing for some ambiguities and accept that knowledge is not finally brought into a standstill through the continuous references to data and information. Instead all definitions of knowledge must recognize its social, emotional, and cultural embedding and therefore all of its definitions are provisional. Thus, more recently, concepts such as *social capital*, anchoring prepositional and tacit knowledge in social relations and shared meaning and sense making capabilities, have been examined by knowledge management theorists and students of innovation work (Nahapiet and Ghosal, 1998; Yli-Renka, Autio, Sapienza, 2001; Inkpen and Tsang, 2005; Subramaniam and Youndt, 2005; Willem and Scarbrough, 2006). In this perspective, knowledge is not what solely derives from data and information but is, to use Orlikowski's formulation, a "social accomplishment" (2002: 252), a jointly produced agreement of how to use collectively shared know-how.

The two schools of knowledge management

Many mainstream knowledge management theorists have been pre-occupied with dividing knowledge into groups, categories, schools, taxonomies, and research traditions. Much of the literature is conceptual and seeks to make knowledge become what is neatly separated into compartments and classes. Sackmann (1992) identifies four types of knowledge:

(1) Dictionary knowledge comprises commonly held descriptions, including labels and sets of words of definitions that are used in particular organizations. What?
(2) Directory knowledge frees to commonly held practices. It is knowledge about chains of events and about their cause-and-effect relationships. How?
(3) Recipe knowledge, based on judgments, refers to prescriptions for repair and improvements strategies. Should?
(4) Axiomatic knowledge refers to reasons and explanations of the final causes perceived to underlie particular events. Why? (Sackmann, 1992: 141)

Tell (2004) speaks of four types of knowledge derived from the procedures of justification in organizations. The forms of knowledge are *personal knowledge, subjective knowledge, institutional knowledge,* and *objective knowledge.* Yanow (2004) distinguishes between what she calls "expert knowledge" and "local knowledge" (see Table 2.3) wherein the former is a based on scientific knowledge embedded in its performativity, its ability to prove itself worthy of the status of knowledge", while the latter form is the practice-based knowledge of everyday life undertakings.

Empson (2001) presents a similar model where knowledge is either regarded as an asset or a process. In the first perspective, knowledge is similar to what Yanow (2004) calls "expert knowledge", forms of objectively useful and widely agreed upon know-how that are employed in

Table 2.3 Two types of knowledge (Adapted from Yanow, 2004: S12)

'Expert knowledge'	'Local knowledge'
theory-based	practice-based
abstracted, generalized	context-specific
scientifically constructed	interactively-derived
academy-based	lived experience-based
technical-professional	practical reasoning
explicit	tacit
scholarly	everyday

the operations. In the second perspective, knowledge is regarded as what is emerging in social interactions and joint collaborations. Here, knowledge is never defined per se or in isolation but is always distributed and collectively constituted (see Table 2.4).

Table 2.4 Alternative perspectives on knowledge in organizations (Adapted from Empson, 2001: 813)

	Knowledge as an asset	Knowledge as a process
Purpose of research	Normative. To identify valuable knowledge and to develop effective mechanisms for managing that knowledge within organizations	Descriptive. To understand how knowledge is created, articulated, disseminated, and legitimised within organizations
Disciplinary foundation	Economics	Sociology
Underlying paradigm	Functionalist	Interpretive
Epistemological assumptions	Knowledge as an objectively definable commodity	Knowledge as a social construct
Models of knowledge transmission	Exchange of knowledge among individuals are governed by an implicit internal market within organizations	Knowledge is disseminated and legitimated within organizations through an ongoing process of interaction among individuals
Main level of analysis	Organization and its knowledge base	Individuals in social contexts

Empson's (2001) two categories capture the difference between the two dominating perspectives on knowledge in the literature. In the first school, conceiving of knowledge as a *stock*, an actual and present body of skills, assets, and resources that can be drawn from in organizational activities; organizations are repositories of knowledge that have over the years proven to have a significant capability in developing, exploiting, and sharing knowledge. In the second school, knowledge is regarded as what is constituted and employed in the actual and joint undertakings and activities within communities and organizations. Rather than assuming that knowledge is already in place, simply located in organizational routines, databases or in the minds of the employees, knowledge is here the outcome from collective collaborations. Knowledge is here metaphorically regarded as a *flow*, that is, what emerges in social practice.

The stock versus flow metaphors present two alternatives traditions of thought. The former tradition is dominated by strategic management theory and questions regarding competitive advantage and the question of how firms compete with one another in a market. The latter tradition is strongly entangled with sociological perspectives on knowledge and addresses the collective constitution of knowledge in organizations. Hedberg and Holmqvist (2001) are representative of the "knowledge as stock" tradition of thinking. They write:

> All organizations are repositories of knowledge, but some organizations are more knowledge-intensive and knowledge-dependent than others. Knowledge is lodged in the brains of organization members as well as in explicit rules, that is, artificial memories, which include files, records, and other documents ... Knowledge is also stored in organizational routines, that is, repetitive modes of acting, and standard operating procedures. (Hedberg and Holmqvist, 2001: 737)

Here knowledge is "lodged in people's brains" and in "files, records, and other documents". Knowledge is in other words located in specific routines, databases, and other organizational resources. Max Boisot (1998: 63) explicitly positions himself within this view: "Assets are stocks rather than flows and we have seen that knowledge assets can be stocked in people's heads, in documents, or in artefacts". A particularly influential model in the stock perspective is Nonaka's (1994) so-called SECI model drawing on a social constructivist framework, suggesting that explicit and tacit knowledge can be translated into the two forms of knowledge through processes of *socialization, externalization, combination*, and *integration* (for a more recent defence of the model, see Nonaka, von Krogh and Voelpel, 2006). Empirical studies using the SECI model (e.g., Schulze and Hoegl, 2006; Dyck *et al.*, 2005) point at some of the shortcomings with this model but also recognizes the usefulness of the model. Gourlay (2006: 1424) is presenting a more critical account, claiming that the model is "flawed" in terms of omitting specific forms of tacit knowledge, enacting a "radically subjective definition of knowledge", and ignoring "scientific forms of knowledge". Gourlay (2006) addresses a number of central concerns regarding the validity and usefulness of the SECI model.

The other perspective, that of knowledge as a flow, is an increasingly recognized view in the organization theory camps affirmative of a more pluralist view of organizations and examining knowledge on the micro level as opposed to the strategic management theorists' meso- or macro level analyses. For instance, Spender (1998: 234–235) is critical of the "stock" metaphor in knowledge management: "[t]o treat knowledge as a mere asset, a static entity like any other of the firm's constituting elements or factors of production, is to miss the opportunity to shift our theorizing into a genuine framework". Tsoukas (1996) argues that organizations are dealing with distributed knowledge in *de-centred* systems, that is, there is no central control over and surveying of the knowledge resources in a firm but all employees must individually use their know-how in a manner they believe is the best for the firm. As a consequence, a firm's knowledge is "not self-contained" and is "inherently indeterminate and continually reconfiguring" (Tsoukas, 1996: 13). In a later paper, Tsoukas and Vladimirou (2001: 990) discuss how knowledge management is "[t]he dynamic process of turning an unreflected practice into a reflective one by elucidating the rules guiding the activities of the practice, by helping give a particular shape to collective understandings, and by facilitating the emergence of heuristic knowledge". Again, knowledge is not what is immediately available for inspection and manipulation and must therefore be managed indirectly, for instance through establishing arenas where knowledge-workers meet and discuss their insights and experiences from their work. Tsoukas and Vladimirou (2001: 991) write: "Managing organizational knowledge does not narrowly imply efficiently managing hard bits of information but, more subtly, sustaining and strengthening social practices ... In knowledge management digitalisation cannot be substituted for socialization". In a similar manner, Sole and Edmondson (2002: S20) speak of "situational knowledge" as knowledge that is "[e]mbedded in the work practices of a particular organizational site". In these views of knowledge, knowledge is grounded in the day-to-day-work, the practices of everyday work life rather than being located in databases and routines in firms and organizations. In this view, all knowledge is, with Castoriadis's (1997: 345) formulation, "co-produced": "All knowledge is co-production; and, in nontrivial cases, we cannot truly separate out what 'comes from' the subject and what 'comes from' the object. This is what I would like to call the 'principle of undecidability of origin'". Empirical studies of for instance project team work and communities of practice show that knowledge is largely locally articulated and enacted, that is, co-produced (Enberg, Lindkvist and Tell, 2006; Lindkvist, 2005). Not only is knowledge socially constructed and embedded in networks of actors, it is also complicated to separate subject from object. For instance, when an architect is working on a sketch of a building using a CAD-program in her computer, it is complicated to separate the agent, the software and the hardware from one another; technology is recursively constituted by and constitutive of practice (Barley, 1990, 1986; Orlikowski, 1992, 2000; Dodge and Kitchin, 2005). The three entities constitute a functional unity including agents and actants, human and non-humans (Michaels, 2000). One must not be too ready to separate humans and non-humans from one another and to locate know-how in either category. Furthermore, to conceive of knowledge as what is always derived from social interactions implies that issues of power and influence need to be addressed. Gherardi and Nicolini (2001: 44) write:

> Every attempt to label something as 'knowledge' is made by a specific social community belonging to a network of power relations, and not by a world consisting purely of ideas. Hence, no knowledge is universal or supreme; instead, all knowledge is produced within social, historical, and linguistic relations grounded in specific forms of conflict and the division of labor. (Gherardi and Nicolini, 2001: 44)

Knowledge is what is anchored in human interests rather than what is existing outside of such conditions and contexts. Therefore, the enfolding of power and knowledge into one another must be continually examined and criticized.

Knowledge and social practice

Etic vocabularies: Meaning, institutionalization, articulation

If we assume that knowledge is more adequately captured by the metaphor of flow rather than the stock, then the notion of social practice is again highly relevant for the analysis of knowledge management

(Gherardi, 2006). Bridging "doing" and "knowing" is then one of the central analytical operations. What bridges these two parallel processes is, Spender (1996) suggests, the notion of *meaning*, one of the most complicated concepts in social theory:

> To know is to be able to take part in the process that makes that knowledge meaningful. Even to feel that confident that one could take part is but a representation of that knowledge, not the knowledge itself, for it is the performance, especially in the face of unanticipated uncertainties and challenges, that is the true test of executive knowing. (Spender, 1996: 59)

Speaking of knowledge in phenomenological terms such as meaning, understanding, and sense-making is shifting of the focus from the mere utility of knowledge to its cognitive, perceptual and emotional constitution qua human skills and capacity. Speaking with Tsoukas and Mylonopoloulos (2004), one must cease to take knowledge for granted and make it become yet again what is not always already in place:

> Unpacking organizational knowledge becomes important the moment we cease to take 'knowledge' for granted, assuming it has already a particular form and content. Indeed, one of the common fallacies concerning organizational knowledge is what we may call the apple-tree fallacy: the knowledge individuals make use of in their work is considered to be a collection of freestanding item waiting out these to be plucked from the tree of organizational knowledge. (Tsoukas and Mylonopoloulos, 2004: S3)

All knowledge work is thus based on collective sense making, the "making of meaning". In addition, speaking of knowledge as what is emerging in social practice emphasizes that the distinction between creating, applying and preserving knowledge becomes fuzzy. In many cases, knowledge is both created and preserved in the very act of applying knowledge: "The distinction between creating knowledge and applying it is often hard to make ... Basic research may have direct applicability, and applied research may contribute fundamental knowledge", Starbuck (1992: 722) writes. He continues:

> Creating, applying and preserving intertwine and complement each other. At least over long periods, merely storing knowledge does not preserve it. For old knowledge to have meaning, people must relate it

to their current problems and activities. They have to translate it into contemporary language and frame it within current issues. Effective preserving looks much like applying. As time passes and social and technological changes add up, the needed translation grow larger, and applying knowledge comes to look more like creating knowledge. (Starbuck, 1992: 722)

Since knowledge is never once and for all stabilized or fixed, one of the key challenges for all knowledge-intensive firms is to institutionalize norms and values regarding what are legitimate and valid forms of knowledge (Kärreman and Alvesson, 2004). Such institutionalization is providing an "epistemological closure" for the available knowledge in a firm. Patriotta (2003) discusses the benefits of institutionalization in a passage worth citing *in extensio*:

Institutionalization is the process by which human agency and knowledge are progressively delegated to the organization and inscribed into stable structures of signification. In this regard, institutionalization produces epistemological closure. By sealing emergent stocks of controversial knowledge, institutionalization produces a stable configuration of background and foreground. But this configuration is susceptible to revision, for example during major episodes of technical breakdown, industrial conflict, or radical change. Current organizational structure or procedure only gives a temporary closure and a 'fixing' to a never-ending, ever evolving process of the reshuffling and restructuring of knowledge (Lanzara and Patriotta, 2001). Institutionalization adds two important aspects to the process of knowledge creation. First, it implies an act of social acceptance whereby certain codes, patterns, structures, and practices become progressively taken for granted within a given community. The legitimization of organizational knowledge points to the importance of reaching a consensus around what is 'valid' knowledge, whilst highlighting a problem of conformity with existing organizational standards. Second, once it has been created and recognized as valid, knowledge needs to be represented and formalized in order to be transferred and diffused at a corporate level. For instance, organizational charts display a formal definition of the division of labour within a certain company which has been socially accepted and legitimized by its members. (Patriotta, 2003: 180–181)

On a more detailed level of analysis, Patriotta (2003) emphasizes the importance of what he calls the "articulation of knowledge" as the process wherein knowledge is connected to cases and concerns and become "visible" for all organization members:

> Through articulation, knowledge is represented and made visible. In fact, articulation can be defined as the act of making knowledge manifest. Controversies recede into the background and legitimate knowledge is sealed into organizational black boxes: organizations create knowledge that can be fitted into purposeful devices. The organization is formally represented and reduced to an abstraction. Only now can we see knowledge lies precisely in this apparent paradox of making manifest while hiding ... as a result of institutionalization, knowledge is inscribed into a system of norms, practices and conventions, and incorporated into stable structures. Knowledge becomes canonical, factual, definite and certain. Institutionalization implies a process of epistemological closure similar to the closure of black boxes. (Patriotta, 2003: 181)

In social practice, knowledge is never wholly self-enclosed but is instead emerging in its application and through the support of various institutions and the articulation of knowledge. Studies of consultants, executives and other professional groups (e.g., lawyers, barristers, etc.) show that such experts need to mobilize a set of resources such as standardized power point presentations, a uniform and carefully elaborated vocabulary, or uniform clothing and other insignia testifying to their status as legitimate professionals and to underline and amplify their authority in and jurisdiction over a particular field (Werr and Stjernberg, 2003; Starbuck, 1992; Goffman, 1959). In other words, expert knowledge is never once and for all removed from discussions and controversies and is certainly not observable through ocular inspections but must be performed and demonstrated through the mobilization of additional resources. A well-dressed lawyer may be expected or even demanded from those employing the lawyer. No knowledge subsists per se but is always constituted in the assemblage of a variety of material and intangible resources. Patriotta (2003) captured this dislocated and distributed nature of knowledge with the phrase, derived from William James, "knowledge in the making":

> [W]e have moved away from a static, commodified definition of knowledge and focused on those phenomena that constitute the essence of knowledge in the making, namely action, context, and time. The analysis performed in the case studies was aimed at deconstructing organizational knowledge as something that is never a perfected

reality but it is always 'in the making'. In particular, knowledge in the making stresses the idea of 'becoming' while pointing to the controversial, ephemeral, and experimental character of both cognitive and practical activities underlying the transformation of organizational knowledge systems. (Patriotta, 2003: 199)

"Knowledge in the making" is thus an epistemological position wherein knowledge is never self-enclosed or self-identical but is always a resource that needs to be embedded in a variety of complementary resources. In addition, knowledge in the making emphasizes all knowledge work as a process of meaning-making and recognizes the entanglement between the creation, application and preserving of knowledge. Knowledge is what is created in the moment of application, to speak with Henri Bergson (1988), in the *actualization* of virtual resources in a specific moment; knowledge is a process drawing together a number of complementary and supporting organizational resources. Speaking of knowledge in such terms is conceiving of knowledge as a flow of activities and resources rather than being what is always already in place. However, this does not mean that the strategic management theory's concern for performance and competitive advantage is mistaken or become obsolete. The issue of using knowledge to safeguard long-term performance and competitive advantage remains legitimate and of central interest.

Emic vocabularies: Knowledge work and knowledge workers

The processes of institutionalization and articulation are *etic* concepts, that is, concepts used by the outsider and the researcher and not by the group of knowledge workers themselves. To use a less abstract and more mundane terms, one may speak of *knowledge work*. Schultze (2000: 5) says that knowledge workers form "a special class of white-collar workers" including a number of different groups such as "professionals, consultants, technicians, intellectuals, and managers". Schultze (2000) lists a number of characteristics of knowledge work:

- It produces and reproduces information and knowledge
- Unlike physical blue-collar work, knowledge work is cerebral ... and involves the manipulation of abstractions and symbols that both *represent the world* and are objects *in the world*.
- Unlike *service work*, which is frequently scripted ... knowledge work defies routinization and requires the use of creativity in order to produce idiosyncratic, esoteric knowledge

- It requires formal education, i.e., abstract, technical and theoretical knowledge. (Schultze, 2000: 5, Emphasis in the original)

One common view of knowledge workers is that they are primarily committed to their work or profession and not their employing corporation. In a study of knowledge workers in three companies in Australia, Japan, and the USA in financial services and telecommunication, Tam, Korczynski and Frenkel (2002: 794) found that knowledge workers were in fact committed to their corporation, but they were even more committed to their occupation. Tam, Korczynski and Frenkel (2002) also found that the knowledge workers to a higher extent wanted to participate in decision-making processes in the firm: "Formal power in decision-making would enable knowledge workers to mobilize corporate resources to protect and advance their interests. Management in our cases, however, relied primarily on extrinsic rewards and job autonomy as the major levers to manage work motivation" (Tam, Korczynski and Frenkel, 2002: 795–796). Knowledge workers may therefore identify more with their corporation if they are given the authority to influence the organization. Blackler, Crump and McDonald (1999: 8) emphasize the need for managing knowledge workers in new ways: "Traditional ways of integrating different domains of expertise do not function well in the fast-moving environments of the present day. Organizations that depend on knowledge work and organizational learning need to move away from co-ordination through rules and hierarchies and to create 'self-managing' systems of collaboration where different specialists interact directly and jointly regulate their shared efforts".

For Schultze (2000: 7), much of the knowledge management literature has been preoccupied with how to transform tacit knowledge and other forms of "non-represented" and "un-coded" know-how into "informational objects". Knowledge work is thus the production and reproduction of informational objects in specific settings; it is a work to code, represent, store, communicate, and disseminate "informational objects". One of the specific challenges for all knowledge workers that is particularly accentuated in scientific milieus is that the knowledge worker is expected to eliminate subjective influences and personal beliefs and assumptions. Schultze (2000) writes:

In scientific inquiry, objectivity is revered and regarded as a sign of excellence ... Objective and universal knowledge is preferred over the subjective and situated. Hard quantification is preferred over soft qualification ... Objectivity is associated with representation that corresponds to an external reality and freedom from the distorting perceptual bias of the individual thinking agent ... Subjectivity, on the other hand, signifies the emotional, personal, individual and idiosyncratic side of human perception and knowledge. It refers to social phenomena which originates and exists within the observer's mind, and which are impossible to check directly. (Schultze, 2000: 6–7)

Knowledge workers are thus trained in being sceptical of all subjective qualities and to regard informational objects as what are essentially cleansed from human "idiosyncrasies". Seen as a social practice, knowledge work is complicated because it is at the same time recognizing and rejecting the social component of knowledge; on the one hand, knowledge work is the structuring and codifying of what are tacit, ambiguous and complex forms of know-how, that is, a categorization and classification of what is fluid and fizzy into stable and compartmentalized "informational objects" made applicable to cases; on the other hand, such structuring and classification is expected to be catered without any decisive influence from the human agents responsible for such activities.

In summary, if *social practice* is an *etic category*, used primarily by academic researchers in theoretical analyses, the notions of *knowledge work* and *knowledge workers* are *emic categories*, used in firms and organizations to capture the nature of the day-to-day work of the professionals, consultants, technicians, intellectuals, and managers listed by Schultze (2000).

The management of knowledge and the quest for sustainable competitive advantage

The strategic management theory tradition is concerned with the question of how firms compete with one another and how they achieve sustainable competitive advantage over time. In what has been called the knowledge-based view of the firm (Foss, 1996), a development from the general resource-based view of the firm (Barney, 1991), it is knowledge that remains the single most important resource underlying sustainable competitive advantage. Davenport and Prusak (1998) speak of knowledge in such terms:

Knowledge ... can provide a sustainable advantage. Eventually, competitors can almost always match the quality and price of a market leader's current product or service. By the time that happens, though, the knowledge-rich, knowledge-managing company will have moved on to a new level of quality, creativity, or efficiency. The knowledge advantage is sustainable because it generates increasing returns and continuing advantage. Unlike material assets, which decrease as they are used, knowledge assets increase with use: Ideas breed new ideas, and shared knowledge stays with the giver while it enriches the receiver. The potential for new ideas arising from the stock of knowledge in any firm is practically limitless—particularly if the people in the firm are given opportunities to think, to learn, and to talk with one another. (Davenport and Prusak, 1998: 17)

Developing, exploiting, and sharing knowledge in firms is for Davenport and Prusak (1998) a self-perpetuating process wherein the knowledge-intensive firm is capable of continuously moving forward through the development of new "knowledge assets". David Teece (2000) is talking about the ability to exploit opportunities in the marketplace through the existing stock of knowledge in a firm as a *dynamic capability* (see also Teece, Pisano and Shuen, 1997). A dynamic capability is defined as "[t]he capacity to sense opportunities and to reconfigure knowledge assets, competencies, and complementary assets so to achieve sustainable competitive advantage" (Teece, 2000: 27). Teece (2000: 29) continues: "The essence of the firm in the new economy is its ability to create, transfer, assemble, integrate, protect and exploit knowledge assets. Knowledge assets underpin competences, and competences in turn underpin the firm's product and service offerings in the market". In order to develop knowledge-based dynamic capabilities, firms need to be capable of codifying knowledge (Boisot, 1998) or orchestrating what Suddaby and Greenwood (2001: 934–935) calls "knowledge commodification". Knowledge commodification "[d]escribes the process by which managerial knowledge is abstracted from context and reduced to a transparent and generic format that can be more easily leveraged within PSF [Professional Service Firms] and sold in the marketplace. Commodification occurs as managerial knowledge products move cyclically between communities of actors within the organizational field". Knowledge commodification is the repackaging of preexisting knowledge in order to make it applicable in new settings. Consultancy firms are excellent examples of firms capable of commodifying their knowledge and applying it to a variety of cases (Berglund and Werr, 2000; Werr and Stjernberg, 2003). Taken together, knowledge is a central organizational resource that can be managed, organized, and administrated in a variety of ways and manners. The management of knowledge-based resources is by no means a self-organizing process but any attempt at managing knowledge involves a series of highly intricate issues pertaining to human cognition, perception, emotionality, and so forth. Therefore, the movement connection between know-how in a firm and long-term competitive advantage is by no means a linear or uncomplicated movement but is on the contrary a process including many substantial managerial challenges.

Managing innovation

Perspectives on innovation

Research on innovation, new product development and the management of R&D in organization is one of the largest empirical domains in organization theory and management studies (for an overview see Dougherty, 1999; Slappendel, 1996; Wolfe, 1994). In a seminal text by Peter Drucker (1955: 32), the management of innovation is introduced as one of the central tasks of the manager, and since the publication of Burns and Stalker's (1961) classic study of Scottish technology industry, innovation has been a part of the management studies agenda. However, the *locus classicus* of the notion of innovation is Joseph Schumpeter's *The Theory of Economic Development* (1934). In a publication from 1939, Schumpeter speaks of innovation in the following terms: "We simply define innovation as the setting up of a new production function. This covers the case of a new commodity, a well as those of a new form of organization such as a merger, of the opening of new markets, and so on ... innovation combines factors in a new way ... it consists in carrying out New Combinations" (Schumpeter, 1939: 87–88). Later on he distinguishes between the enterprise and the entrepreneur: "For actions which consists in carrying out innovation we reserve the term Enterprise; the individuals who carry them out we call Entrepreneurs" (Schumpeter, 1939: 100). The two fields of innovation management and entrepreneurship studies are therefore both indebted to Schumpeter's work.

Today, there is a massive research literature on innovation in organizations; a rich variety of theoretical perspectives in this body of literature is ranging from a narrow micro level of individuals to the analysis of industrial clusters and regions. Wolfe (1994) identifies three distinct research questions and research tradition within the innovation literature (see Table 2.5).

Table 2.5 Schools of innovative research (Adapted from Wolfe, 1994: 407)

Research question	Research approach	Research focus
1. What are the patterns of diffusion through a population of potential adopter organizations?	Diffusion of innovation (DI) research	Addresses the *diffusion of an innovation* over time and/or space
2. What determines organizational innovativeness?	Organizational innovativeness (OR) research	Addresses the *determinants of innovativeness* of organizations
3. What are the processes organizations go through in implementing innovations?	Process theory (PT) research	Addresses the *process of innovation* within organizations

The first research question has engaged a number of researchers to explore how innovations have been diffused in markets and industries. The second research question has produced a number of studies regarding the determinants of innovation, and the third research question deals with the actual innovation process. For Wolfe (1994), these three perspectives are complementary because innovation is too complex a practice or event to be captured by one single, unified model or perspective. Wolfe (1994) therefore suggests a pluralist view of innovation. Similarly, Slappendel (1996) talks in her review of the innovation literature about three complementary perspectives on innovation: (1) the *individual perspective*, emphasizing the individual actors that are the principal agents in innovative work, (2) the *structural perspective*, "assuming that innovations is determined by organizational characteristics" (Slappendel, 1996: 113), and (3) the *interactive perspective*, studying innovation as the outcome from the joint collaboration between groups of individuals, organizations, and relevant resources. The three perspectives are summarized in Table 2.6.

For Slappendel (1996: 122), the three perspectives have evolved over time and consequently it is the interaction perspective that is the most recent contribution to the analysis of innovation. Both Wolfe's (1994) and Slappendel's (1996) reviews of the literature suggest that innovation is a substantial field of research that cannot be boiled down into

Table 2.6 The main feature of the three perspectives (Adapted from Slappendel, 1996: 109)

	Individualist	Structuralist	Interactive process
Basic assumption	Individuals cause innovation	Innovation determined by structural characteristics	Innovation produced by the interaction of structural influences and the actions of individuals
Conceptualization of an innovation	Static and objectively defined objects or practices	Static and objectively defined objects or practices	Innovations are subject to reinventions and reconfigurations. Innovations are perceived.
Conceptualization of the innovative process	Simple linear, with focus on the adoption stage	Simple linear, with focus on the adoption stage	Complex process
Core concepts	Champions Leader Entrepreneurs	Environment Size Complexity Differentiation Context Formalization Centralization Strategic type	Shocks Proliferation Innovative capability
Research methodology	Cross-sectional survey	Cross-sectional survey	Case studies Case histories
Main authors	Rogers March and Simon	Zaltman *et al.*	Van de Ven *et al.*

one single unified model or theory. Thus the literature needs to be approached as a heterogeneous body of texts.

In the innovation literature, some contributions have bearings on adjacent theoretical fields such as knowledge management (e.g., Subramaniam and Venkatraman, 2001; Von Hippel, 1998), human resource management (Bunce and West, 1996), or philosophy (O'Shea, 2002). Among the various perspectives pursued, researchers have studied the impact of local cultures on innovation (Jassawalla and Sashittal, 2002), the ability to share knowledge within new product development teams (Leonard-Barton, 1995) as well as between business units and firms (Spencer, 2003; Jones, 2000; Hage and Hollingsworth, 2000; Nobel and Birkinshaw, 1998; Powell, Koput and Smith-Doerr, 1996), the capacity to implement and use new technology (Cardinal, 2001; Dodgson, 2000; Hargadon and Sutton, 1997; Tushman and Nelson, 1990), the role of managerial control (Feldman, 1989), organization size (Damanpour, 1992; Romano, 1990), slack (Nohria and Gulati, 1996), the ability to interrelate heedfully in work team (Dougherty and Takacs, 2004), and the influence of managers' cognition, identities and conceptualization of innovation (Greve, 2003; Salaman and Storey, 2002; Harrison and Laberge, 2002; Greve and Taylor, 2000; Scott and Bruce, 1994). Different contributors suggest that innovation is an outcome from a superior ability to combine existing resources (Galunic and Rodan, 1998; Hargadon, 1998), the establishment of a culture that supports experimenting and innovative thinking (Thomke, 2001; Kamoche and Pina e Cunha, 2001), or the capacity to manage expert knowledge (Blackler, Crump and McDonald, 1999). Some researchers have claimed that innovation is of necessity at least partially chaotic (Cheng and Van de Ven, 1996) or challenge predominant beliefs and institutions (Dougherty and Heller, 1994) and therefore large organizations are poorly equipped for managing innovation work (Dougherty and Hardy, 1996). Others have stressed that innovation is co-dependent with the institutional milieu in which the firm is located (Hargadon and Douglas, 2001; Whitley, 2000). Furthermore, Argyres and Silverman (2004) show that organization structures determine innovation. In firms with a central R&D function, innovations were more general and of the "basic research type" while in firms with divisionalized R&D functions, innovation work was more focused on applications: "We find that firms with centralized R&D organization structure (i.e., corporate-level R&D labs only) and centralized R&D budget authority (i.e., funds coming from corporate headquarters) generate innovations that are significantly different along several dimensions from those generated by firms with decentralized R&D organizations", Argyres and Silverman (2004: 930) conclude.

For the sake of clarity, in this book the definition of innovation formulated by Andrew Van de Ven (1986: 591) will be adhered to. Here innovation is conceived of as "[t]he development and implementation of new ideas by people who over time engage in transactions with others in an institutional context". This is a broad and general definition but it captures the long-term commitment to a specific practice or objective. In addition, Van de Ven (1986: 591) speaks of innovation as a *combination of ideas*: "An innovation is a new *idea*, which may be a recombination of old ideas, a scheme that challenges the present order, a formula, or a unique approach which is perceived as new by the individuals involved". Van de Ven points at the managerial consequences of innovation work: "From a managerial viewpoint, to understand the process of innovation is to understand the factors that facilitate and inhibit the development of innovations. These factors include ideas, people, transactions, and context over time" (Van de Ven, 1986: 591). Needless to say, Van de Ven's definition is accompanied by a number of different definitions and perspectives on innovation. Damanpour (1992: 376) defines innovation rather loosely as "[t]he adoption of an idea or behaviour, whether a system, policy, program, device, process, product or service, that is new to the adopting organization". Dougherty and Hardy (1996: 1121) talk about "sustained product innovation": "We define sustained product innovation as the generation of multiple new products, as strategically necessary over time, with a reasonable rate of commercial success". This definition is of interest because it points at the commercial effects as being an integral component of innovation. Harrison and Laberge (2002: 498) emphasize the distinction between technological and social innovations: "Studies of innovation generally distinguish between technological resources and social innovation. Technological innovation is often the result of a deliberate creation or invention while social innovation most often consists in the codification of a specific type of interaction". Hellström (2004) criticizes what he calls "naively functionalist process frameworks of innovation" for portraying innovation work as a linear process aimed at producing some artefact as its principal outcome. Instead, Hellström (2004) suggests that innovation is to be conceived of as a form of "social action":

> The key lesson from this analysis should be that, whereas in common usage innovation may exist *qua* artefactual representation, in the context of social action the actual thing could never be understood as having 'a life of its own'. Rather, reification should be conceived of as a parallel movement of continuous physical representation that acts eventually to reinforce the innovating actor in a Parsonian norm structure, as well as creatively set the foundations for practical consciousness. (Hellström, 2004: 644)

Innovations are then not solely a matter of producing artefacts but prior to that, the ability to integrate a number of relevant actors and make them engage in social activities is of central importance for any innovation process. In the perhaps largest integrated innovation research program, The Minnesota Innovation Research Program directed by University of Minnesota in the 1980s (Van de Ven, Angle and Poole, 2000), the *process* of innovation was strongly emphasized. Van de Ven and Poole (2000) distinguish between *innovation* and *process of innovation*:

> A theory of innovation is fundamentally a theory of change in a social system. While *innovation* is defined as the introduction of a new idea, the *process of innovation* refers to the temporal sequence of events that occur as people interact with others to develop and implement their innovation ideas within an institutional context. *Events* are instances when changes occur in the innovation ideas, peoples, transactions, contexts, or outcomes while an innovation develops over time. *Change* is an empirical observation of differences in time on one and more dimensions of an entity. (Van de Ven and Poole, 2000: 32)

It is therefore important to integrate the broader organizational and institutional context into account when studying innovation work. In the same volume, Schroeder, Van de Ven, Scudder and Polley (2000) are critical of the functionalist orientation of much innovation research:

> [T]he innovation process has traditionally been viewed as a sequence of separable functional stages (such as design, production, and marketing) sequentially ordered in time and linked with transition routines to make adjustment between stages. These simple unitary stage-wise progression models are increasingly being discredited because of their lack of empirical validity or correctness. (Schroeder, Van de Ven, Scudder and Polley, 2000: 113)

They continue: "The tendencies to reduce complex innovation processes to simply unitary stages and their lack of empirical substantiation suggest that many of the process models in the literature are suspect of simply inadequate (Schroeder, Van de Ven, Scudder and Polley, 2000: 113). Hung (2004) is formulating a similar critique of the innovation literature and suggests that most models of innovation are either voluntaristic or deterministic in their design. As opposed to these two positions, Hung (2004) advocated a path-dependency model called a *technology path* mediating the actor-structure problem inherent to all innovation activities. Hung writes:

> The power to innovate ... derives not so much from individual actors, but from their identification with, and appropriation of, the structural context. These distinctive notions in characterizing the structure are particularly identified: 'regime' as a knowledge base; 'paradigm' which embodies a model and a pattern of enquiry; and 'tradition', which is cognitively based. The spread of regime, paradigm or tradition comes partly through the emergence of dominant designs and partly through the prevalence of technological guideposts. (Hung, 2004: 1481–1482)

However, the success of a particular innovation is not solely a matter of activities and the deployment of resources internal to the firm (see e.g., Powell, Koput and Smith-Doerr, 1996: 118). Innovations need to be favourably received by external stakeholder such as investors and customers in order to become viable. Therefore, Hargadon and Douglas (2001: 476) speak of the "cultural determinants" of innovation: "One cultural determinant of an innovation's value is how well the public, as both individuals and organizations comprehends what the new idea is and how to respond to it". Other researchers reject the dominant image of the innovation process as a voluntaristic, purposeful and consciously managed process and conceives of innovation work as a distributed, haphazard, and non-linear event. For instance, the sociological view of innovation advocated by Akrich, Callon and Latour (2002a) stresses the heterogeneity of innovation: "An innovation in the making reveals a multiplicity of heterogeneous and often confused decisions made by a large number of different and often conflicting groups, decisions which one is unable to decide a priori as to whether they will be crucial or not" (Akrich, Callon and Latour, 2002a: 191). Innovation is here not simply located in certain departments but ideas may evolve from all kinds of settings. In addition, the innovator needs to be able to mobilize a variety of stakeholders to make an innovation become a final product launched in the market. They exemplify with the perhaps most emblematic figure in innovation, Thomas Alva Edison: "Edison is everything but a handyman of genius. He is an organizer, an entrepreneur, a strategist, a researcher, a public relations man and if there is any genius, it is in this ability to pass from one role to the another and to play each of them with equal delight, that it must be situated" (Akrich, Callon and Latour, 2002b: 215. See also Hargadon and Douglas, 2001; Gitelman, 1999). Akrich, Callon and Latour (2002a) thus speak of the importance of mobilizing interested and influential individuals or groups of individuals that support the new innovation (see also Harrison and Laberge, 2002; Latour, 1996; Bijker, 1995):

> Since the outcome of a project depends on the alliances which it allows for and the interests which it mobilises, no criteria, no algorithm, can ensure success a priori. Rather than to speak of the rationality of decisions, we need to speak of the aggregation of interests which decisions are capable or incapable of producing. Innovation is the art of interesting an increasing number of allies who will make you stronger and stronger. (Akrich, Callon and Latour, 2002a: 205)

Innovation is then not solely a matter of effectively integrating intellectual and technical skills, competencies and experiences but equally a matter of making the specific innovation become a desirable object for investment, an object that heterogeneous groups can collectively collaborate around. Subramaniam and Youndt show in their quantitative study of innovative capabilities that social capital, operationalized as "[t]he knowledge embedded within, available through, and utilized by interactions among individuals and their networks of interrelationships" (2005: 451), was the strongest determinant for innovation. Somewhat surprisingly, Subramaniam and Youndt (2005) found that human capital, defined as "[t]he knowledge, skills, and abilities residing within and utilized by individuals" was *negatively* related to innovative capabilities. Subramaniam and Youndt (2005: 459) draw their conclusions:

> To effectively leverage investments in human capital, it may be imperative for organizations to invest in the development of social capital to provide the necessary conduits for their core knowledge workers to network and share their expertise. Organizations that neglect the social side of individual skills and inputs and do not create synergies between their human and social capital are unlikely to realize the potential of their employees to enhance organizational innovative capabilities.

A similar argument is made by Nahapiet and Ghosal (1998: 260) saying that "we see the roots of intellectual capital deeply embedded in social relations and in the structure of these relations. Such a view contrasts strongly with the relatively individualistic and acontextual perspectives that characterize more transactional approaches for explaining the existence and contributions of firms".

In everyday life in innovating organizations, there is rarely too *little* innovation; on the contrary, managers and project leaders have to made decisions all the time regarding what innovations to prioritize. Knorr Cetina (1981: 60) writes: "Generally speaking, the interest of an 'innovative idea' is not that it is new, but that it is *old*—in the sense that it draws on available knowledge as a source for producing knowledge". Innovations are then rarely, if ever, as the romantic image suggests, a bolt from out of the blue but are rather ideas that are forged together with other ideas, material resources, laboratory practices, and so forth, into assemblages that may qualify as innovations under favourable conditions.[4] The "aggregation of interests" is one of the central functions herein because it provides the social embeddedness the innovation demands to become viable (Latour, 1995).

In addition to the notion of innovation, the notion of *new product development* will be employed in the book (see e.g., Lindkvist, Söderlund and Tell, 1998). The definition of Sheremata (2000: 392) points at the major traits of new product development: "New product development includes all activities needed to conceive, design, produce, and deliver a product to market. It is a specific type of innovation, defined here as the commercialization of invention, where invention is an act of insight". To distinguish the two terms one may say that innovation is the activities prior to commercialization, while new product development is the commodification of an innovation.

In summary, innovation work contains intellectual, technical, and social components and has cognitive as well as emotional consequences. Innovation is then never strictly a matter for engineers and scientists but engages a broader set of functions within as well as outside of the organization. Since innovation today, at least in the pharmaceutical industry, is largely a matter of communicating and collaborating across functions, departments, expertise groups, and company boundaries, innovation processes are never solely located in one place but is always the outcome from collaborations between various organizational units or departments. Such collaborations increasingly demand large-scale operations and the integration of a number of functions. Therefore, the bureaucratic organization form is a fruitful domain for innovation work.

Innovation in large organizations

In the vocabulary of March (1991) and followers of March's framework (e.g., Holmqvist, 2004; Gupta, Smith and Shalley, 2006), large firms need to be capable of simultaneously exploiting existing knowledge bases and exploring new domains. In practice, research suggests, this is complicated for large firms (Sharma, 1999). In their study of 15 large firms, Dougherty and Hardy (1996: 1121) found poor capacities for sustained product innovation: "We found that most of these firms were not organized to facilitate innovation: occasionally innovation did occur, but it occurred in spite of the system, not because of it". In general, large, bureaucratic firms are regarded poor performers in terms of innovation work. A similar argument is out forth by Collinson and Wilson (2006), discussing Japanese industry. In Blau and McKinley's (1979) study of innovation—operationalized as the number of awards received by the firm—in 152 architecture firms, it was found that differentiation of tasks where negatively correlated with innovativeness:

> At least in architectural firms, a high degree of differentiation does not have the beneficial consequences for innovation that it has in other types of organizations. This implies that excessive subdivision of tasks and responsibilities reduce the flexibility and openness that are required for highly creative work. Moreover, social integration may be impaired by excessive differentiation. In architectural firms working relations must be so close that suggestions can be readily filtered through diverse channels and consultation networks easily maintained. If excessive differentiation impedes such close relations, contributions become fractionated, making it difficult to implement an integrated design. In short, organizations that create original products may require integration through personal contact; in these organizations, structural differentiation, by adversely affecting integration, is detrimental to innovation and creativity. (Blau and McKinley, 1979: 212)

Moreover, Blau and McKinley (1979: 214) report that a close match between the organization and its environment did not guarantee any significant improvement terms of the number of innovations: "Our data show that there is little relationship between the complexity of the environment and that of the organization regardless of how innovative the firm and that a better match between environmental and organizational complexity is not more likely in successful firms". In general, Blau and McKinley (1979) conclude that firms that standardize their activities and work procedures are less likely to establish an innovative milieu:

> Firms with routine production emphasizes satisfying a relatively uniform market demand, and principals, in an effort to maximize

profit and reduce risks, may seek to standardize further, for example by promulgating criteria for a widely accepted style ... But award-winning firms stress maximizing efficiency and profit less than they do turning out unique, aesthetically or technically notable projects. These firms rarely standardize design concepts from project to project, and attempt to continually to evolve new and creative solutions to particular problems. In this 'uniform' situation, it is necessary to look beyond an individual building project to find a stable set of values in which a permanent means-ends hierarchy and a continuously organized structure can be anchored. (Blau and McKinley, 1979: 216–217)

In a similar vein, Hlavacek and Thompson (1973: 371) predicted that large organizations would develop new organization forms to promote innovative work procedures: "In conclusion, it appears that firms in complex, rapidly-changing technology fields, where expenditures on research are relatively high, are beginning to experiment with new, non-bureaucratic forms of organization to manage the problem of new product innovation". Speaking in terms of the bureaucratic organization form, Dougherty and Hardy (1996), Blau and McKinley (1979), and Hlavacek and Thompson (1973) suggest that large, functionally organized firms are less capable of innovating and have poorer skills in organizing innovative work. As opposed to this view, Damanpour (1992: 389) found "[a] positive and statistically significant relationship between size and innovation". In other words, large firms demonstrate a more significant capacity to innovate than small and medium sized firms. Damanpour suggests that this may be related to the actual size of innovative departments within large firms:

A survey of 4,000 innovations and innovative firms in the U.K. over four decades has shown that the average size of innovative firms is increasing, but the average size of divisions within those firms is decreasing (Pavitt *et al.*, 1989). Therefore, it appears that large innovative organizations are creating the required flexibility and autonomy needed for innovation by founding smaller (more specialized) divisions, while maintaining the advantages associated with large size. (Damanpour, 1992: 395)

This proposition is also supported by the research of Nohria and Gulati (1996) suggesting that there is an inversed U relationship between slack and innovation; organization with little or no slack and organizations with excessive resources are poorer performers in terms of innovation than firms that have a reasonable amount of slack (see also Feldman, 1989 on control vs. autonomy in innovation work). Since the organization's size probably influences the amount of slack, it may be that large firms effectively organizing smaller units are better equipped to successfully manage innovative work.

In addition to the parameter of size, innovation is also strongly affected by mergers and acquisitions of the focal firm. Consequently, it is important to take into account the effects of such major organization changes. Hitt, Hoskisson, Johnson and Moesel (1996) found in their analysis of Compustat company statistics that firms that underwent a merger or an acquisition displayed a lower degree of innovation: "These results strongly suggests that firms actively buying or selling businesses, or both, are likely to produce less internal innovation and rely more heavily on external innovation for a variety of reasons, including the structure and implementation of the internal control system derived from their strategic actions" (Hitt, Hoskisson, Johnson and Moesel, 1996: 1110). They continue:

> Our results suggest that an active acquisition strategy has direct, negative effects on the internal development of firm innovation. This effect is likely due to the transaction costs involved and to acquisition-related activities that absorb managers' time and energy. Because of these transaction costs, managers have little time left to manage other important projects, and target firm managers in particular become strongly risk averse. Thus, managers of acquiring and target firms may postpone major decisions regarding long-term investments such as R&D and thereby reduce the innovative capabilities of their firms. (Hitt, Hoskisson, Johnson and Moesel, 1996: 1110)

It is therefore not only the organization form and size as such that influence the capacity to innovate. Also strategic objectives such as mergers and acquisitions have a decisive influence on the innovative capacities of the firm.

Summary and conclusion

Knowledge is portrayed as the perhaps single most important production factor in the contemporary society. This is equally true for individuals, work teams, departments, companies, industries, regions and nations; knowledge is, to draw on Bateson's (1972: 381) definition of information, a "difference which makes a difference". The main challenge for today's firms is to develop, manage, and exploit sources of knowledge internal and external to the firm. One principal "context of application" (Reichenbach, 1938) is innovation work. Since both the literature on knowledge management and innovation is extensive and include many different theoretical orientations, methodological approaches, and epistemological positions, it is complicated to articulate what Rorty (1989) calls "a final vocabulary" on the management of knowledge in innovation work. Therefore, there is no "one best way" of managing and controlling knowledge work and innovation work. Instead, a series of contingencies and local conditions need to taken into account. To complicate things further, the type of innovation examined in this book is based on scientific expertise. Scientific disciplines are assemblages comprising theoretical, technological, ideological and practical resources, capabilities, and artefacts and are in many cases not possible to fully monitor and control through conventional managerial methods and techniques. In the next chapter, the concept of science-based innovation will be examined in greater detail.

3
What Do Scientists Do?: Components of Scientific Work

Introduction

The perhaps most spectacular achievement of modernity is techno-science, the totality of the heterogeneous social, material and symbolic resources engaged in the exploration of natural, social or cultural systems. The concept of technoscience is a complex one, first coined by Jean-François Lyotard (1984) and later used by actor-network theorists like Bruno Latour to grasp the technological constitution of contemporary science. Today, scientific work in disciplines such as physics, biology and chemistry is inconceivable without modern technology. Hence, the neologism technoscience. Even though technoscience is one of the most complicated and complex human endeavours, highly structured around standard operating procedures, regimes of control and evaluation, scientific ideologies, and the influence of advanced technology, technoscience remains what is primarily a standardized methodology or approach to the investigation of (in our case) natural (and more specifically, biological systems) systems. Schopenhauer (1995: 101) declares: "What distinguishes science from ordinary knowledge is merely the form, the systematic, the facilitation of knowledge by the inclusion of all particulars in the universal (by means of the subordination of concepts) and the completeness of knowledge gained this way". A few decades later, Max Weber (1948) emphasized its systematic approaches as the principal characteristic of scientific activities. As a consequence, the scientists have to accept a few conditions serving to delimit the authority of scientists. Rabinow (2003), commenting on Weber's argument, writes:

> Science is not wisdom, science is specialized knowledge. A number of important consequences follow from this situation. First, 'scientific work is chained to the course of progress'. All scientists know

that, by definition and in part of their own efforts, their work is destined to be outdated. Every scientific achievement opens up new questions. One might say that a successful scientist can only hope that his or her work will be productively and fruitfully outmoded rather than merely forgotten. Second, the knowledge worker must live with the realization that not only are the specialized advances the only ones possible but that even small accretions require massive dedication to produce. Dedication or enthusiasm alone, however, are not sufficient to produce good science, nor does hard work guarantee success ... The calling for science thus must include a sense of passionate commitment, combined with methodical labor and a kind of almost mystical passivity or openness. The scientific self must be resolutely willful and persistent, yet permeable. Androgynous, if you will. (Rabinow, 2003: 99)

The insistence on small contributions and the inevitable progress of the sciences are predicaments all scientists have to endure. They also have to be aware that even though scientists are dealing with the ultimate matters of being and its constitution on various levels (e.g., the physical level of elementary particles, the biochemical level of molecules and proteins, and the biological level of phenotypes), their contribution will always be evaluated peers in a social context. Science, therefore, has to simultaneously transcend and draw on social conditions; science moves one step beyond the social but return to it to gain legitimacy.

Since the evaluation of scientific results is embedded in the cognitive and perceptual capabilities of the researchers, the credible scientists of a particular field and discipline, all scientific results, no matter how accomplished and finished they may appear, are of necessity provisional and (to use Popper's, 1959, term) corroborated, rendered true "for the time being" and until new evidence emerges. Research is not primarily based on metaphysical necessities but always implies a *choice* on the part of the researcher of what theoretical system he or she pledge allegiance to. Cilliers (2005: 25), speaking of complexity theory, writes: "There is no stepping outside of complexity (we are finite beings), thus there is no framework for frameworks. We *choose* our frameworks. This choice needs not be arbitrary in any way, but it means that the status of the framework (and the framework itself) will have to be continually revised. Our knowledge of complex systems is always provisional. We have to be modest about all claims we make about such knowledge". Ludwik Fleck (1979) speaks of communities of "witnesses" as a "thought collective" demonstrating an adherence to a particular "thought style" (German, *Denkstile*).

In summary, then, scientific ideologies prescribe detailed rules for how to distinguish science from non-science and quasi-science (Canguilhem, 1988), assuming that science would be possible to conceive of as a thing on its own, removed from all-too-human faculties and interests. In practice, in the day-to-day operations in laboratories and scientific milieus, scientific work is a more complicated matter than the outsider may suggest. In the daily practices, machinery, technology, "specimens of nature" of reproduced or simulated natural environments, theoretical frameworks, and human perceptual and analytical skills are brought together into a functional unit that in many cases are complicated to fully understand for the outsider. The main point is that no matter how much the formal scientific rhetoric emphasizes the "extra-social" qualities of scientific endeavours, it remains what is conducted by humans and is therefore open for interpretations, negotiations and controversy.

In this chapter, science-based innovation will be examined in greater detail. While the last chapter emphasized organizations and firms as knowledge-based systems capable of managing innovation work, this chapter will show under what conditions science-based innovation is operating. The perspective on scientific work is heavily indebted to the social studies of science and technology research tradition and the actor-network literature, in many respect an outgrowth from the first tradition of science studies. Rather than assuming that science is operating in accordance with formal rhetoric and textbook presentations, scientific work is regarded a social practice including a variety of theoretical, technological, and emotional inconsistencies, ambiguities and concerns that are not possible to anticipate or account for in formal documents. Laboratory life is not a seamless web of inherently rational and optimal solutions to scientific problems but is instead an everyday work life engagement to bring order in what is heterogeneous and complex and to achieve legitimacy for such an imposed order among peers and authorities in the field. In this chapter, we therefore move from the level of the *conceptual* elaborations in the knowledge management and innovation management literature to the level of *practice* constituted by an interrelated series of resources, assets, capabilities, experiences, skills and know-how.

The emergence of modern science: sense-perception, thought experiments, and modest witnessing

The emergence of modern science is following a trajectory including many controversies, conflicts and debates. Ideas that today have become part of common sense thinking may have been originally formulated as most daring hypotheses by creative thinkers. Alexandre Koyré (1968), talking about the emergence of modern science as a "Galilean and Cartesian revolution", writes: "Modern science did not spring perfect and complete, as Athena from the head of Zeus, from the minds of Galileo and Descartes. On the contrary, the Galilean and Cartesian revolution—which remains, nevertheless, a revolution—had been prepared by a strenuous effort of thought" (Koyré, 1968: 1). For Koyré, Galilei and Descartes's decisive contributions to modern science lie in their ability to overcome the predominant doctrine of their times, that of Aristotelian physics. De Landa (1992: 129) points at the importance of breaking with such doctrines and emphasizes the immediate limitations for scientific practice that doctrines erect: "Unlike the Chinese astronomers, who had been able to observe the occurrence of sunspots centuries before Galileo simply because their cosmological beliefs did not preclude celestial change, early Western astronomers were unable to 'see' changes in the cosmos. Sunspots, for example, remained 'invisible'—that is, insignificant and anomalous—until Copernicus's idea changed the ways in which European astronomers could look at the heavens". What plays a central role here is the notion of "sense-perception". Koyré (1968) writes:

> Aristotelian physics is based on sense-perception, and is therefore decidedly non-mathematical. It refuses to substitute mathematical abstraction for the colourful, qualitatively determined facts of common experience, and it denies the very possibility of a mathematical physics on the ground (*a*) of the nonconformity of mathematical concepts to the data of sense-experience, (*b*) of the inability of mathematics to explain quality and to deduce movement. There is no quality, and no motion, in the timeless realm of figures and number. (Koyré, 1968: 5)

For Aristotelians, the motion of a body—the problem that preoccupied Galilei and eventually was formulated in his law of inertia stating that a body, left to itself, remains in its state of rest or in motion as long as it is not interfered with by some external force—implied a "change" in the body, a process of "actualization" or "decay" (Koyré, 1968: 5). Butterfield (1962) explains the Aristotelian position:

> On the Aristotelian theory all heavy terrestrial bodies had a natural motion towards the centre of the universe, which for medieval

thinkers was at or near the centre of the earth; but motion in any other direction was violent motion, because it contradicted the ordinary tendency of a body to move to what was regarded as its natural place. Such motion depended on the motion of a mover, and the Aristotelian doctrine of inertia was a doctrine of rest—it was motion, not rest, that always required to be explained. (Butterfield, 1962: 3)

Among other things, this doctrine produced a set of what Thomas S. Kuhn would call *anomalies*—events observed that could not be fully explained by the dominant theory. One such anomaly was *acceleration*; in Aristotelian doctrine, a constant force produced constant motion; thus accelerating bodies observed could not be explained (Butterfield, 1962: 6). Galilei's physics, today celebrated as a major contribution to scientific thinking, is thus formulated in opposition with the authorities of his days: "Galileo is well aware of the tremendous difficulty of his task. He knows perfectly well that he has to deal with powerful enemies: authority, tradition, and effort—worst of them all—common sense. It is useless to present proof to minds not able to grasp their value", Koyré (1968: 12) argues. Butterfield adds:

It was supremely difficult to escape from the Aristotelian doctrine by merely observing things more closely, especially if you had already started off on the wrong foot and were hampered beforehand with the whole system of interlocking Aristotelian ideas. In fact, the modern law of inertia is not the thing you would discover by mere photographic methods of observation—it required a different kind of thinking-cap, a transposition in the mind of the scientist himself. (Butterfield, 1962: 4–5)

For us moderns, accustomed to the empirical sciences, it is complicated to see the full scope of Galilei's proposals since the very idea of science and truth had fundamentally different connotations in medieval times. Alexander (2002) describes how scientific authority was accomplished in scholastic thinking:

Traditionally, true knowledge was based on the interpretation of a canon of ancient texts, which included scripture and the corpus of the ancient philosophers and church fathers. The underlying assumption was that all relevant knowledge was already in existence and was contained within prescribed canon. The search for truth, therefore, consisted of the proper application of the wisdom contained within the bounds of these volumes to the problem at hand. If, as was often the case, the canonical texts were in conflict with each other, the difficulties would be resolved through the scholastic practice of disputation. Truth, in other words, was arrived at not through new discoveries but through hermeneutics—the detailed interpretation of authoritative texts. (Alexander, 2002: 99)

Galilei's genius lies in his emphasis on what the Austrian physicist Ernst Mach would later call "thought experiments" (German, *Gedankenexperimente*) (Koyré, 1968: 45), a "physics *a priori*" not primarily relying on experiments but on careful thinking. For Galilei, "experiment is useless because before any experiment we are already in possession of the knowledge we are seeking for" (Koyré, 1968: 12). Such a downgrading of experimentation and sense-perception (Mandelbaum, 1984, 1964) was no less than a provocation for Galilei's contemporary Aristotelian scholars. In addition to the emphasis on "thought experiments", Galilei made use of mathematics (and more specifically geometry) to formulate his theses in an exact language. Galilei's well-known statement that "the book of nature is written in mathematical characters" (expressed in his *Il Saggiatore, The Assayer*) is a Platonist declaration. Koyré points at the differences between a Platonist and Aristotelian epistemology:

If you claim for mathematics a superior status, if more than you attribute to it a real value and a commanding position in physics, you are a Platonist. If on the contrary you see in mathematics an abstract science, which is therefore of lesser value than those—physics and metaphysics—which deal with real being; if in particular you pretend that physics needs no other basis than experience and must be built directly on perception, that mathematics has to content itself with the secondary and subsidiary role of a mere auxiliary, you are an Aristotelian. (Koyré, 1968: 36–37)

For the Aristotelian, a physicist should investigate "real things", while the geometer "reasons about abstractions" (Koyré, 1968: 28). Therefore, one must not, Aristotelians claimed, mingle physics and geometry. The importance of the recognition of mathematics cannot be overrated. "Without the achievement of the mathematicians the scientific revolution, as we know it, would have been impossible", Butterfield (1962: 89) contends. For astronomers like Johannes Kepler, himself an excellent mathematician, mathematics was the regime of signs wherein God reveals himself to man; here mathematics takes on an almost mystical meaning (Hallyn, 1990):

> God signifies and communicated to man through nature. Consequently, the practice of astronomy becomes a means of following the contemplative path that leads man to God ... Understanding the world is ultimately to find the Meaning and the Author in signs. The calculations with which the astronomer discovers his laws or supports his hypotheses contribute to making man more God-like: For the resemblance between man and God is as much a task as a fact. We construct the resemblance by constructing internally the laws that govern Creation. (Hallyn, 1990: 173)

Therefore, Galilei's Platonist standpoint caused a series of challenges for his scientific project. Koyré writes:

> They [Galilei, Descartes, and other followers of modern science] had to destroy one world and to replace it by one another. They had to reshape the framework of our intellect itself, to restate and to reform its concepts, to evolve a new approach to Being, a new concept of knowledge, a new concept of science—and even to replace a pretty natural approach, that of common sense, by another which is not natural at all. (Koyré, 1968: 21)

There were thus a number of implications from the scientific projects formulated by Galilei. For the first, the Aristotelian doctrine dominating Western thinking since the medieval times had to be confronted. Its emphasis on experiments and its denial of mathematical expression were substituted for "thought experiments" and geometry. This does not suggest that Galilei was hostile towards experimentation as such. Not so. Galilei conducted a great number of experiments, but he was also aware of their limitations. "Real experiments", Koyré (1968: 45) says, "are often very difficult to carry out; and just as often involve complicated and expensive equipment. Furthermore, they are necessarily attended by a certain lack of precision, and so by a certain element of doubt". He continues:

> Perfection is not of this world: no doubt we can approach it, but we cannot attain it. Between empirical facts and theoretical concept there remains, and will always remain, a gap that cannot be bridged. That is where imagination appears on the scene. It cheerfully closes

the gap. It is not embarrassed by the limitations imposed on us by reality. It achieves the ideal and even the impossible. It operates by means of theoretical perfect concepts, and these are the very concepts that are brought into play by the imaginary experiments. (Koyré, 1968: 45)

With Galilei (and Descartes, Kepler, Leibniz, Newton and a few more major thinkers), modern science is born as a theoretical enterprise supported by advanced mathematics. It is also a scientific doctrine devoid of deities and spirits which in turn paves the way for modern science and its material and mechanistic *Weltanschauung*: "The modern law of inertia, the modern theory of motion, is the great factor which in the seventeenth century helped to drive the spirits out of the world and opened the way to an universe that ran like a piece of clockwork" (Butterfield, 1962: 7). Modern science must always think outside of the theoretical systems erected by authorities such as Aristotle and seek new ways for thinking. Physics is for Galilei "made *a priori*" and therefore, Koyré (1968: 17) says, modern science is "created and developed neither by engineers nor technicians, but by theorists and philosophers".

The first step towards modern science taken by Galilei and Descartes, emphasizing abstract thinking and geometry as a system of representation was later complemented by an increased emphasis on experiments and what Robert Boyle called "modest witnessing". Shapin (1994) speaks of scientific procedures as the outcome from a particular gentlemanly culture of the English social elites of the seventeenth century, relying on mutual trust and what was in general regarded as civic behaviours of the gentlemen given their prerogative to pursue scientific interests. Today, the institution of trust is not very legitimate in scientific discourses, because trust is regarded as what is in essence "unscientific". Shapin (1994: 16) writes: "[m]uch modern epistemology has systematically argued that legitimate knowledge is defined precisely by its rejection of trust. If we are heard to say that we know something on the basis of trust, we are understood to say that we do not possess genuine knowledge at all. It is unwise to take the world on trust". "Trust and authority stand against the very idea of science", Shapin concludes (1994: 16). In the early modern period, trust did however play a pivotal role in the establishment of scientific procedures. The new regime advocated by empirical researchers like the Irish aristocrat Robert Boyle emphasized "sense-experiences" at the expense of authority. Shapin argues: "The rejection of authority and testimony in favour of individual sense-experience is just what stands behind our recognition of seventeenth-century practitioners as 'moderns', as 'like us', and, indeed, as producers of the thing we can warrant as science" (Shapin, 1994: 201). Such "sense-experiences" were however not randomly collected but where accounted for by a specific group of men, namely "honorable men" belonging to scientific association such as the Royal Society, and capable of transcending their own beliefs and preferences for the greater good. Women, generally regarded as having stronger "powers of imagination" but "weaker reasoning faculties" (Shapin, 1994: 88–89) were for instance excluded from this group. Shapin here speaks of the witnesses as "selfless selves": "Experimental truth ... was to be sought by selfless selves, seeking not celebrity or private advantage but the civic good. This was a conception of the gentlemanly civic actor thoroughly familiar from early modern ethical writing, and English scientific practitioners proposed to reconstitute the natural philosopher on just that civic model" (Shapin, 1994: 124). "Sense experience or perception" gradually became part of regular scientific procedures. Francis Bacon argued for instance in *Novum organum* (1620) that "nature should be interpreted through the senses, aided by experiments 'fit and apposite'" (Hackman, 1989: 35). This emphasis on collective witnessing and reliance on "sense-experience" is today instituted in all scientific procedures. For instance, Haraway (2000: 160) argues: "[S]cientific knowledge *is* about witnessing. That is what the experimental method is about, the fact of being there".

The roots of modern science is, of course, to be found among the Greeks (Schrödinger, 1954; Whitehead, 1967), but modern science, made operational as a set of a scientific procedures and a number of various institutions and mechanisms for the control and monitoring of scientific work, is demonstrating a trajectory that includes a few giant leaps and a great many small steps. What is characteristic of modern science is the emphasis on what Ian Hacking (1983) calls "representing and intervening", the combination of the formulation of theoretical frameworks and conceptual elaborations and the use of experiments and other forms of interventions into natural or social systems. To simplify a most complicated matter, one may say that eminent theorists such as Galilei and Descartes emphasized new modes of representation (i.e., mathematical expressions), breaking with the Aristotelian doctrine of taxonomies, and an empiricist like Robert Boyle contributed to methodologies for more systematic interventions.

The development of disciplines

While various forms of scientific speculations and experimentation have taken place since the birth of human civilization, it is the renaissance and the scientific revolution in the sixteenth and seventeenth centuries that mark the beginning of modern science. However, since much scientific work remained the prerogative of wealthy amateurs and a smaller number of professional scientists employed by the European courts, it is not until the nineteenth century that the core of the natural sciences (physics, chemistry, mathematics, and the emerging discipline of biology) are attaining their modern forms. For instance, Harman (1982) examines the period 1800–1850 as the period wherein physics was transformed into a mathematical science. Harman emphasizes four significant individual contributions during the period:

1. P.S. de Laplace and his followers formulated a mathematical theory of interpraticulate forces, to be applied to mechanical as well as to thermal and optical phenomena.
2. The publication of Joseph Fourier's mathematical theory of heat in 1822 brought the study of heat within the framework of mathematical analysis previously applied only to mechanical problems.
3. A.J. Fresnel's wave theory of light, which supposed that light was propagated by the vibrations of a mechanical ether, brought optics within the framework of the mechanical view of nature.
4. The formulation of the law of the conservation of energy in the 1840s stressed the unity of physics, subsuming the phenomena of heat, light, electricity, and magnetism within the framework of mechanical principles. (Harman, 1982: 2–3)

Similar to Butterfield (1962), Harman (1982) also emphasizes the new applications of mathematics as being a pivotal step towards "universal physics". Harman (1982: 13) writes: "The separation of analysis from geometry in the eighteenth century led to the development of flexible methods for the mathematical expression of physical quantities. Mathematical symbols were stripped of their geometrical foundations and employed directly to represent physical quantities, a procedure that enabled complex physical concepts to be represented mathematically". During the next hundred years, the combination of advanced mathematics and physics produced some of the most astonishing scientific theories.

In the case of chemistry, a similar pattern of standardization could be observed. Arabic and Alexandrian chemistry established a detailed stock of know-how in the period of 800–1000 AD and alchemy was a major domain of investigation and expertise in the medieval and early modern period (Tomlinson, 1993), but until the eighteenth century there is no shared vocabulary or denotative system in use. Bensaude-Vincent and Stengers (1996: 46) point out the difficulties when reading an eighteenth century chemistry book:

> One becomes lost, without landmarks, in a jungle of exotic and obscure terminology. Some products were named after their inventor (Glauber's salt, Libavius's liquor), others after their origin (Roman vitriol, Hungarian vitriol), others after their medicinal effects, and yet others after their method of preparation (flower of sulfur, obtained by condensing vapor, precipitate of sulfur, spirit or oil of vitriol, depending on whether the acid was more or less concentrated). On every page: what is he talking about? What substance is he describing? (Bensaude-Vincent and Stengers, 1996: 46)

In Germany and Sweden, chemistry found its early applications in the mining industry. Elsewhere, "it was more a science of amateurs—of experimental demonstrations in salons or public and private courses—than a university discipline" (Bensaude-Vincent and Stengers, 1996: 64). Chemistry was still the first discipline to form international association; the first international scientific conference was held in Karlruhe in Germany in 1860 by an association of chemists. From the middle of the eighteenth century, a number of "simple bodies" (chemical elements)[5] were quickly identified and they grew quick in number: "The table Lavoisier made in 1789 contained 33 simple substances (i.e., elements). In 1834 Thénard named 54 simple bodies in his textbook, and in 1869 Dmitri Mendeleev counted 70" (Bensaude-Vincent and Stengers, 1996: 111). In addition, an "arsenal of laws" (Bensaude-Vincent and Stengers, 1996: 119) was formulated in the discipline.

A specific branch of chemistry that would later prove to be of great importance was what was named *Zymotechnology*, a name coined by Prussian court physicist Georg Ernst Stahl (1659–1734)—one of the two frequently named "fathers of chemistry" beside Lavoisier—in his *Zymotechnia Fundamentalis* (1697). Zymotechnology (from the Greek word for "leaven") dealt with all sorts of "industrial fermentation", for instance the brewing of beers. Although zymotechnology may appear obscure a discipline, it is the foundation of what today is referred to as biotechnology. "Zymotechnology … constitutes a vital stage in bridging the gap between biotechnology's ancient heritage and its modernist associations", Bud (1983: 3) writes. In 1828, the German chemist Friedrich Wöhler managed to synthesize urea, thereby eroding the difference between natural and chemical products (Bud, 1983: 10). In modern biotechnology and pharmaceutical industry, such differences are no longer of any vital importance. Today, biotechnology is one of the most important industries and the one holding the greatest potential in the eyes of the public and investors.

In summary, the growth and institutionalization of modern science suggests that standardization and what Lynch (1988) calls mathematization are the two principal mechanisms for establishing clearly demarcated disciplinary boundaries and for sharing regimes of representation and vocabularies across communities, schools and nations. A standardized morphology of science is then not fallen from the sky but is the outcome from centuries of scientific practice and debate.

The morphology and components of scientific work

Science-based work is based on the integration of a number of resources. Robert Merton, representing a "sociology of science" perspective, addresses science in the following terms: "Science is a deceptively inclusive word which refers to a variety of distinct though interrelated items. It is commonly used to denote (1) a set of characteristic methods by means of which knowledge is certified; (2) a stock of accumulated knowledge stemming from the application of these methods; (3) a set of cultural values and morals governing the activities termed scientific; or (4) any combination of the foregoing" (Merton, 1973: 268). Science is thus always already an assemblage of heterogeneous resources, tied together by institutions, culture, values, and beliefs. More recently, Merton's sociology of science has been criticized for resting on "the cornerstones of realism, objectivity, disinterestedness, and autonomy" (Lenoir, 1997: 5), that is, for underrating the very constitution and maintenance of scientific communities. Lenoir (1997) uses Bourdieu's concept of field to examine science. In a field, agents need to possess and make use of various forms of symbolic and economic capital; "[T]he positions occupied by individuals in a specific disciplinary field ... depend upon the specific capital they can mobilize within the field" (Lenoir, 1997: 16). In this view, scientific communities are not given from the outset but must be explained per se prior to any engagement with their output, the scientific work. For Lenoir, then, scientific practice is a cultural practice "[i]mbricated in a seamless web with other forms of social political, even aesthetic practices" (Lenoir, 1997: 3). Jasanoff (2005) here uses the term co-production to underline the co-evolutionary dependencies between science (as forms of systematic

knowledge production) and society: "Knowledge and its material embodi-
ments are at once products of social work and constitutive of forms
of social life; society cannot function without knowledge any more
than knowledge can exist without appropriate social support. Scientific
knowledge, in particular, is not a transcendental mirror of reality. It
both embeds and is embedded in social practices, identities, norms,
conventions, discourses, instruments and institutions—in short, in all
the building blocks of what we term the social. The same can be said
even more forcefully of technology" (Jasanoff, 2005: 2–3). Seen in this
view, there is no proper inside and outside of science vis-à-vis society,
but science is intrinsically formed on basis of social objectives and
expectations. The co-productionist framework advocated by Jasanoff
(2005) is therefore a critique of realist epistemologies that "persistently
separates the domain of nature, facts, objectivity, reason and policy from
those of culture, values, subjectivity, emotions and politics" (Jasanoff,
2005: 3). Following the arguments of Lenoir (1997) and Jasanoff (2005),
one must refrain from portraying scientific work as what is capable of
holding a detached and isolated position vis-à-vis broader social interests. Instead, even the most mundane scientific procedures derive from
negotiations and collaborations between various and often heterogeneous interest; there is no science removed from and operating in
isolation from the broader social community.

Lynch (1993) introduces the useful term *epistopics*, "discursive terms"
that often are referred to in scientific and practical reasoning and that
are—to borrow a term from Lacan—the "anchoring points" (French,
points de caption) for scientific conversations and disputes. Such
epistopics include processes and terms such as "observation, description, replication, measurement, rationality, representation, and explanation" (Lynch, 1993: 299). Each such epistopics in turn embodies a
range of skills, purposes, texts, materials, routines, and modes of
agency that are employed in scientific procedures. The ethnomethodological study of scientific work that Lynch (1993) advocates aims at
revealing how these epistopics structure everyday research life. In the
following we will talk about scientific work as the integration of a
number of epistopics and resources that we here refer to as *conceptual
frameworks* (theories, theorems, images of the object of investigation,
and so forth), *material resources* (technologies, laboratory equipment,
etc.), *practices* evolving in the course of action, bringing the material
resources and conceptual scheme together into a functional unit, and
narratives, storytelling and *writing practices* representing the outcome
from the scientific process (Fujimura, 1995, 1992; Schaffer, 1996; Law,

1986). This model is embedded in the ideology of science, the collective beliefs and expectations of practising researchers. The integration of conceptual frameworks, material resources, and practices is serving to provide scientific "facts", that is, corroborated and jointly agreed upon statements about the empirical reality. Such facts are inextricably entangled with the use of oral and written narratives, both *en route*, in the very production of such facts, and when presenting facts to a broader community of scientists in scientific papers and texts. Scientific work is therefore a most complex and diverse field of activities operating to integrate ideological, material, cognitive, and storytelling resources and skills.

Intangible resources: conceptual schemes

Science is a *social* practice; it is based on the interactions of certain groups of individuals and the various resources at hand (Fuller, 2002; Fuchs, 1992; Fujimura, 1996; Merton, 1973; Reichenbach, 1938). Barnes, Bloor and Henry (1996: 28) explicate this idea: "The mind of the individual scientist is the point of contact between our physical environment and our social environment. Interpretations are where nature and culture meets". The world of the scientist is a fabricated reality aimed at providing a firm ground for systematic investigation: "The 'natural world' of the scientist is an artefact no less than the world of practical activity", Oakeshott (1991: 506) says. Fuchs (1992), speaking of science as "fact-making", argues: "Facticity is always a cultural artifact. Consequently, the interactions and negotiations between scientists are shown to resemble very closely the practices of accounting for reality studied by ethnomethodologists in mundane settings" (Fuchs, 1992: 4). As a consequence, science-based work is to be regarded as a form of making things fit together rather than aiming for some transcendental truths. Such a pragmatist view is advocated by Nelson Goodman (1978: 21): "Discovery often amounts, as when I place a piece in a jigsaw puzzle, not to arrival at a proposition for declaration or defence, but to finding a fit. Much of knowing aims at something other than true, or any, belief". This image of science is for Goodman a *pluralist view* or what Richard Rorty (1999: xxxii) calls an *antifoundationalist view*. Goodman continues: "The pluralist, far from being antiscientific, accepts the sciences at full value. His typical adversary is the monolithic materialist of physicalists who maintains that one system, physics, is preeminent and all-inclusive, such that every other version must eventually be reduced to it or rejected as false or meaningless" (Goodman, 1978: 4).

For Weber (1948), science provides the tools for making connection between different "pieces in the jigsaw puzzle" and must therefore be examined as such. One of the consequences is that scientific communities have developed a certain outlook on the world giving priority to "scientific rationalities" seeking value-neutral, law-regulated knowledge, often presented in the form of mathematical formulae or statistics. Nevertheless, this favoured rationality represents one particular form of rationality: "Scientific rationality is an extreme ideal type that has been constructed through centuries of discussions by philosophers and scientists implanted in researchers through education and socialization ... We seek scientific rationality because it pleases our minds, but what gives our minds please may not give us insight or useful knowledge", Starbuck (2004: 1239) remarks. One of the consequences of the scientific rationality is the denial of subjective influences on the research process; science is supposedly value-neutral and therefore there should be no trace of the researching subject in the "facts" provided by the systematic research. Stengers (1997) argues:

> All of the phenomena that we know of are overloaded with multiple meanings, capable of authorizing an indefinite multiplicity of readings and interpretations, that is, of being utilized as evidence in the most diverse situations, and thus also of being disqualified as evidence. The whole situation is thus, for the scientist, to produce testimony that cannot be disqualified by being attributed to his or her own 'subjectivity', to his biased reading, a testimony that others must accept, a testimony for which he or she will be recognized as a faithful representative and that will not betray him or her to the first colleague that come along. (Stengers, 1997: 86)

The ideology of science is therefore portraying scientific work as what is essentially detached from the subject of research, while at the same time being of great importance for society in a broader perspective. Whitehead (1978) here speaks of the *sensationalist principle* of science: "The sensationalist principle is, that the primary activity in the act of experience is the bare subjective entertainment of the datum, devoid of any subjective form of reception. This is the doctrine of *mere* sensation" (Whitehead, 1978: 157). This denial of subjectivity makes the ideology of science paradoxical in terms of being detached from the researcher in the first place while simultaneously being firmly embedded in legitimate social problems. Such paradoxes are part of what Bourdieu calls *illusio*, the necessary degree of self-denial or illusion that is needed for making society operate properly. The *illusio* of science is its denial of the subjective influence and the provisional and transient nature of scientific facts.

However, in practice such inconsistencies do not constitute any major concerns for the scientists because the distinction between subjective and objective is complicated to maintain. Instead, the boundaries between what is known and not known, what is real and what is conceptual, remain obscure in the early phases of a research program. Hans-Jörg Rheinberger (1998: 285) speaks of a move from a Kuhnian perspective on science as theory, emphasizing the discontinuity and relativity of science, to a "post-Kuhnian engagement with science as experimentation". Rheinberger (1997) presents a study of biochemistry research wherein he talks of as *epistemic things* as the principal outcome from the "experimental situation". Rheinberger (1997) positions his work accordingly:

> [I] am not looking for a 'logic' in the relationship between theory and experiment. I am not looking for a logic behind experiment. Rather I am grappling with what must be seen, irreducibly, as the 'experimental situation'. In this situation, which is irrevocably local and situated in time and space, there are scientific objects and the technical conditions of their coming into existence, there is differential reproduction of experimental systems, there are conjunctures of such systems, and graphematic representations. All these are notions related to the process of producing what I shall call epistemic things. (Rheinberger, 1997: 21)

For Rheinberger, all studies of scientific work must start with the experimental situation because the experimental activities draw together a series of resources and knowledge into one single practice:

> Experimental systems are to be seen as the smallest integral working units of research. As such, they are systems of manipulations designed to give unknown answers to questions that the experimenters themselves are not yet able clearly to ask ... They [laboratory machinery] are not simply experimental devices that generate answers; experimental systems are vehicles for materializing questions. They inextricably cogenerate the phenomena of material entities and the concepts they come to embody. (Rheinberger, 1997: 28)

The "material entity" that Rheinberger talks about is the "epistemic thing" becoming the object of inquiry. Rheinberger emphasizes that epistemic things are vague because they have not yet been fixed by systems of verification or further materialized by the laboratory equipment and technologies:

> They are material entities of processes—physical structures, chemical reactions, biological functions—that constitute the objects of inquiry. As epistemic objects, they present themselves in a characteristic, irreducible vagueness. This vagueness is inevitably because, paradoxically, epistemic things embody what one does not yet know. Scientific objects have the precarious status of being absent in their experimental presence; they are not simply hidden things to be brought into light through sophisticated manipulations. (Rheinberger, 1997: 28)

Rheinberger (1997) also points at the mutual dependencies between experimental systems and epistemic things through the use of the metaphor of "hardware" and "software" in scientific work:

> Experimental systems grow slowly into a kind of scientific hardware within which the more fragile software of epistemic things—this amalgam of halfway concepts, no-longer techniques, and not-yet-values-of-standards—is articulated, connected, disconnected, placed, and displaced. Certainly they delineate the realm of the possible. But as a rule, they do not create rigid orientations. (Rheinberger, 1997: 36)

One good illustration to Rheinberger's (1997) thesis is Joan Fujimura's (1996) study of the onto-gene research, one of the emerging scientific fields of the 1980s. For Fujimura, biological representations are products of collective arrangements and therefore a concept such as "the gene may have different meanings on situated practices: "Currently, a new set of commitments and practices have created new technical definitions of genes and genetics in molecular terms. 'Gene', then, is not an abstract concept when situated in the work of biologists, their research tools, the purposes and themes that framed their work, and the uses to which the work is applied" (Fujimura, 1996: 65). As new techniques and research methods develop, new epistemic things are being produced. Keller (2000: 67) points at the diversity of genes in the expanding domain of genetics: "Techniques and data from sequence analysis have led to the identification not only of split genes but also of repeated genes, overlapping genes, cryptic DNA, antisense transcription, nested genes, and multiple promoters (allowing transcription to be initiated at alternative sites and according to variable criteria). All of this variations immeasurably confound the task of defining the gene as a structural unit". Thus, the gene has "[b]ecome many things—no longer a single entity but a word with great plasticity, defined only by the specific experimental context in which it is used" (Keller, 2000: 69). Expressed differently, conceptual scheme and technologies, techniques and methods mobilized in the scientific procedures are not separated but follow shared trajectories; new techniques produce new epistemic things. However, since all theory is underdetermined by data (i.e., systematic observations), that is, theories are rarely if ever falsified even though observations do not support theories (Lenoir, 1997: 22)—the so-called Duhem thesis—it is more common that new epistemic things complement the previous ones rather than displacing them. Fujimura (1996) argues that the rapid adoption of oncogene theory can be explained by the limited challenge it posed to other established theories: "[T]he proto-oncogene theory did not challenge the theories to which the researchers had made previous commitments. Indeed, the new research provided them with ways of triangulating evidence using new methods and a new unit of analysis to support earlier ideas. These views of oncogene research were 'realized' through the efforts of these researchers and, in turn, this realization further extended the reach of oncogene research and the complexity of the theory" (Fujimura, 1996: 151). Conceptual schemes are then continuously altered in the face of new challenges such as new data and observations of conflicting theories.

Rheinberger (1997) points out that new epistemic things cannot be developed and conceptualized in isolation. Instead, there is a continuity between preexisting "phenomena" and newly produced "epistemic things". Scientific work is therefore not what is disruptive and discontinuous but is on the contrary in most of the cases evolving as a string of interconnected experiments. On the other hand, experimental results are in many cases not compatible and explained by theoretical frameworks and therefore there is a continual "misfit" between laboratory results and the theoretical frameworks that needs to be overcome: "A research process is a procedure in which, eventually, new things happen to emerge that cannot be predicted by a 'theoretical system' and that likewise are not inevitably generated by the 'practical system' of experimentation. Thus, the design of experiments is not necessarily determined by theory, and the design of theories is not necessarily constrained by experiments. Thus mutual nonfitting is exactly what makes the experimental process an explorative endeavor" (Rheinberger, 1997: 56). The work of the skillful and experienced researcher is closing the gap between new results and the theoretical framework. Seen in this view, "scientists are first and foremost, *bricoleurs* (tinkerers), not engineers" (Rheinberger, 1997: 32). Clarke and Fujimura (1992: 11) say: "Tinkering involves a kind of 'indexical' (local or situational) logic and opportunism—using what is at hand, making-do, using things for new purposes, patching things together, and so on" (see e.g., Schaffer, 1989). Fujimura (1996) advocates an "ecological approach" wherein different accomplishments of the scientific community are embedded in the interaction of a number of registers or orders:

> In my approach, scientific facts, theories, routines, rules, standards, and conventions are achieved in orders; they are constructed of the organizations of scientific work commitments and perspectives at particular times and in particular spaces. Every instance, kind, and scale of order is achieved through complex daily interactions— conflicts, agreements, abdications, force, negotiations, manipulations, persuasion, education—among many actors working under specific local conditions. Routines are orders to be explained and not assumed. Constructing scientific facts, theories, artifacts, and procedures are temporally located collective processes. (Fujimura, 1996: 13)

In a study of Louis Pasteur's research on microbes and his massive impact on nineteenth-century society, Latour (1988: 262, n. 7) points at the importance of understanding the innovator's crossing of the boundaries between nature and society. Great scientists are not bounded by either domain but are successful exactly because they manage to bridge laboratory research and pressing social problems and to demonstrate solutions to social problems. The microbes examined by Pasteur caused a range of diseases in the nineteenth-century Europe, for instance anthrax attacking the cattle and diseases affecting humans such as the plague. On the one hand, hygienists sought explanations in factors pertaining to what Latour (1988: 103) calls the "*external* agents on the macroscopic scale" such as cities, climate, soil, air, and "*social* agents" such as "poverty, overcrowding, and the laws of governing commerce". On the other hand, doctors were interested in "*internal* and above all *individual* practices" such as bodily constitutions and the treatment of infected wounds. In-between these two perspectives or scientific programs, the Pasteurians found a new domain not yet explored:

> Between the external and the internal, the crowd and the individual, there was little contact. The biologist or physiologist was concerned with internal agents that were sometimes microscopic, sometimes functional, which had no necessary relations with physicians, still less with hygienists. They spoke of organs, of the glycogenic function of the liver, of breathing, of cells. This was a huge world that had nothing directly to do with the doctor-patient relationship of the sanitization of cities. (Latour, 1988: 103)

Speaking with Rheinberger (1997) and Clarke and Fujimura (1992), Pasteur's brilliance lies in his ability to explore what is in-between the external and the internal, the regime of *internal agents*, the microbes. Pasteur sought for solutions to social problems and offered laboratory experiments that proved that the microbes were the explanation for a range of diseases (Latour, 1988: 85). For Latour, the Pasteurians were "[n]o more numerous, no more brilliant, no more rigorous, and no more courageous than the others, but they followed a different agent, the cultivated-microbe-whose-virulence-they-varied". That is, they followed another path than the hygienists and the doctors and found new relations and associations between the microscopic and the macroscopic levels, between various agents, practices, conditions, and beliefs. The Pasteurians were in short bricoleurs transgressing the boundary between nature and society.

Scientists, then, to speak with Hacking (1983), *intervene* and *represent*; they conduct experiments (i.e., manipulate nature) and they account for their experiments in theoretical terms. Scientific work is therefore a sort of cartography where new places (research results) are to be integrated into the existing "map" (i.e., a theoretical system). Actor-network theorists speak of the process of rendering the scientific object intelligible and open to inspection and analysis *inscription*. The inscribing of the scientific object presupposed a shared and uncontested regime of representations. For Rheinberger (1997: 111) however, "temporally and spatially, the object *is* a bundle of inscriptions. It displays only what can be handled in this way". Similarly, Lenoir (1998: 8) argues that inscriptions are the very essence of "fact-making" in laboratory sciences: "[L]aboratory studies observe the striking congruence between literary inscriptions and 'facts': discussions about facts are inseparable from their inscriptions; the acceptance of a scientific fact is tied to the strength of its links to layers of texts; the ostensibly factual nature of a statement can be undermined by drawing attention to the process of its inscriptions". Rheinberger (1998), drawing on Jacques Derrida's *Of grammatology*, uses the concept of *graphematic space* to capture the dual function of inscriptions as what both represents and constitutes the epistemic thing:

> What goes on when the experimentalist produces a chromatogram, a protein sequence, an array of tubes, to which pieces of filter paper are correlated, on which, in turn, counts per minute of radioactive decay are superimposed? All these epistemic procedures are the object on an ongoing process of materialized interpretation. They represent certain aspects of the scientific object in a form that is manipulable in the laboratory. The arrangements of these graphematic traces or graphemes and the possibility of their being articulated in a particular space of representation constitute the experimental 'writing-game'. Out of these units the experimenter composes what he calls his model. (Rheinberger, 1998: 296)

The same idea expressed by Lenoir (1998):

> The instrument is no longer regarded as simply an extension of theory, a mere supplement, useful for exteriorising an ideal meaning contained within theory. When we treat the experimental system as a model of the theory, we no longer tend to regard it simply as an expression, an unproblematic translation of the ideal relations and entities of the theory into the representative hardware-language of the experimental system. Furthermore, if we consider the web of instrumentalities that mediate and stabilize our interactions with nature, then rather than treating knowledge as stabilized by reference to an independent, objective reality antecedent to scientific work, we are free to develop a pragmatic realism based on the representation of nature as articulated through the technologies of experiment and intervention. From this perspective, it is through our machines that practices and simultaneously a nature capable of being theorized are stabilized. (Lenoir, 1998: 6)

Procedures and routines for inscriptions is thus a *sine qua non* for all scientific work.

Scientific work is what is embedded in the experimental system and is aiming at producing scientific objects that are turned into epistemic things. The epistemic things are not yet fully enclosed and rendered legitimate but are located in a liminal position halfway in-between entity and representation. Speaking in the vocabulary of Bergson (1988), one may argue that epistemic things are virtual multiplicities on the verge of being actualized. Scientists inscribe scientific objects as the first attempt of making them become epistemic things and advocate that the epistemic thing must be examined in such and such way and rendered theoretically legitimate in specific ways. In Rheinberger's account of scientific work, most activities and entities elaborated upon are provisional and open for critique and negotiation. The insistence on portraying scientists as "tinkers", or "bricoleurs", a community of handy-men rather than engineers of "fact-making", underscores the idea that scientific work is not a matter of controlling a self-enclosed machinery but of making many parts fit together. The epistemology of science is one of becoming, fluidity and processes rather than fixed, immobile entities, it is, in François Jacob's phrase, "a machine for making the future" (Rheinberger, 1998: 288). What is of particular interest is how such a mobile and fluid environment is anchored in material resources and actual practices.

Tangible resources: material resources and laboratories

In addition to the conceptual resources mobilized in scientific practice, material resources such as technology and laboratory equipment are a *sine qua non* for modern science; "no science without technology, without machines", Michel Serres (1995: 15) says. Historical studies of scientific instruments (e.g., Gooding, Pinch and Schaffer, 1989) suggest that instruments and machinery helps "stabilizing" the relations between scientific practices. For instance, Hackman (1989: 34) argues that scientific instruments brought together experimental and mathematical sciences in the seventeenth century and made them co-evolve in the coming period. Alluding to Latour (1991), technology can be said what makes science durable. In addition, instruments and their performances and, in some cases, even sheer size and advanced technological content may help promoting the acceptance of certain theoretical frameworks. Hackman exemplifies with the Dutch scientist Martinus van Marum's electrostatic generator, which qualifies as what Hackman (1989) calls a "heroic device":

> Scientific instruments were (and still are) used as arbiters between contending theories, and sheer size could give a psychological

advantage. A celebrated example from the eighteenth century is the giant electrostatic generator made for the Dutch natural philosopher Martinus van Marum by the English instrument maker John Cuthbertson. It fulfilled all the requirements of a heroic device ... it was large and constructed to the limits of what was technically possible. This awesome machine with its two glass discs five feet in diameter, produced discharges twenty-four inches long; in modern terms, between 300 000 and 500 000 volts. It was not difficult to understand why Van Marum's fellow scientists could be persuaded by his experimental results. These were the main factors for the early acceptance of Lavoisier's combustion (oxidation) theory in the Netherlands. No apparatus is, however, self-evidently superior. Its value, like that of the experiment, lies in its power of persuasion. Bachelard has likened the instruments to *un théorème réifié*. (Hackman, 1989: 32)

Today, after centuries of systematic scientific research, technology is an indispensable component in any scientific undertaking. Numerous students of science and technology use the notion of technoscience because it is epistemologically complicated to draw a line of demarcation between science per se and the technologies employed in scientific endeavours (Bachelard, 1984). However, it is still a risk that one takes the instruments and the materiality of the scientific procedures for granted. For instance, not even computers and their functioning (e.g., the code of the machine language employed or their software) are devoid of controversy or are as uncomplicated as common sense thinking might suggest (MacKenzie, 1995: 165). Scientific work is resting on technologies temporarily agreed upon and stabilized to enable a proper functioning.

What is of particular interest for some researchers is the laboratory setting as such as being at the center of scientific inquiry. Karin Knorr Cetina (1992) describes the laboratory:

The laboratory is an enhanced environment which improves upon the natural order in relation to the social order. How does this improvement come about? Laboratory studies suggest that it rests upon the malleability of natural objects. Laboratories use the phenomenon that objects are not fixed entities which have to be taken as they are or left to themselves. In fact, laboratories rarely work with objects as they occur in nature. Rather they work with object images or with their visual, auditory, electrical, etc., traces, with their components, their extractions, their purified versions. (Knorr Cetina, 1992: 116)

Also Fujimura (1996) emphasizes that scientists do not, in general investigate *natura naturans* ("nature per se") but *natura naturata* ("natured nature"), i.e., created, artificial nature. As a consequence, the distinction between science and technology is permeable and fluid:

> Scientists 'create' nature in laboratories just as they create 'intelligence' in computers. They create 'nature' along the lines of particular commitments and with particular constraints, just as computer scientists create computer technologies along the lines of particular commitments and with particular constraints. Thus, the boundary between science and technology is blurred. To bring the theoretical discussion back to the case of inbred mice, geneticists employed experimental technologies and protocols to create novel techno-scientific objects. These objects *are* nature, at least as nature is described in scientific narratives. (Fujimura, 1996: 31)

Hilgartner (2005: 133) emphasizes that laboratories are not to be conceptualized as producers of "research results" but as producers of stream of entities such as "a wide range of inscriptions, processes, materials, skills, techniques, and other resources". These entities are only eventually forming what Rheinberger (1997) refers to as epistemic things, that is, entities become "neatly packaged and clearly bounded". In this view, the laboratory is a complex social institution capable of forming administrative routines that are capable of handling "processes of inquiry, methods for securing credibility, and mechanisms for airing and managing dissent (Jasanoff, 2005: 40); the laboratory is the site where a long range of heterogeneous interests and concerns are negotiated. Fujimura (1996: 204) emphasizes this point: "There is no outside and inside in the research laboratory. Both university administrators and biotechnology stockholders were often present, often in spirit and sometimes in embodied form. The world is in the laboratory, and the laboratory is in the world minute by minute. There is no micro-, meso-, and macro-sociology in the laboratory".

In these accounts, the laboratory serves to simulate something that resembles nature but that still remain distinctly separated from nature. One may say that the nature investigated in the laboratory is *hyperreal*; it is more real than reality, more natural than nature itself. Hacking (2002: 3) contrasts modern laboratory science, inextricably bound up with laboratory practices and equipment, and the archaic forms of research: "In ancient times men studied, observed and speculated about phenomenon. In modern times we make phenomenon, or isolate or purify them". Knorr Cetina (1992) also points out that the laboratory serves as the infrastructure of scientific work, a sort of anchoring point for the more innovative research activities: "Organizationally, science is conducted in experiments, while laboratories provide the (infra) structure for the conduct of science—they supply office space, computer time, living quarters, means of transportation, a local management that recruits financial resources, and above all, particle collisions" (Knorr Cetina, 1992: 133). "*[S]cientific statements are anchored in working pieces of technical equipment.* Laboratories are behind the numbers, graphs, and figures displayed in scientific texts", Fuchs (1992: 67. Emphasis in the original) writes. Clarke and Fujimura (1992) list a the variety of resources mobilized in scientific work:

> The *elements* (our generic term) of the situation generally include *workplaces* (laboratories or other work sites and their basic infrastructure); *scientists* (including their individual career issues); *other workers* (graduate students, technicians, clerical staff, artists, computer programmers, etc.); *theories, models, and other representational entities* (both tacit and explicit); *research materials, instruments, technologies, skills, and techniques*, and *work organization* (of the immediate work site, of the larger local administrative unit such as a university or federal agency, and of disciplines and specialties through professional organizations and other means of communication); *sponsorship and its organization* (of both intramural and extramural fiscal support); *regulatory groups* (local, national, international); and both desired and unintended *audiences* and *consumers* of the work. (Clarke and Fujimura, 1992: 5)

Even though the laboratory is the primary site for scientific investigation, several writers emphasize the integration of laboratory equipment and technology with conceptual frameworks and jointly agreed upon theories as the most important connection in scientific work. Fujimura's (1996) study of oncogene research suggests that research problems, theory, and practices were stabilized and rendered ontologically certain through the establishment of technology and scientific procedures in the laboratories. Fujimura here speaks of the *concretization* of abstract theoretical frameworks: "By reconstructing oncogene research in these new sites, a variety of research laboratories locally *concretized* the abstract protooncogene theory in different practices to construct new problems and new laboratory artifacts. Suddenly, novel entities such as *myc*, *abl*, *ras*, and other oncogenes were named and defined, and novel organisms were created through gene transfer techniques" (Fujimura, 1996: 7); "[T]he standardized tools themselves", Fujimura (1996: 7) continues, "became agents for the standardization of the laboratories in a process of *co-concretization*". Therefore, the technological standardization contributed to "theoretical robustness of oncogenes".

Similarly, Hacking (1992) talks about the "matériel of an experiment" and "the ideas" as being closely bound up:

> I think of the matériel of an experiment as more central to its stabilization than do writers in the tradition of social studies of science. By the matériel I meant the apparatus, the instruments, the substances or objects investigated. The matériel is flanked on the one side by ideas (theories, questions, hypotheses, intellectual models of apparatuses) and on the other by marks and manipulations of marks (inscriptions, data, calculations, data reduction, interpretation). (Hacking, 1992: 32)

In fact, it is the ability to bring ideas and materials together and make sense out of the inscriptions provided that "stabilizes science": "The process of modifying the workings of instruments—both materially (we fix them up) and intellectually (we redescribe what they do)—furnishes the glue that keeps the intellectual and material world together. It is what stabilizes science" (Hacking, 1992: 58). Similarly, Griesemer (1992) speaks of the integration of "tools" including heterogeneous resources into an "assembly" in biology research:

> Tools are objects designed as aids to articulation (or disarticulation) of parts into (or from) an assembly ... Tools in science are more heterogeneous [than the 'carpenters' tools']: theorems and rules of interference are tools in the assembly of mathematical and logical proofs; biological materials can serve as tools the hands of biologists to construct theories and test hypotheses. By assembling materials in a certain way, biologists can elaborate theories as descriptions or materials. (Griesemer, 1992: 54)

Fujimura (1996: 79) lists some of the tools and materials being used in oncogene research: "Some of the most obvious materials include restriction enzymes, plasmids, DNA probes, herring sperm DNA, reverse transcriptase, long-passed cell lines, antibiotics, many kinds of chemical reagents (ethidium bromide, ammonium acetate, and cesium chloride to name a few), agarose and polyacrylamide gels, and more". All these materials demand their own specific expertise for their handling and use. Even though scientific ideologies obscure the situated and contingent use of tools and portray tools as what is essentially unproblematic, studies of the use of particular techniques and tools show that not even the skilled laboratory researcher can fully account for every detail of "backbone methods". Jordan and Lynch (1992) study the use of the "plasmid purification and isolation" method (in most cases referred to as the "plasmid prep") used for "[a] variety of purposes and in combinations with various instruments, specimen materials, and other techniques" (Jordan and Lynch, 1992: 80). The plasmic prep is not associated with any single experiment but is a "[d]etachable phase of a wide variety of disciplinary routines and experimental recipes". Rather than being what is wholly unproblematic and detached from any scientific concern, the plasmic prep erects a number of problems for the practitioner: "What our ethnographic materials make perspicuous ... is not a process of closure and stabilization of initially 'flexible' technological designs. Rather, we are alerted to the conditions of instability and fragmentation in routine laboratory practice" (Jordan and Lynch, 1992: 84). Jordan and Lynch continue: "Novices discover that even within the confines of a particular laboratory, a variety of methods are used. By 'novices' we mean practitioners who have yet to learn particular procedures, but are not necessarily 'complete novices'" (e.g., graduate and doctoral students) (Jordan and Lynch, 1992: 88). Contrary to common sense belief, the laboratory practices that serve as the infrastructure of the laboratory is not of necessity uncontested and unproblematic (Schaffer, 1989). Instead, the most generic techniques may be bound up with contingent, local, and even personal skills and competencies. Therefore, it is important for the student of scientific practice to pay close attention to the sleight-of-hand and dexterity of individual laboratory researchers. Even though they draw on the same scripts— often in the form of "classic textbooks" used in the community of researchers—the performances differ between individual researchers. Therefore, tools are not the "black boxes" they are presented as in the scientific literature but are more permeable, "porous", and contingent than is generally recognized.

As a consequence, researchers do not run experiments solely on basis of their conceptual schemes but also actively engage in adjusting laboratory equipment, inscriptions, and theories to one another so they constitute a credible, yet somewhat fluid assemblage (Lynch, 2002). This particular perspective is also shared by Andrew Pickering: "[S]cientific knowledge should be understood as sustained by, and as part of, interactive stabilizations situated in a multiple and hetero-geneous space of machines, instruments, conceptual structures, dis-ciplined practices, social actors and their relations, and so forth. This is my version of Serres's idea that 'nature is formed by linkings'" (Pickering, 1995: 70). In Pickering's vocabulary, science is constituted by the "interactive stabilizations" of two resources, the "machinic per-formances" and "conceptual strata"; "these alignments of the material world with the world of representation are what sustains specific facts and theories and give them their precise form" (Pickering, 1995: 182). In Pickering's account, the machines and technologies plays a central role in scientific work in terms of being "the balance point, liminal between the human and nonhuman worlds" (Pickering, 1995: 7). The liminal position of the machine as being neither human, nor non-human, calls for, in Pickering's view, a radical reconceptualization of science as a *posthuman space*, that is, "a space in which the human actors are still there but now inextricably entangled with the non-human, no longer at the center of action and calling the shots" (Pickering, 1995: 26. See also Hayles, 1999). For Pickering, science is no longer solely a matter for humans but is equally a matter for machines. Humans still constitute the most important component in scientific work but it is accompanied by various resources that are on the verge of humanity; intelligent machines, genetically designed laboratory animals—for instance the patented OncoMouse developed at Harvard University examined by Haraway (1997)—and a great many other entities (Braidotti, 2006: 101).

Laboratory work is the essence of scientific work in terms of its con-finement of a domain dedicated to the production of a specific form of knowledge. In addition, the laboratory has an emblematic status in today's society as being the black box from which all sorts of amazing findings are delivered, capable of healing humans and providing various scientific wonders. But once one enters into the laboratory, the black box proves to be constituted by a multiplicity of heterogeneous resources and assets, material, technical, and cognitive.

Bridging the tangible and the intangible: scientific practice

Fuchs (1992) advocates the view that it is the organization of techno-science that constitutes its authority—its ability to influence the everyday life of human beings (see e.g., Collins and Pinch, 2005, critical account of medicine as field of expertise):

> The authority of science is not simply grounded in its texts, but rather in its organization. The important consequence is that science deserves no more and no different type of respect than other powerful organizations. People are willing to surrender to the experts because they are in awe of the privileged rationality of their science. So we, accept the experts telling us what to eat, who we are, how we should live, and how to raise our children ... Once we stop being too impressed by the experts and their science, and once we realize that their power is simply that of their organization, we can begin to loosen their tight grip on our lives. (Fuchs, 1992: 18)

What Fuchs (1992) calls "science-in-the-making" is then neither magic, nor the work of autonomous geniuses, but rather the everyday work life "mangle of practice" (Pickering, 1995), the tinkering and bricolage of practising scientists supported by ideology, technology, and social organization. Fuchs (1992: 89) also argues that disciplines characterized by a certain degree of *density*, that is, a high degree of resource concentration and mutual dependence between individual researchers and research groups, is more likely to produce scientific facts that are corroborated over time. All scientific work is based on the ability of the practising researchers to serve as what Selznick (1957) called an *institutional leader*, or what may be called an "institutional entrepreneur", a person that actively aligns tangible and intangible resources with the dominant beliefs and strategic agendas being adhered to for the moment in an organization (Garud, Jain and Kumaraswamy, 2002; Garud and Rappa, 1994). Similarly to the shaping of technology through practices, such institutional actors are actively pursuing their ends through the means at hands, be they ideological, political, or technological. Expressed differently, scientific work and science-based innovation do not subsist in a social vacuum, but are rather continuously related to other activities in the firm. Institutional actors then impose ideologies, beliefs and modes of thinking on their co-workers, thereby reinforcing certain behaviours and beliefs.

While the scientific ideology underlines the separate components of theory, experiment, technology, and outcome (e.g., data, conceptual schemes, theories, epistemic things), the practice of scientific practice is far messier. Ethnographies of scientific work underline the partly chaotic nature in any research laboratory. Lynch (1993), examining molecular biology research, stresses the ability of the researcher to navigate between standards of exactness and "what actually works" in the day-to-day work:

> [T]he languages games of … molecular biology are not bound up by a closed set of disciplinary skills and/or a corpus of knowledge but that … are permeated by an immense variety of discursive and embodied practices, some of which seem no more or less rigorous, distinctive, and precise than turning an engine or preparing a soufflé. Moreover, standards of exactness, strict sequentiality, and tolerance for variation are assessed 'for all practical purposes' in laboratory work just as they are in various other crafts, literary art, and household activities. Sequences of laboratory work is not always 'unforgivably strict', nor, as many studies in sociology of science have documented, are issues necessarily 'settled' in the natural sciences without lingering dispute (perhaps mathematicians do, after all, 'come to blows'). (Lynch, 1993: 297–298)

The practising scientists is then someone capable of mediating the vision of finalized and cleaned-up version of scientific work being showcased and demonstrated in public in journal papers and the less ordered and linear life world inside the laboratory. Even though scientists at times reject such a vocabulary, Fujimura (1996) speaks of the "productivity" of certain methods and technologies:

> Scientists, like technocrats and business people, attribute properties of 'productivity', 'speed', and 'efficiency' to the technologies with which they work. Nevertheless, these properties—standardization, speed, efficiency and productivity—also are outcomes of the commitments made by various parties to the production and maintenance of these technologies. A technology is efficient only when it is part of a network of commitment to particular practices, that is, not until, it is formalized and standardized. (Fujimura, 1996: 104)

As a consequence, the success not only of certain technologies but also for entire theoretical frameworks such as the oncogene theory depends on the ability to investigate what Fujimura (1996) calls "doable problems" within the new field. Fujimura also points at the relatively mundane and practical nature of much of the laboratory practices. She uses the term *articulation work* to denote a variety of activities such as "purchasing chemicals for reagents, negotiating with sponsors, and collecting information about the latest results of competing laboratories" (Fujimura, 1996: 186). The articulation work is the backbone of any scientific program or individual laboratory; without mechanisms for handling the everyday work life activities, there would be no or little scientific breakthroughs to showcase.

One of the most important practices in scientific work is to render the scientific objects identified and visualized by the laboratory equipment intelligible and open for inspection and analysis through the act of inscription. Inscription is here a broad-ranging term capturing a variety of practices aiming at making what is obscure for the outsider become structured and organized, preferably in the form of graphs, diagrams, mathematical formulae, or symbolic representations (e.g., vernacular language). Pierre Duhem, the great French physicist and philosopher of science, emphasized the importance of a shared vocabulary among physicists and defended a nominalist position: "[P]hysical definitions construct what may be truly called a vocabulary: Just as a French dictionary is a collection of conventions making a name correspond to each object, so, in physical theory, the definitions are a group of conventions making a magnitude correspond to each physical concept" (Duhem, 1996: 4). On the other hand, Niels Bohr, the Danish physicist and one of the major contributors to quantum physics, is defending a strict nominalist position: "[T]here is no quantum world. There is only an abstract quantum mechanical description. It is wrong to think that the task of physics is to find out how Nature *is*. Physics concerns what we can say about Nature" (Niels Bohr, cited in Norris, 2000: 44). However, for Duhem, advocating a cultural and social view of the laboratory sciences as opposed to the positivist view that science should be removed from specific interests, points at three "phases" in the development of physics (or any other scientific discipline): "the observations of facts", "the discovery of laws", and "the construction of theories" (Duhem, 1996: 30). These three phases imply different activities and regimes of representations but share the quality of being based on inherently social and agreed upon systems of representation. A philosopher of science like Ian Hacking (2002) speaks of the inscriptions of scientific objects as an act of "naming". Naming is not happening in isolation but is, in the Oxford philosopher John Austin's (1962) vocabulary, a perlocutionary statement mobilizing the scientific authority in a field. Hacking (2002: 8) writes: "Naming alone is never enough to create ... naming occurs in sites, particular places, and at particular times. For a name to do its creative work, it needs authority. One needs usage within institutions. Naming does its work only as a social history works itself out". Similarly, Collins (1990: 5) emphasizes that the accounting for what is observed is a disciplined activity: "Like, the face, scientific facts do not speak for themselves. Disputes in science are not settled by broad agreement about what *ought* to be seen when one looks in a certain way and at a certain time and location. Thereafter, anyone who looks and does not see what everyone agrees ought to be seen is blamed for defective vision (or defective experimental equipment)". Scientists must learn to speak of his or her empirical material in certain ways, otherwise the legitimacy of the research may be at stake.

The act of naming is the end of a rather complicated process including many operations and activities. Krieger (1992) identifies the following tools in the "physicist's toolbox" enabling physicists to "take hold of the world":

1. Mathematical Tools
   a. counting and approximation: statistics and combinatorics
   b. pattern: geometry, symmetry, conservation laws
   c. linearity: calculus and optimisation procedures
2. Diagrammatic Tools
   a. geometric and spatial: vectors and graphs
   b. patterned algebraic expressions
3. Rhetorical Tools
   a. media: spacetime vacuum, crystal, hydrogen atom, gas
   b. objects: particles, oscillators, fields, waves
   c. interactions: collisions, Lagrangians, response functions
   d. strategies of address: find a good vacuum, or ground state, or equilibrium; group objects into families; find nicely separable parts; divide the labor among specialists
   e. commonplace or qualitative methods, such as using a classical picture supplemented by quantum rules. (Krieger, 1992: 116)

Such "tools" heavily determine the physicist's outlook on the world. Lynch (1988: 153) talks about the two operations of *selection* and *mathematization* when representing a scientific objects or epistemic object: "Selection concerns the way scientific methods of visualization simplify and schematize objects of study. Mathematization concerns how such methods attribute mathematical order to natural objects". Selection is the choice of method to visually illustrate and "purify" the graphics, diagrams and other output from the laboratory equipments (see Lynch, 1985). In many cases, there are ambiguities and inconsistencies in the photos or graphs that need to be eliminated to make the image become intelligible. Amann and Knorr Cetina (1988: 90) argue that it is important that visual data does not speak for itself. Instead, visual data partially represent the *modus operandi* per se, partially represent the scientific object as such, and therefore all visual data demands an "exegesis", an act of interpretation: "The distinguishing characteristic of visual data is that they are not ... treated as unproblematic displays of visual objects. Data act as a *basis of sequences of practice* rather than observation at a glance. They are subject to extensive visual exegeses, rendering practices which attempts to achieve *the work of seeing what the data consists of*". Thus, to achieve the demanded degree of legitimacy, scientists must "aesthetically enhance" what is claimed to be an evidence of a favoured theoretical hypothesis or framework: "Evidence is the aesthetically enhanced, carefully composed rendering of flexible visual objects that, through the meandering interrogatory process of image analyzing talk, have been 'embedded' and entrenched in procedural reconstruction, local experiences and in the landscape of data display" (Amann and Knorr Cetina, 1988: 115–116). In other words, there are few *factum brutum* in scientific work but instead a series of filtered, selected, modified, and aesthetically enhanced images are presented to the outsiders. Scientific work is not, contrary to common sense thinking, devoid of aesthetic components.

The next phase is to account for the first crude images in the regime of representation of choice in the discipline. In the natural sciences, mathematics is the most generally applied form of representation. Duhem (1996: 25) speaks of the physicists' work to *"mise en équation"* the laboratory findings—to put the results "into equations" as a central activity for achieving scientific legitimacy. For various reasons, mathematics has entrenched a position where it is regarded a social practice separated from interests and politics. This common belief is of Platonist origin: "For Plato, mathematics is a condition for thinking or theorizing in general because it constitutes a break with *doxa* or opinion ... Everything else that exists remain prisoner to opinion, but not mathematics", Badiou (2004: 29) says. As a consequence, mathematics is still the "queen of the sciences", a regime of representation that offers enormous opportunities for sharing and distributing information effectively. Lynch says that the mathematization of sets of selected data is the final outcome from the research processes: "The details of laboratory work, and of the visible products of such works, and largely organized around the practical task of constituting and 'framing' a phenomenon so that it can be measured and mathematically described" (Lynch, 1988: 170). Lynch (1988) concludes:

> Research teams use laboratory practice to transform invisible or unanalyzable specimens into visually examined, coded, measured, graphically analyzed, and publically presented data. Such ordering of data is not solely contained 'in perception' but is also a social process—an 'assembly line' resulting in public access to new structures wrested out of obscurity or chaos. Instruments, graphic inscriptions, and interactional processes take the place of 'mind' as the filter, serving to reduce phenomena of study into manageable data. (Lynch, 1988: 156)

Speaking with Fleck (1979), scientific communities—"through collectives"—are constituted not only by shared interests and concerns but also their ability to evaluate and judge contributions within a particular field. For Rheinberger (1997), scientific communities are inextricably bound up with the languages mobilized and used:

> Languages, scientific ones not exempted, do not describe the world, they inscribe themselves into practices—whence their power, their seductive force, and the cross-fertilization hubbub to which they give rise. Science does not work in spite of the fact that there are different languages on different operational levels, it works *because* there are many of them, thus creating the possibility for differential context, for unexpected hybridization, and for all sorts of effects of interference and intercalation without which the thing we call research would not exist. (Rheinberger, 1997: 142)

In summary, scientific practices are both producing scientific results and other forms of output, and making such output open for inspection, analysis and evaluation through a number of inscriptions routines and operations. Some of these routines imply a filtering, re-shaping and modulation of the original visual material provided from the laboratory machinery and equipment. Speaking again with Hacking (1983), scientific work is not only a matter of intervention into natural systems and environments but also of representing what is found in credible and intelligible manners.

Narrating scientific work

In the following, we will examine two types of narratives: verbal and written accounts of research procedures and outcomes.

Verbal accounts of scientific work: Once scientific facts (e.g., in the form of data inscribed into a protocol) are provided, they are subject to continuous and ongoing discussions within scientific communities, both locally and globally (Turner, 2001). The everyday life of the practising scientist is guided by such collective and systematic reflection and speculation and controversies regarding scientific interpretation are "the normal accidents" of scientific work (Fuchs, 1992: 102). Traweek (1988), studying the work of particle physicists, points at the importance of oral communication: "Oral communication is fundamental to the operation of the particle physics and successful senior physicists are the masters of the form" (Traweek, 1988: 117). She continues:

> Physics and its culture is produced and reproduced through talk which is storytelling, talk which is judgmental, talk which punishes and rewards. In short, by gossip ... talk accomplishes diverse tasks for physicists: it creates, defines, and maintains the boundaries of this dispersed but close-knit community; it is a device for establishing, expressing, and manipulating relationships in networks; it determines the fluctuating reputations of physicists, data, detractors and ideas; it articulates and affirms the shared moral code about the proper way to conduct scientific inquiry. Acquiring the capacity to gossip and to gain access to gossip about physicists, data, detractors, and ideas is the final and necessary stage in the training of a high energy physicist. Losing access to that gossip as punishment for violating certain moral codes effectively prevents the physicist from practicing physics. (Traweek, 1988: 122)

Narratives and oral communications are then what integrates the geographically and institutionally disperse community of physicists together; without the ability to jointly determine what is a good contribution and what is not, they would be unable to advance their discipline as one single and unified scientific field. Therefore, narratives and storytelling is of immediate importance for scientific work. Lynch (1985) supports this view:

> '[T]alking science' or 'shop talk', is an integral part of the ordinary work of doing science. As such, it is not to be treated as a casual or leisurely activity as, for example, idle chatter during coffee breaks, or as talk which relieves the boredom of routine tasks which can be done 'without thinking'. Although much of the talk that occurs in the lab is

such an 'idle' character, 'talking science' is talk which is directly part of the collaborative achievement of inquiry. (Lynch, 1985: 155)

Research *en route* is embedded in continuous and ongoing communication. Owen-Smith's (2001) ethnography of a multidisciplinary biology laboratory, H-lab in a major American research university, examines the mechanisms for control and evaluation of the research activities. The director of the lab is rarely giving orders or direct instruction but is instead relying on what Owen-Smith calls *premise-based control*, a form of what Perrow (1986) calls "unobtrusive control". During the weekly "muffin meetings" on Wednesday mornings in the H-lab, the director interrogated the co-workers during the presentations of their ongoing research. These interrogations were firmly based in a sceptical attitude and are thus "[s]imultaneously a method of control, a path of resistance, and an evaluative mechanism" (Owen-Smith, 2001: 429). Owen-Smith speaks of such peer-based review procedures as being central to the control of the lab:

> A skeptical encounter is any public conversational exchange in which critical or directive comments are made about the technical, substantive, or theoretical details of a scientific claim. By monitoring outcome quality, such skepticism underpins decisions about what claims 'make it out' of the lab to the wider evaluative arena of peer review and public presentation.

During the weekly meetings, the scientists of the lab were expected to tell stories about the progress of their research and their findings. The premise-based control is what holds "diverse, uncertain, and loosely coupled organizations" (Owen-Smith, 2001: 434) such as the laboratory together and provides a shared culture and mechanisms for peer control. Owen-Smith also points at the various mechanisms for resistance used by the junior faculty, for instance the drawing on status orders external to the lab, using group-oriented rhetoric to emphasize collective motivations for individual projects, and relying on nonconformist presentations styles to "defuse skeptical attacks". Since there is a strong formal and informal hierarchy in the laboratory, researchers are to a varying degree exposed to the scepticism of the director and the colleagues. For instance, the three post-doc "stars" are treated more like peers while the so-called "hired-hands" researchers are scrutinized in greater detailed and their claims are examined with greater scepticism. In Owen-Smith's (2001) ethnography, researchers are not only trained in conducting actual research procedures in laboratory but also to respond to critical examinations in-house in verbal communication and externally in written form.

Written accounts of scientific work: Research that is "getting out the door", that is, being submitted to academic journals and conferences, is no less subject to storytelling capacities and skills (Cantor, 1989). "There is no science without fiction and there is no fiction without passion", Stengers (1997: 150) argues. Knorr Cetina (1981: 95) continues: "If we define literary skills in terms of a repertoire of techniques for persuasion, there is no shortage of such devices in natural and technological science writing". In more specific terms, written accounts of scientific work are supposed to cover up any doubt that there is something ambiguous about a particular piece of research: "Scientific papers are not designed to promote an understanding of alternatives, but to foster the impression that what *has been done* is all that *could be done*" (Knorr Cetina, 1981: 42). French molecular biologist and Nobel laureate François Jacob (cited in Rheinberger, 2003: 315) testifies to the use of such rhetoric and says that when the scientist, when going public, "describe their own activity as a well-ordered series of ideas and experiments linked in a strict logical sequence. In scientific articles, reason proceeds along a high road that leads from darkness to light with not the slightest error, not a hint of bad decision, no confusion, nothing but perfect reasoning". Such accounts represent what Jacob calls "day science" which is contrasted against "night science"; while day science is the official and formal account of successful and legitimate scientific work, night science is what precedes day science and is what must remain hidden for the public gaze: "[N]ight science wanders blind. It hesitates, stumbles, recoils, sweats, wakes with a start. Doubting everything, it is forever trying to find itself, question itself, pull itself together. Night science is a sort of workshop of the possible where what will become the building material of science is worked out", Rheinberger (2003: 315) writes. Researchers must also pay attention to the power inherent to *ex post facto* storytelling and scientific representations: "Scientific representations are not ethereal or inconsequential because they are human (and nonhuman) constructions. Representations are real in terms of their consequences", Fujimura (1996: 18) reminds us. Rhetorical or narrative skills were developed by Galilei—"Galileo's innovativeness was not confined to redefining the relationship between mathematics and physics, his literary technology was also innovative", Cantor (1989: 171) argues—but it was Robert Boyle, Shapin and Schaffer (1985) claim, who championed the new "literary techniques" giving the reader the impression of "virtual witnessing" the reported experiments. Rhetoric and narrative skills became after Boyle an indispensable resource for the scientist.

When writing a scientific paper, a number of literary devices are employed or developed. Metaphors and other tropes, narratives, analogies, and a great many writing skills are mobilized in order to defend a thesis or a scientific result presented in a particular paper. Yet, authors need to carefully avoid becoming too personal or speculative in their texts; scientific texts effectively muddle through potential concerns that may undermine the arguments advanced. The text must then be a credible account of the research work, yet it needs to point at the potential implications and consequences of the research findings. Hilgartner's (2000) analysis of the National Academy of the Sciences (NAS) and the report *Diet, Nutrition, and Cancer* (1982), published by the National Research Council, one of 17 reports on diet and cancer published between 1977 and 1989, shows how scientific credibility is invoked to undermine criticism and concerns regarding the content of scientific reports. In the 478 pages report, a great number of "semiotic entities" ranging from "'epidemiologists', to 'mucosal cells', from 'broiled beef' to 'alcoholics admitted to mental hospitals in Massachusetts', from 'Marshall *et al.*' to '2-aminofluerene'" (Hilgartner, 2000: 45) are enrolled to support its arguments. The basis for legitimate scientific advice is then distributed between a variety of events, evidence, and entities. In addition, the report makes use of references to "the literature" and "evidence" to stabilize the ensemble of "semiotic entities":

> The team that produced the report also uses many other 'props' to bolster its authority. The most important are 'the literature' and 'the evidence', formally invoked by 1,738 citations ...These references have a complex character: not only do they tie report to establish knowledge, but they simultaneously link to prestigious institutions, such as well-known journals, and to reliable procedures, such as peer review. Facts, reputations, and procedures are all deployed to attest the credibility of the report. The team's overall narrative about the authority of the report is thus grounded in a widely distributed, mutually reinforcing network of assurances about the credibility of the elements of its story. (Hilgartner, 2000: 50)

However, scientific authority does not come for free but is instead the outcome from negotiations between opposing or even conflicting views. Hilgartner (2000: 53–54), drawing on Erwin Goffman's dramaturgical sociology, argues that NAS "backstages" such negotiations, that is, discussions and omissions that would "complicate, call into question, or otherwise muddy" the clean narrative of credibility of the report are not accounted for. NAS reports need to be staged as unified, formal statements wherein science speaks with one single voice. Among other things, such a unified view is necessary because scientific reports are often criticized and called into question by adversaries—often equipped with relevant resources, experience and rhetorical skills, thereby being capable of producing damaging critiques of formal reports. In such critiques, the mass media and various political bodies in Washington are used to advance alternative or even opposing views on the matter. Hilgartner (2000) points out a number of approaches when formulating such critiques. Taken together, formal scientific reports are, above all, no matter how much "evidence", "literature", and "expertise" they are invoking, at the bottom line rhetorical texts filled with statements that claim to be objective. Managing to bring a variety of heterogeneous resources together at the same time as a façade of unity is erected is certainly demanding fine-tuned rhetorical skills. Staging science in the role of adviser is in Hilgartner's (2000) account not a trivial operation but is instead a veritable *mise-en-scène* involving many risks and concerns.

Summary and conclusion: scientific work as the integration of conceptual strata, materials, practices and narratives

In this account, scientific work—accumulating into technoscience—is bringing together four types of resources into one seemingly unified or coherent process: conceptual strata or frameworks, material resources, actual practices, and verbal and written narrative skills. Conceptual strata are the theoretical frameworks that the researcher is simultaneously adhering to and aims at making a contribution to; material resources are the tools used in the scientific experiment; practices are the actual use of various resources and their "interactive stabilizations"; the narrative skills are both the ability to engage in oral interactions in the course of action and the ability to formulate credible accounts of the entire research process and the key findings in scientific papers and other media. Each practising researcher needs to, in various ways and very much dependent upon the local conditions and other contingencies, make use of these four resources and sets of skills. The outcome from scientific work are different types of "facts", data that are inscribed into protocols and other forms of procedures of witnessing (see Haraway, 1997; Shapin and Schaffer, 1985), that are more or less legitimate, more or less corroborate, more or less jointly constituted. Some researchers are part of vast international networks of researchers, while others operate along their own idiosyncratic routes. The life world of researchers could differ significantly as an effect of the local access to relevant equipment, venture capital and know-how. Even though the ideology of science states that research should be undertaken regardless of personal interests, the influence of capitalist interests on a scientific field has decisive effects.

The field of biotechnology, for instance, a field of research that was formed in the 1970s, exploded in the 1980s and 1990s as an effect of the influence of commercial interests. The anthropologist Paul Rabinow (1999, 1996) has explored the world of biotechnology researchers in the U.S. and in Europe. The first move towards a field of scientific research heavily influenced by commercial concerns was the elimination of the difference—a most ideological line of demarcation— between "applied" and "pure" bioscience (Rabinow, 1996: 10). Once leading researchers agreed that it was possible to bridge the commercial and scientific interests, biotechnology firm could attract venture capital. In Rabinow's account, the alliance of venture capitalists and researchers is a curious one in which venture capitalists initially did not really know how to evaluate scientific contributions such as journal publishing and conference presentations. Eventually, the investors found out a correlation between scientific prestige in a field and the amount of patents: "The gold standard of legitimacy for investors was scientific prestige" (Rabinow, 1996: 28). What is of great importance in Rabinow's studies is the central importance of venture capital for the growth and political interests for a particular scientific discipline. Today, biomedicine and biotechnology have displaced physics—which in turn took the place of chemistry—as the dominant scientific discipline. Biology may be a young discipline (Keller, 2003) but is today regarded as a field of systematic knowledge that can solve a variety of perceived social problems related to ageing population in the Western world and various diseases and illnesses causing much human suffering. Therefore, one may add capital or venture capital to the first four resources; capital is not only providing a more safe and firm ground for particular groups of researchers, it is also boosting interest among politicians and in the media. In Foucault's formulation, there is a "political economy of truth" inherent to all discourses; in the field biotechnology such political economy includes a rich variety of concerns and interests. For instance, in his book *French DNA*, Rabinow

(1999) points at the heterogeneity and diversity in such "political economies of truth": "French DNA is about a heterogeneous zone where genomics, bioethics, patients groups, venture capital, nations and the state meet. Such a common place, a practical site, eruptive and changing yet strangely slack, is filled with talk of good and evil, illness and health, spirit and flesh. It is full of diverse machines and bodies, parts and wholes, exchanges and relays" (Rabinow, 1999: 4). A wide variety of interests (such as for instance that of the French state, as Rabinow clearly points out) are then mobilized in the course of action. Speaking with Bruno Latour (1993), science is always already a narrative infested with political, epistemological, and practical concerns and aspects. If it is one thing science is not, it is not detached from its social environment and practical concerns.

4

From the Laboratory to the Pipeline: New Drug Development in the Pharmaceutical Industry

Introduction

While the last two chapters addressed the literature on knowledge management and innovation management and examined the various resources mobilized and put into action by practising laboratory researchers, this chapter will discuss how science-based innovation is organized in practice, and more specifically in the case of new drug development in pharmaceutical industry and in the British-Swedish major pharmaceutical company AstraZeneca. Prior to a more detailed review of such activities, a sociological perspective on science will be discussed, pointing at all-too-human characteristics such as peer recognition and social hierarchies as influencing and even in cases determining what we come to deem as proper science and proper knowledge. Rather than assuming that scientists and individuals managing science-based innovation are capable of overcoming their own preconceived ideas— their "prejudice" if you will, to speak with Gadamer (1975)—one must assume that previous experiences and past trajectories affect how individual researchers and research groups are capable of promoting and gaining recognition for their research efforts. In the end of the chapter, the methodology of the study reported in the second part of the book is accounted for.

For a sociology of science: the all-too-human nature of science

Peer-recognition and the Mathew effect

Science is often struggling to maintain the image of being detached from personal interests and individual agendas. The social studies of science literature and other social and behavioural theory perspectives on scientific work show that this insistence on objectivity and value neutrality is poorly supported by empirical evidence. For instance, rather than being value neutral, scientific work is an immersing and highly emotional activity exposing the individual researcher to a great deal of anxiety whether he or she is pursuing the right ends with the right means in the research. Consequently, peer-recognition is the true gold standard of all scientific work; researchers crave the recognition from peers to be able to pursue any scientific projects over time. For instance, Hans Selye, a pioneer within the study of stress, addresses peer recognition as being some kind of feature in conflict with the objectivity standards of scientific procedure:

> Many of the really talented scientists are not at all money-minded; nor do they condone greed for wealth either in themselves or in others. On the other hand, all the scientists I know sufficiently well to judge (and I include myself in this group) are extremely anxious to have their work recognized and approved by others. Is it not below the dignity of an objective scientific mind to permit such a distortion of his true motives? Besides, what is there to be ashamed of? (Hans Selye, cited in Merton, 1973: 400)

To put it in terms of a truism, scientists are nothing but humans; they are often navigating in little known domains and any indication that they may be on the right track or are working on legitimate problems is greatly appreciated. Moreover, scientific disciplines are characterized by an uneven distribution of resources, credibility and scientific recognition. This condition is captured by what Robert Merton calls "the Matthew effect": In the Gospel According to St. Matthew, it is written: "For unto every one that hath shall be given, and he shall have abundance: but for him that hath shall be taken away even that which he hath" (cited in Merton, 1973: 445). For scientists, this harsh message is a brute reality encountered on everyday basis. Merton says that Nobel laureates "[r]epeatedly observe that eminent scientists get proportionately great credit for their contributions to science while relatively unknown scientists tend to get disproportionately little credit for comparable contributions" (Merton, 1973: 442). In other words, one substantial scientific contribution may give additional, comparatively less well deserved, attention for other scientific contributions. Since the 1970s, Merton's "sociology of science" has been under fierce criticism by a range of scholars (Yearley, 2005: 8–12) regarding Merton as a proponent of positivism, and Cole (2004) shows that there is in fact little empirical evidence supporting Merton's idea of a "Matthew Effect": "The Matthew Effect described a pattern that did not exist. It was wrong", Cole (2004: 840) states. Still, one may examine some of the social consequences of the influence of authority and eminence in science work. Kay's (2000) history of the breaking of the genetic code in the period of 1953–1967 offers a fine illustration of how such beliefs regulate scientists' behaviour and reactions. When the relatively unknown scientists Marshall W. Nirenberg and J. Heinrich Matthaei identified the genetic code of a protein (phenylalanine) in 1961, the result was immediately attended to but was also met with scepticism: One leading scientist complained he was not quoted in the paper; some viewed it as being a "lucky strike"; others—for instance a well-read textbook—implied it was an "unintentional" accomplishment. In comparison to the "high priests" of molecular biologists, for instance Francis Crick, Jacques Monod, or François Jacob, Nirenberg and Matthaei were not yet scientists of the highest rank, but the news regarding their findings "spread like a brushfire" in the community, Kay (2000: 254) says. Still, their contribution was received in terms informed and shaped by the Matthew effect. Nirenberg was eventually awarded a long series of prestigious prizes including the Nobel Prize in Medicine in 1968 (shared with Robert Holley and H. Gobind Khorana).

Expressed in more affirmative terms, reputation is what reduces the cognitive complexity for the operating scientists: "No scientists listen to all statements. Reputation reduces complexity for scientists whose limited span necessitates decisions about whom to listen to, whom to ignore, whom to ridicule, and whom to take very seriously" (Fuchs, 1992: 72). The name of a well-known researcher is then working like a brand that attracts attention. In many cases, well-known scientists are respected for their work for good reasons, but occasionally, new and creative thinking is being turned down just because the ideas are advocated by lesser known researchers or researchers not recognized by the major authorities in the field. Merton (1973) lists a number of examples:

> The history of science abounds in instances of basic papers having been written by comparatively unknown scientists, only to be neglected for years. Consider the case of Waterson, whose classic paper on molecular velocity was rejected by the Royal Society as 'nothing but nonsense'; or of Mendel, who, deeply disappointed by the lack of response to his historic papers on heredity, refused to publish the results of the research; or of Fourier, whose classic paper

on the propagation of heat had to wait thirteen years before being finally published by the French Academy. (Merton, 1973: 456–457)

Such stories may be a consolation for mediocre scientists, not yet (in his or her mind) sufficiently recognized for their contributions, but for Merton it is an evidence of the discrepancies between the scientific ideology emphasizing that scientific work is allowing for new ideas to emerge, and the actual experience of a long series of researchers. For Merton, the Matthew effect and the uneven distribution of authority are potentially negative for a scientific discipline:

> When the Matthew effect is thus transformed into an idol of authority, it violates the norm of universalism embodied in the institution of science and curbs the advancement of knowledge. But next to nothing is known about the frequency with which these practices are adopted by the editors and referees of scientific journals and by other gatekeepers of science. This aspect of the workings of the institutions of science remains largely a matter of anecdote and heavily motivated gossip. (Merton, 1973: 457)

In some cases, important contributions previously neglected are re-evaluated—for instance the case of the biochemist and Nobel laureate Barbara McClintock accounted for by Stengers (1997: 120ff)—while others (Mendel is the example *par excellence* here) are, in Nietzsche's apt phrase, "born posthumously". Anyway, such stories make us learn that one cannot perhaps anticipate and foresee what future generations of scientists may regard as a valuable and credible. Past generations of theorists embracing concepts like phlogiston, miasma, or corpuscles and experts such as the phrenologists (having the skill of evaluating a person's qualities through an examination of the shape of the skull) may have been credible during their lifetimes but are today regarded as representing antiquated research programs. Robert Merton's emphasis on authority and peer-recognition defamiliarizes the view of science as the value-neutral and strictly instrumental matter that scientific ideologies often inscribe into scientific practice. Instead, science work is conducted by humans unable or even unwilling to transcend their own humanity—their curiosity, their demand for companionship and peer-recognition, and their struggle to entrench a credible position within a particular field. Hence the importance of understanding social conditions and outcomes such as the Matthew effect when examining scientific work as social practice.

Boundary-work in scientific disciplines

Scientists are not only engaging in establishing the hierarchical structure of the individual disciplines but are also concerned with safeguarding a neat separation between science and non-science, and between more and less credible sciences. Gieryn (1983: 782) is talking about the "boundary-work" of scientists as "their attribution of selected characteristics to the institution of science (i.e., to its practitioners, methods, stock of knowledge, values and work organization) for purposes of constructing a social boundary that distinguishes some intellectual activities as 'non-science'". Science and non-science need to remain separated. What is at stake is authority, professional identity, access to resources, and jurisdiction over the individual domain of expertise. Gieryn (1999, 1983) makes use of a number of examples of how proponents of science has drawn a line of demarcation between domains of expertise. One such example is the rejection of the emerging practice of phrenology, represented by a certain George Combe, by the intellectual elite in Edinburgh in the middle of the nineteenth century. According to Gieryn (1983), phrenology could not be accepted as a science for a number of reasons:

> First, phrenology challenged orthodox theories and methods, and anatomists may have suffered losses to professional reputations and opportunities had Combe been successful in his claim to science ... Second, Combe's democratic ideal certifying truth by popular opinion challenged the authority of scientific experts. Third ... phrenologists' desire to meld science and Christianity could have inspired a religious backlash against other scientists, at a time when religion may had greater hold on public sympathy than science. (Gieryn, 1983: 789)

In order to become widely accepted and recognized, new scientific fields and theories must not, as for instance Fujimura's (1996: 151) study of oncogene theory shows, challenge the predominant order *in toto*. Gieryn (1983: 792) concludes that "science is no single thing". Instead, "characteristics attributed to sciences vary widely depending upon the specific intellectual or professional activity designated as 'non-science', and upon particular goals of the boundary work. The boundaries of science are ambiguous, flexible, historically inconsistent, and sometimes disputed". Sciences are in this view territories that need to be guarded against potential intruders. Within the disciplinary territories, regimes of authority, mechanisms for the distribution of resources, and

means for resolving disputes are instituted, and privileges and responsibilities are enacted. The boundary-work is the day-to-day reproduction of such predominant regimes. Sommerlund's (2006) study of a
microbiology department at a major Danish University shows that
boundary-work is not what is abstract or solely conducted by credible
spokesmen and spokeswomen of the discipline, but that boundary-
work is an ongoing activity bound up with the day-to-day research
work. Sommerlund (2006: 912) was struck by the insistence among the
researchers to tell stories about conflicts, both historical and contemporary, especially between the sub-disciplines of *molecular microbiology*,
drawing on the dominant "genetic system" of classification, and *microbial ecology*, using the older "naturalist system". Such stories of conflicts
and controversies helped the researchers to reconcile the two dominant theoretical systems in the discipline, the taxonomic system in
the tradition of Linneaus and Darwin and the genetic system advanced
by modern genetics. In addition, the stories of conflict served, Sommerlund (2006) argues, as incentives for the work. In addition, the boundary-
work of the researcher helped reiterating predominant ideas and virtues
in the community. For instance, the epistemic ideal of "exactness" was
widely regarded as the principal quality of an accomplished scientific
discipline: "[T]he idea of 'exactness' seems to be so deeply embedded in
the way the researchers regard their own work that it has become synonymous with 'science'; their comments was not 'that's not very
exact', but rather 'that's not very scientific'", Sommerlund (2006: 918)
notices. For both Gieryn (1983) and Sommerlund (2006), scientific
work involves a continuous attention to the boundaries between
science and non-sciences or the less prestigious sciences. Scientists are
then self-surveilling communities regulating their own behaviour and
actions. They are very aware of the costs and risks involved when
transgressing the borders between disciplines. For instance, alternative
or traditional medicine advocated by "amateurs" is often severely criticized by medicine authorities. As an effect, as Mol's (2002) ethnographic study of atherosclerosis treatment in a Dutch hospital shows,
strict disciplinary boundaries may produce illnesses that are "multiple", many things at the same time regarding of what discipline is
examining the patient. Mol explains:

> Ontology in medical practice is bound to a specific site and situ-
> ation. In a single medical building there are many different athero-
> scleroses. And yet the building isn't divided into wings with doors
> that never get opened. The different forms of knowledge aren't

divided into paradigms that are closed off from one another. It is one of the great miracles in hospital life: there are different athero-scleroses in the hospital but despite the differences between them they are connected. Atherosclerosis enacted is more than one—but less than many. The body multiple is not fragmented. Even if it is multiple, it also hangs together. (Mol, 2002: 55)

The effective boundary-work produces clearly demarcated domains of expertise. Since the boundaries are prohibited from intersecting, it is the illnesses that have to be translated and molded. Contrary to common sense thinking, an illness is not a singularity, an *immutable mobile* to use Latour's (1987) phrase, but becomes "many different things" when it is passed around over the disciplinary boundaries. Illnesses are then, Mol argues, *enacted*: "[n]o object, no disease, is sin-gular. If it is not removed from the practices that sustain it, reality is multiple. This may be read as a description that beautifully fits the facts. But attending to the multiplicity of reality is also an *act*. It is something that may be done—or left undone. It is an intervention. It intervenes in the various available styles for describing practices" (Mol, 2002: 6). One of the surprising effects of boundary-work is then, in some cases and under certain conditions, that scientific objects become multiple and lose their status as a singularity.

Science and its social values

A sociology of science may also be capable of theorizing and examin-ing the less flattering aspects of scientific work. While for many scien-tists and the broader public, science stands out as one of the most honorable and extraordinary accomplishments of mankind, represent-ing the domination over nature and an improvement of the human condition. Contrary to this view, sceptics like Figueroa and Harding (2003) speak of the "exceptionalism" and the "triumphalism" in scien-tific ideologies:

Modern science and technologies have been claimed as the mark of the superior intellectual and cultural character of dominant groups and mark of socially progressive cultures. Such an evaluation invokes both exceptionalist and triumphalist assumptions. Exceptionalist holds that only modern science could ever achieve such an exalted status and that they alone escape permeation by religious and cultural values that infest other culture's knowledge system. Triumphalism holds that the history of 'real science' has been a story only of increasing achievements; any errors or bad effects have been the consequence of not real science but only bad science or of politics. (Figueroa and Harding, 2003: 9)

Similarly, Daniel Greenberg's—a former editor of the prestigious journal *Science—The politics of pure science* (1999, first published in 1967), examining what he calls "the politics of pure science", suggests that scientists are demonstrating traits of "chauvinism, xenophobia, and evangelism" and that they take on a role as a group of distinguished experts expecting full funding from the state, yet are reluctant to submit to any kind of control or review by individuals or institutions outside of the domain of "pure science". Early defences of science in the Victorian age such as that of John Tyndall (1820–1893) insisted that science had "a cultural value beyond practical utility" (Gieryn, 1983: 787). Such sentiments are still predominant in scientific communities; one must not be too ready to dismiss scientific work not leading to practical uses. In Greenberg's (1999) critical account, scientists advocate a *laissez-faire* ideology wherein their contributions must not be questioned by outsiders, paired with the demand for public funding:

> [T]he scientific ideology can be seen as bound together by a twofold ideology: first the desire for society to support, but not to govern, science; and second, for the community of science to exist as a loosely organized—meritocratic anarchy may best describe it—in which hierarchy and tables of organization bear little relation to the realities of power. This dual ideology is important, not because it governs events, but rather because it affects the vision of scientists and influences the stances that they adopt, both in relation to each other and in their dealings with nonscientists. (Greenberg, 1967/1999: 5)

Greenberg (1999) offers a series of statements wherein outstanding scientists demonstrate a rather complacent and arrogant view of the outsider's ability to understand the contributions, actual as well as potential, of scientific endeavours. Science is therefore not only a human blessing, a social resource at hand solving a range of problems; it is also a domain wherein privileged elites and influential individuals are struggling to attract financial resources safeguarding a future of scientific work (for a critique of science from a feminist and post-colonial theory perspective, see Harding and Hintikka, 2003; Anderson, 2002; Jordanova, 1989; Keller, 1985). Concepts like "exceptionalism", "triumphalism", "chauvinism", "xenophobia", and "evangelism" are not regularly associated with "pure science". If nothing else, they are indication of the hegemony of scientific ideologies. A sociology of science may reveal some of the less flattering traits scientific ideologies.

Technoscience in action: the case of new drug development

New drug development is a lengthy and costly process, taking an average of 15 years (Yu and Adedoyin, 2003). On average, it costs a company more than US$800 million to get one new medicine from the laboratory to the pharmacist's shelf (DiMasi, Hansen and Grabowski, 2003). Pharmaceutical research is a complex science-based innovation process wherein a whole spectrum of major scientific disciplines are intertwined such as organic chemistry, biochemistry, pharmacology, toxicology, molecular genetics, analytical chemistry are integrated in the course of action. New drug development is generally divided into three phases: (1) The discovery phase (or the pre-clinical development) is a stage in the development of a new drug that begins before clinical trials (testing in humans) can begin where the active molecule (new chemical entity, NCE) is identified together with the corresponding biological target and mode of action. If an NCE for a particular biological target thought to be important in disease, has demonstrated sufficient efficacy and safety it progresses to become (2) a candidate drug (CD). (3) In the development phase the CD is tested, further refined and tested in larger populations of patients, the launch and marketing phase where the new drug is sold on the market. In this book, it is primarily the first phase, the discovery phase that is examined. Hara (2003) speaks of the drug discovery in the following terms:

> A drug discovery is here defined as a discovery of the 'fact' that a natural or synthesized chemical has a particle of biological activity which can be applied to the treatment of diseases. However, from the viewpoint of the social shaping of science and technology, I do not intent to suggest that the 'fact' is an objective matter, which exists independently of social processes. (Hara, 2003: 7)

Hara emphasizes that the notion of "discovery" is a somewhat misleading term: what is referred to as a discovery is in fact a fabrication, the "mutual adjustment" of the chemical and the biological systems to one another: "[I] use the word discovery, referring to ... the causal relationship between chemical and the biological activities, not to the chemical itself" (Hara, 2003: 19). In other words, molecules are not "discovered" like diamonds in the rough but are instead continuously modified and tested against the biological system (biological organisms such as a mouse or a human being) and therefore undergo several transformations and changes during the development phase. Abraham and Reed (2002) explain the process:

> The discovery phase of drug innovation involves finding a 'lead compound'—that is, a chemical with therapeutically interesting biological activity. Once a pharmaceutical firm has identified a lead compound, it must test its toxicity in animals to meet safety regulations. If a compound is not discarded at this stage because of its toxicity, then the manufacturers will probably conduct clinical evaluations of the drug's safety and efficacy in humans. Such toxicological and clinical testing is, of course, the essence of the regulatory science of pharmaceuticals. The new discovery has been developed into a drug product innovation when, after completing their review of the manufacturer's drug-testing data on the compound, the regulators approve it for marketing. (Abraham and Reed, 2002: 341)

In the discovery and development process, the molecule is being what Barry (2005) calls "informed"—inscribed with meaning and functions. Barry (2005) explains:

> Pharmaceutical companies do not produce bare molecules—structures of carbon, hydrogen, oxygen and other elements—isolated from their environment. Rather, they produce a multitude of informed molecules, including multiple informational and material forms of the same molecule. Pharmaceutical companies do not just sell information, nor do they sell material objects (drug molecules). The molecules produced by pharmaceutical companies are more or less purified, but they are also enriched by pharmaceutical companies through laboratory practice. The molecules produced by a pharmaceutical company are already part of a rich informational material environment, even before they are consumed. This environment includes, for example data about potency, metabolism and toxicity and information regarding the intellectual property rights associated with different molecules. (Barry, 2005: 58)

The molecules are therefore never isolated entities but are instead the center of a texture of relations—be they chemical, biological, and pharmacological—between series of processes, events, and entities.

Hara (2003) points at the various resources mobilized in the process of "informing molecules":

> [T]he process of drug discovery and development can be regarded as involving heterogeneous elements including:
> 1. human actors such as chemists, pharmacologists, toxicologists, different functions in the company, corporate managers, academics, doctors, patients, government officers, politicians, activists and the general public
> 2. non-human entities such as drugs, materials, instruments and facilities; and
> 3. institutional and structural factors such as strategies, organizational linkages, human networks, organizational capabilities, funds, markets, regulations, sciences and clinical trials. (Hara, 2003: 32)

Hara concludes:

> [T]he shaping of drugs is the process of heterogeneous engineering. Various human actors, non-human entities and institutional and structural factors are involved in the process. In some cases, we can see interpretative flexibility about the properties of compound, a diversity of candidate drugs and different closure mechanisms ... In addition, actors are not isolated from wider and quite stable social relationships. Institutions and structures such as organizational structures, organizational capabilities, corporate strategies, regulatory systems, clinical trials, patent systems, production economies and market structures affect the process of shaping drugs. (Hara, 2003: 182)

As a complex social practice, new drug development is notorious for the large costs and long development times involved. Several authors point at this condition. Barry (2005: 58) writes:

> Although pharmaceutical companies may be able to identify potential drug molecules through a variety of methods, there is no guarantee that active molecules will work effectively and safely as drugs in living bodies. During development many active molecules fail, whether because they are poorly absorbed or metabolized, or are subsequently shown to have toxic effects. Moreover, in the context of the growing concern of consumers, regulators have become more

cautious about drug approvals ... In these circumstances, research and development costs have escalated. Pfizer, for example, the world's largest drug company, has warned that its $5bn annual research budget will yield only about two major new drugs per year. The average pre-clinical trial development cost of new chemical entities is said to be $30m per molecule. Perhaps 90 percent of chemical entities is said to fail such trials. The cost of generating a single approved medicine is claimed to be over $600million. (Barry, 2005: 58)

Abraham and Reed (2002: 341) add: "The cost to bring a new chemical entity to market can be as high as US$350 million, and it is estimated that the time from first synthesis of a new drug to its marketing quadrupled from 1960 to 1989". Gassman and Reepmeyer (2005: 235) report the following figures regarding the increased costs for new drugs: In 1976, the cost for developing a drug was US$54 million; in 1987 US$231 million; in 1991 US$280 million. In addition to the high costs involved in developing the drug, pharmaceutical companies also have to select what drugs they believe have the largest potential to actually to make it to the market, and, in the later phases, select the drugs with the largest market potential. Substantial resources are spent on substances that never make it to the market. Needless to say, the production of substances to choose from is enormous—"since the beginning of synthetic chemistry, some ten million different molecules have been 'invented'", Bensaude-Vincent and Stengers ([1993] 1996: 255) say—and the number grows by "more than a thousand a day" Bensaude-Vincent and Stengers (1996: 255) continue: "For one substance used by the pharmaceutical industry, nearly ten thousand have been tested and declared without intrinsic or commercial value". Nightingale (1998: 704) speaks of the medicinal chemists work as "number reduction": "[T]here are: 10^{180} possible drugs, 19^{18} molecules that are likely to be drug like, 10^8 compounds that are available in libraries, 10^3 drugs, but only 10^2 profit making compounds. Drug discovery involves reducing the 'molecular space' that profitable drugs will be found in, to a small enough volume that empirical testing can take place". In order to manage to handle such a large number of potentially interesting molecules, the medicinal chemist develops, Nightingale (1998) argues, a "chemical intuition":

The medicinal chemist uses this build up knowledge to select molecules that are potentially similar to the desired molecule. This sense of similarity is termed 'chemical intuition' and is a form of tacit knowledge that allows some medicinal chemists to recognize potential drug-like molecules for testing. While the novice might see a simple molecule, a medicinal chemist with years of experience and built up tacit 'chemical intuition' can recognize the same molecule as more or less drug-less, and therefore as a more or less likely candidate for testing. Just as the electronic engineer can see components 'as' things, the tacit knowledge allows the medicinal chemist to relate to function. (Nightingale, 1998: 704)

The skill of "chemical intuition" may be useful for medicinal chemists but what Walters, Stahl and Murcko (1998) call the "virtual chemistry space"—made up by Nightingale's (1998) "10^{180} possible drugs"—needs to be radically reduced to a more manageable number of targeted molecules. To identify promising chemical entities, computer-aided screening, so called *virtual screening* (Walters, Stahl and Murcko, 1998; Eckert and Bajorath, 2007), is employed in the industry. However, the use of these new advanced methods has not produced an output in parity with the speed of the methods of analysis. Drews (2000) writes:

The advent of genomic sciences, rapid DNA sequencing, combinatorial chemistry, cell-based assays, and automated high-throughput screening (HTS) had led to a new concept of drug discovery. In this new concept, the critical discourse between chemists and biologists and the quality of scientific reasoning are sometimes replaced by the magic of large numbers ... So far, this several hundredfold increase in the number of raw data has not yet resulted in a commensurate increase in research productivity, As measured by the number of new compounds entering the market place, the top 50 companies in the pharmaceutical industry collectively have not improved their productivity during the 1990s. (Drews, 2000: 1962)

As a consequence of the vast number of potential compounds, the dead ends are many and terminated projects are part of the industry: Blau, Pekny, Varma and Bunch (2004: 228) address this concern: "[A]lmost half of the resources that U.S. industry devotes to NPD are spent on product that fail or are cancelled. In the pharmaceutical industry this problem particularly is challenging because of long development times, low success rates, high capital requirements for building a manufacturing facility, and broad uncertainty in sales estimates". One of the principal challenges for the industry is to be able to predict what substances have promising therapeutical effects and can be effectively distributed in the human body. One industry representative expresses this challenge accordingly:

> Large pharmaceutical companies are very good at the front end of drug discovery, which often involves capital-intensive screening of compounds, They are also very good at the later stages of drug development—running large clinical trials. It is in the important middle ground of this process—converting promising compounds into viable products—where the flexibility and responsiveness of smaller biotech firms is essential. (GlaxoSmithKline CEO Tachi Yamada, cited in Birkinshaw and Mol, 2006: 84)

Blau, Pekny, Varma and Bunch (2004) argue that pharmaceutical firms must manage their product pipeline so that they maximize expected economic returns, minimize risk, and maintain diversity in the product portfolio. This product portfolio management includes many complicated decisions, predictions, and estimations:

> The portfolio must be selected in such a way that the competition among drug candidates for limited resources does not result in unusually long average product development times and hence late commercialization ... Further, the portfolio must be large enough to compensate for product failures yet must not be too large to over-extend resources. (Blau, Pekny, Varma and Bunch, 2004: 230)

Today, pharmaceutical firms are no longer enclosed organizational structures but try to become "[n]odes in large-scale scientific networks that include biotech firms as well as universities" (Gassman and Reepmeyer, 2005: 235); pharmaceutical companies seek to become "knowledge–brokers" struggling to overcome their reliance on a few blockbuster drugs. Gassman and Reepmeyer (2005: 237) point at the differences in importance of blockbuster drugs between companies. While Pfizer "generates 80 percent of total sales from its eight blockbuster products", other major pharmaceutical companies like Bristol-Myers Squibb, Novartis or Aventis "have a rather balanced product portfolio". One approach to make large pharmaceutical firms become more innovative is to buy biotech firms. However, studies (Schweizer, 2005) show that the integration and effective use of biotech know-how is not easily accomplished.

In addition to all the tradeoffs, ambiguities, and unpredictable events in the new drug development process and the large costs and long development times such conditions imply, there is a number of contextual factors that pharmaceutical companies must relate to. One such factor is the so-called good clinical practice standard operating procedures that pharmaceutical companies adhere to. Rather than being once and for all fixed and immutable, there is a standing conference called International Conference on Harmonisation of Technical Requirements for Registration of Pharmaceuticals for Human Use (in brief, ICH) that enacts good clinical practice standards. Abraham and Reed (2002) show that rather than being "unidirectional"—standards are specified regardless of technical and scientific innovations—regulation is in fact negotiated on basis of such new technical and scientific opportunities. Thus, regulatory practice that is officially detached from politics and social interests is actually partially shaped by new opportunities for innovation (see also Fox, Ward and O'Rourke, 2006).

Recent developments

Another contextual factor strongly affecting the pharmaceutical industry and the community of scientists is the recent development in domains of biotechnology, for instance genomics and proteomics. Hedgecoe and Martin (2003: 333) sketch the development of new biotechnologies in the 1990s:

> Coming into the 1990s, a number of new technologies such as polymerase chain reaction and high-throughput screening gave scientists greater understanding of genetic variation and increased the interest in pharmacogenetic studies. In addition to these technical developments, there were also ideological changes which, in the wake of the Human Genome Project, started to restructure medicine in terms of genetics (Bell, 1998). Perhaps most importantly, pharmacogenetics finally aroused the interest of the new genetic technologies with a focus on drug discovery and development. Around this time a new term began to be used to describe the discipline: Pharmacogenomics.

The value of genomics is that a large number of new targets can be identified. Gassman and Reepmeyer (2005: 239) write: "Genomic technologies will enable the identification of 3,000 to 10,000 new drug targets, compared with the current number of 5,000 (Pfeiffer, 2000). The integration of genomics and other technologies will lead to a shift from broadly targeted drugs to more focused medicines with higher therapeutic value for the target population allowing for mass-

customization of drugs". Pharmacogenomics, defined as the integration of "[t]raditional pharmaceutical sciences such as biochemistry
with annotated knowledge of genes, proteins and single nucleotide
polymorphisms" (Gassman and Reepmeyer, 2005: 239), is of interest
for pharmaceutical companies for similar reasons as genomics is: They
can identify "[a]ssociations between genetic markers for drug response
and those genes directly involved in the development of different
forms of pathology" (Hedgecoe and Martin, 2003: 337). That is, if a
strong correlation between a genetic marker and a drug response can
be proved, then the drug can be modified in terms of e.g., the dose of
the active substance or its distribution to suit the individual patient or
the group of patients demonstrating similar responses to the drug.
Pharmacogenomics thus enables the production of genetically designed
drugs, what Sowa (2006) calls "personalized medicine". Gassman and
Reepmeyer (2005: 239) write: "Pharmacogenomics integrates traditional pharmaceutical sciences such as biochemistry with annotated
knowledge of genes, proteins and single nucleotide polymorphisms
and thus combines the disciplines of pharmacology and genomics.
Hence, pharmacogenomics deal with the production of tailor-made
drugs for individuals". During the last 15 years period, a number of
new techniques such as *in silico testing* (testing of a substance in a com-
puter-simulated environment) and *high throughput screening* (the automatization of the testing of substances against a biological target) have
been developed and gradually adopted by pharmaceutical companies.
Still, research shows that pharmacogenetics/pharmacogenomics remains
contested among researchers. Hedgecoe's (2006) study of the reception
of such new techniques shows that not everyone is celebrating the new
concept: "I have to say that I don't think pharmacogenetics is at the
moment playing any part in, certainly, clinical practice", one clinical
researcher says (cited by Hedgecoe, 2006: 728). Still, as Sowa (2006: 16)
reports, in July 2005, no less than four "personalized" anticancer drugs
were registered and sold in Japan, namely Herceptin (breast cancer),
Rituxan (B cell non-Hodgkin's lymphoma), Glivec (chromic myeloid
leukaemia CML and gastrointestinal stromal tumor GIST) and Iressa
(lung cancer). The vision of being able to design individual drugs on
basis of pharmacogenomics and proteomics is still a venture for the
future. In general, the traditional ways of developing drugs, relying on
close collaboration between synthesis chemists, pharmacologists and
biologists and *in vivo* testing in laboratory animals is being contested
when new techniques are developed. This makes the pharmaceutical
a dynamic industry, serving as the testing ground and context of

application for a variety of highly innovative technologies and techniques. Still, such new technologies and techniques add to the complexity managers and co-workers have to handle in their day-to-day work and decision-making.

An overview of the new drug development process in AstraZeneca

The company

AstraZeneca is a major international pharmaceutical company engaged in the research, development, manufacture and marketing of prescription pharmaceuticals and the supply of healthcare services (astrazeneca.com). The company is one of the world's leading pharmaceutical companies with healthcare sales of $26.47 billion (2006) and leading positions in sales of gastrointestinal, cardiovascular, neuroscience, respiratory, oncology and infection products. AstraZeneca discovers, develops, manufactures and markets medicines for important areas of healthcare—cancer, cardiovascular, gastrointestinal, infection, neuroscience, respiratory and inflammation. In 2006, the company employs over 66,000 people worldwide and has 16 R&D centres in eight countries. Each working day, AstraZeneca spends $16 million on discovering and developing new medicines.

The research process in discovery

For the pharmaceutical industry, the discovery of a new drug presents an enormous scientific challenge, and consists essentially in the identification of new molecules or compounds. Ideally, the latter will become drugs that act in new ways upon biological targets specific to the diseases requiring new therapeutic approaches. The drug discovery (preclinical) process can be divided into five stages (Sams-Dodd, 2005) separated by milestones to indicate significant progress, according to Figure 4.1. Moving from one phase to the next depends upon meeting different criteria. It normally takes three to five years to produce a CD.

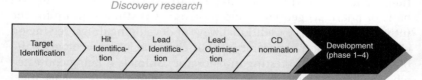

Figure 4.1   The drug discovery research process

Target identification and validation

The identification of therapeutic targets requires knowledge of a disease's etiology (the study of the causes of a disease) and the biological systems (e.g., the nervous system, the cardio-vascular system, or the respiratory system being part of the human body) associated with it. The duration of this phase may range from several months to several years. Target identification attempts to identify new targets, normally proteins, whose modulation might inhibit or reverse disease progression. The role of target validation is to demonstrate the functional role and biological relevance of the potential target in the disease phenotype (that is, the physical manifestation of the organism such as cells, structures, organs or reflexes and behaviors; anything that is part of the observable structure, function or behavior of a living organism). Target validation facilitates the identification and timely progression of lead molecules to provide effective improvement of diseases and, at the same time, it helps reducing the risks of failures from incorrect biological hypothesis. In many instances, however, drug targets are newly discovered and thus their full biological role is not known. This demands constant updates of the connectivity of a target throughout the lifecycle of a drug discovery project.

Hit and lead identification

Once the therapeutic target has been identified, scientists must then find one or more leads (e.g., chemical compounds or molecules) that interact with the therapeutic target so as to induce the desired therapeutic effect. In order to discover the compounds whose pharmacological properties are likely to have the required therapeutic effects, researchers must test a large variety of them on one or more targets. The term "hit" refers to when a compound has sufficient activity to warrant it being a candidate for clinical studies, provided it meets toxicity and other peripheral requirements. Many pharmaceutical companies have large libraries of synthetic or natural compounds, ready to be tested. To test the chosen compounds in large numbers, scientists use an entirely automated process known as high throughput screening (HTS). In general, of the thousands of compounds tested, barely 1 percent will qualify for further and more probing analysis. An important task is to ensure that the chosen compounds have the desired therapeutic effect on the target and to check relative toxicity bioavailability *in vivo* on animals.

Lead optimization

Lead optimization is defined as those activities that are required to optimize a screening hit to a pre-clinical candidate. The purpose of this stage is to optimize the molecules or compounds that demonstrate the potential to be transformed into drugs, retaining only a small number of them for the next stages. To optimize these molecules, scientists use very advanced techniques. For example, data allow the medical chemists to modify the structure of the selected molecules or compounds, if necessary, by screening, thereby creating structural analogues. The creation of hundreds, possibly thousands, of analogues, is aimed at, for example, improving the effectiveness, diminishing the toxicity or increasing the organism's absorption of the drug. This phase requires close collaboration between the biologists and chemists, who form a feedback loop. In this phase biologists test the biological properties of compounds on biological systems while the chemists optimize the chemical structure of these compounds in the light of information obtained by the biologists. This optimization stage aims at developing new substances that are more effective than known compounds. The latter are then subjected to a specific evaluation involving broader biological tests such as preliminary toxicology, computer-aided drug design, *in vitro* and *in vivo* studies which aim for testing in man.

CD nomination

The development potential of a candidate molecule depends essentially on its capacity to be administered to humans and show therapeutic effectiveness, with an acceptable level of side-effects (Hara, 2003). Before testing candidate molecules on humans in clinical trials (Development), scientists must show that the candidate drug (CD) does not present an unacceptable level of risk, given the expected therapeutic benefit. Regulatory authorities require pharmaceutical companies to demonstrate the safety of the drug for humans and to prove that the therapeutic advantages of the compound greatly outweigh any associated undesirable side-effects (e.g., migraine or high blood pressure in the case of cancer treatment). These studies are conducted in conformity with the rules of the regulatory bodies. During this stage scientists (e.g., biochemists, pharmacologists and toxicologists) continue to evaluate the phamaco-kinetic, pharmaco-dynamic (i.e., how the drug affects the body and how the drug is affected by the body, respectively) and toxicological properties of the compound *in vitro* and *in vivo* (on animals).

Development and clinical trials

If the CD is found safe, an application (investigation of a new drug, IND) is filed with drug regulatory authorities and ethical committees to obtain approval for testing on humans. After authorities approve the IND, clinical studies can begin. The required three-part clinical trials process (the clinical research program continues after the product's launch—commonly named Phase 4—by collecting data from outcome research and epidemiology data from patients; this might lead to new indications for the product), which judges the efficacy and safety of potential treatment, is a major undertaking. After completion of Phase 3 studies, the final documentation can be compiled and submitted to the appropriate national regulatory agencies (e.g., the FDA) for review (new drug application, NDA; Hullman, 2000). After approval, the product can be marketed. Adverse effects are followed meticulously through all clinical phases and after approval of the drug for launch. In the entire new drug development, the discovery process is the most complex and unpredictable and involves many factors that could influence the successful outcome (Zivin, 2000).

To conclude, the Discovery organization is accountable for the drug developing projects in the first five stages after which accountability transfers to Development organization. However, Discovery involvement does not end at CD Nomination, but must partner the Development organization into the sixth stage—the Proof of Principle Testing phase (containing pre-clinical development and initial clinical testing) aiming for the successful delivery of each drug project.

As we have seen, the literature on scientific and laboratory work, pointing at the interrelationships and intersections between technology, tolls, theoretical frameworks, practices, and narrative skills, and political *savoir-faire* may be useful when understanding how science-based innovation takes place within organizations competing on open markets, thus relying not so much on the scientific liberties of free investigation into the ultimate matters of organisms but on the capacity to manage and organize a totality of resources providing drugs that are both demonstrating adequate therapeutic effects and market viability. As we will see in the next three chapters, the management of this process is depending on a number of managerial practices and procedures. Prior to this investigation, the connections between knowledge management theory and the innovation management literature and what we here call science-based innovation are recapitulated. Thereafter the methodology of the study is accounted for.

Science-based innovation and knowledge management and innovation management theory: a summary of arguments

As suggested by for instance Scarbrough and Swan (2003), the emergence of knowledge management theory may be examined in terms of a discursive formation that is dependent upon a variety of changes in today's society and its organizations. Knowledge management is therefore the outcome from a number of interrelated changes, to name a few significant changes over the last 15 years, such as the access to information and communication technology, corporate governance policies, corporate strategies, and human resource management practices. Still knowledge management theory tends to treat knowledge as some kind of quasi-tangible asset that is firmly located within the firm. In addition, knowledge is often regarded as what is objective, "thing-like", and largely unproblematic once it has qualified as a form of legitimate knowledge within a community or in a particular setting. In many cases, such view of knowledge does not have far-reaching consequences. In other cases, though, this reification of knowledge and "black-boxing" of knowledge work may have decisive influence on organizational performance. Here, science-based innovation is not treated as some unified and coherent system simply providing output on basis of comparative amount of input of researchers, capital, technology and machinery, research management skills, and other important factors in scientific work. Instead, science-based innovation is portrayed as a specific form of social practice wherein a community of scientists jointly constitutes a set of legitimate research problems, a number of applicable methodologies, and a shared conceptual framework guiding the laboratory work. In brief, the community of scientists establishes a *modus operandi*, often strongly affected by individual political interests and concerns, within their particular field of research. Science-based innovation is here always a social practice characterized by ambiguities, elusiveness, ongoing negotiations and bargaining, and periods of little or limited visual progress. In other words, it is a social practice aiming at constituting scientific findings under the conditions of limited resources, competing interests, and time pressure. Science-based innovation is therefore not the one-dimensional machinery conveniently providing new findings and results dominating common sense thinking, but is instead a domain of creative work wherein new thought and images of reality are in the making.

Knowledge management is making claims to provide theory that creates an understanding of and guide management practice in knowledge-intensive organizations. Yet, it has not showed sufficient interest in what is happening in scientific communities and under what conditions science is actually being produced. A significant number of the companies and organizations that are categorized as knowledge-intensive are inextricably bound up with their ability to manage science-based innovation. As a consequence, knowledge management literature may be fruitfully informed by research in the fields of science and technology studies in sociology, and studies in disciplines presenting ethnographies of scientists' day-to-day practices. For instance, in the pharmaceutical industry, an industry firmly based in the biomedical and biotechnology sciences, a field integrating a rich variety of disciplines, there have been two recent cases of drugs being subject to critique from the Food and Drug Administration (FDA), the U.S. authority dealing with the licensing of drugs and monitoring of the pharmaceutical industry. In September 2004, the British-Swedish multinational pharmaceutical company AstraZeneca was asked to provide additional research to prove that its drug Exanta, the new oral anticoagulant drug preventing the blood from clotting, did not have undesirable side-effects. In January 2005, The French Drug Monitoring Authority declared the need for similar information. In the same day the FDA declared its decision, the AstraZeneca stock value fell by 7 percent and £2.5 billion was wiped off the stock market value. During the same period, the American pharmaceutical company Merck had to recall the arthritis pain drug Vioxx after the FDA had collected reports about lethal incidents—so called "adverse events"—connected with using the drug. The immediate financial effects from this recall of the drug were, Forbes reported in October 1, 2004, a reduction of ongoing pretax income of about $2 billion. Such incidents are devastating for pharmaceutical companies in terms of loss of income, market share, and scientific prestige in the industry. The decision of the FDA is here, at least officially, based in strictly scientific concerns. Medical and pharmacological expertise and leading experts are serving as autonomous reviewers making evaluations of what is acceptable and what is not in terms of side effects. Again a certain political economy of truth is played out in the negotiations between FDA and the focal pharmaceutical companies; new confirmatory studies and additional information are decided upon on basis of what is a joint agreement of what is required to safeguard a proper scientific procedure. Expressed differently, such incidents are grounded in competing social interests and opposing political agendas and thus must be examined as such.

Knowledge management theorists not paying close attention to the functioning and ideologies of scientific procedures and the deliberate actions of their significant agents have fewer opportunities for understanding the management of companies dependent on their capabilities in science-based innovation. The knowledge management literature has not been very concerned about moving inside the laboratories and experimental milieus wherein scientific works are being produced, and, consequently, knowledge management theory does not adequately address the role of science-based innovation in knowledge-intensive companies. Rather, the mainstream knowledge management literature is filled with general statements about themes such as the emergence of the knowledge society, the knowledge-based firm, or even "knowledge capitalism" (Burton-Jones, 1999). Besides being statements bringing knowledge management theory per se into the limelight, this literature neither provides guidelines, nor really enables for understanding of how science-based companies are operating. As long as the insight into scientific communities is scattered, knowledge management literature is at risk to remain dependent on the belief in what Feldman (2004) calls "objective knowledge", knowledge that is never the outcome from the mangle of social practice but is always ready-made and packaged. As has been suggested by the science and technology literature, no knowledge may claim such a pristine position. Knowledge is the outcome from practices, negotiations, politics, storytelling, and the operating of laboratory machinery, not what is found like a pearl at the bottom of a river—perfected and finished and from the beginning a true wonder of nature.

Methodology of the study

Epistemological disputes

Before the data collection and data analysis of the study are accounted for, some epistemological issues are addressed. Following Latour's (2004: 221) statement that "[a]ny epistemology is a political epistemology", it is important to position the study within the broader theoretical debates in the field of organization theory and management studies. One of the standing ontological and epistemological concerns regarding research methodology is the ongoing debate between schools of realism and schools of anti-realism (often portrayed by its antagonists as *relativists*). Realism is, Tsang and Kwan (1999: 761) say, "[t]he philosophical thesis that a mind-independent reality, which has its own inherent order, exists" (for an extended philosophical argument, see Dummett, 1978a, b). While a realist position is often defended in terms of speaking of the search for an ultimate matter that can be examined through scientific methods, anti-realists believe that there are few opportunities for identifying such a reality per se, detached from human interests, the influence of laboratory equipment and other "vision machines" (Virilio, 1994), and devoid of jointly agreed upon interpretative and theoretical frameworks. Instead, anti-realists say that realities are constructed on bases of a variety of resources including material, cultural, and social resources. In several cases, such anti-realist arguments are vehemently criticized by realists suggesting that such a denial of ultimate matter implies a "slippery slope argument" wherein the distinction between right and wrong, good and bad, and so forth become obscure or neglected. For instance, Schmidt (2001: 149) argues that "the normative indifference" of contructivists is a smug position: "[R]elativists sometimes claim not to be judging at all. They are simply more tolerant than their universalistic counterparts, more willing to live with the cognitive and evaluative pluralism which is so characteristic to modernity". Harding (2003), defending a standpoint epistemology, speaks of such accounts as being representative of a "relativism panic":

> [T]he threat of a damaging relativism drives people back into the absolutes of the unity ideal in spite of plausible arguments against the latter. Unity idealists generate a 'relativism panic' when faced with criticism that the standards of modern science are too weak, as has been argued by feminists, the multicultural and postcolonial science studies, and elements of postpositivist philosophy of science. (Harding, 2003: 54)

While allegations of "normative indifference" may be shrugged off as some moralist raving not worthy of responding to, more tempered realists have sought to reconcile the realist/anti-realist positions. One such attempt is the critical realism school taking social structures as "real" while maintaining the belief that human beings are free (at least in principle) to act on such structures. Mandelbaum (1964) distinguishes between a direct (or naïve) and a critical realism:

> I should like to define epistemological *realism* as holding that there exists independently of perception a world of physical objects whose nature can be known by human beings. Direct, or 'naive' realism would hold that the actual qualities of such objects are not different from those which we ascribe to them on the basis of sense-perception; in other words, independent physical objects as they appear to us to be. (Mandelbaum, 1964: 118)

Mandelbaum (1964: 119) continues: "In contradistinction to naïve or direct realism, a critical realist would hold at least some of the types of qualities which physical objects appear to possess are not actually possessed by them". A critical realist like Mutch (1999) speaks of this epistemological position accordingly:

> Critical realism retains a central place for human choice, arguing it is always open to humans to act in manners which are not suggested by the situations in which they find themselves. However, it is not their immediate actions which create those situations. although they might well contribute to their reproduction. Rather, such situations, and the constraints on activity which they impose, are the consequences, intended or otherwise, of previous human activity. In a similar fashion, our actions in the present can change or reinforce current structures which will go on to form the constraints or opportunities for another set of actions. (Mutch, 1999: 328)

Reed (2001) also advocates a realist position in similar terms:

> Critical realism is grounded in an objectivist social ontology in that it focuses on social reality as consisting of objectified social structures that exists independently of the various ways in which they can be discursively constructed and interpreted by social scientists and other social actors located in a wide range of socio-historical situations. (Reed, 2001: 214)

Reed (2001: 214) thus emphasizes the recognition of enduring social structures in critical realism: "Realism, both ontologically and methodologically, gives far more explanatory weight to enduring generative mechanisms and social structures that are even minimally accommodated within constructionist ontology and epistemology". Reed (2005) even talks about a "critical realist turn" in organization and management studies, a position thoroughly criticized by Contu and Willmott (2005). However, for anti-realists, the critical realist program does not succeed in addressing the difference between what is "mind-independent" and what is not, thus falling back into a realist position. Mir and Watson (2001: 1169) argue:

> While critical realists indeed focus on the contingent relationships between phenomenon and structures, they still subscribe to the realist notion that the inherent order of things is 'mind-independent' ... On

the other hand, constructivists attribute structures not to a mind-independent reality, but rather to the generative (and therefore constructive) act of researchers and theorists. (Mir and Watson, 2001: 1169)

For anti-realists such as constructivists and pragmatists and what Richard Rorty calls anti-foundationalists, arguments put forth within the philosophy of science literature pointing at the value of a non-realist perspective are virtually ignored. Such arguments include *inter alia*, the writing of Pierre Duhem pointing at the inability to falsify central hypothesis but merely supporting hypotheses (an idea further developed by Imre Lakatos, 1970), Gaston Bachelard's emphasis on the laboratory equipment as a set of artifacts always already laden with and embodying scientific assumptions, and Ludwik Fleck's view of scientific work as being community-based and thus being situational and contingent. Realists then believe that the ultimate matter of being is accessible *as such* without any distortion derived from laboratory equipment, scientific procedures, theoretical frameworks, and other resources mobilized in the research activities. Anti-realists believe this is a simplistic and ideological view of scientific work. For instance, Wylie (2003), advocating a standpoint epistemology, argues:

Under some conditions, for some purposes, observer neutrality—disengagement, strategic affective distance from a subject—may be an advantage in learning crucial facts or grasping the causal dynamics necessary for understanding a subject. But at the same time, considerable epistemic advantage may accrue to those who approach inquiry from an interested standpoint, even a standpoint of overtly political engagement. (Wylie, 2003: 33)

Willmott (2005), speaking of management studies, is pointing at two implications from the (critical) realist program. First, it is the natural sciences that are assumed to serve as some generally applicable model for all scientific activities: "At the heart of the critical realist project is a belief that (a realist view of) the logic ascribed to natural science provides the basis for investigating the social world. The distinctiveness of scientific method is conceived to reside in its capacity to discern the operation of causal laws in the patterning of events" (Willmott, 2005: 756). Second, he emphasizes that (critical) realists assume a voluntarist model of action wherein individuals are free to act as they like and that any critique of such a voluntarist view is becoming subject to harsh critique:

> Critical realists assume that 'structure' identifies a force that conditions action; and therefore are bewildered if not outraged when it is said to be 'illusory'. Their outrage is associated with a second assumption: that describing structure as 'illusory' announces an idealism and/or voluntarism in which actors are unconstrained (an un-enabled) by the forces conceived as 'structure'. This reaction is symptomatic of dualistic, zero-sum thinking where the seeming denial of determinism, 'structural' forces is interpreted and endorsing an extreme voluntarism. (Willmott, 2005: 761)

By the end of the day, then, realism and anti-realism remain unreconciled and both camps are defending their position in rather polemic terms. The methodology of this study is located in the anti-realist domain of research. While the idea of an ultimate matter makes sense as a guiding principle for a number of natural and life sciences, in practice such "physical", "chemical", or "biological" "truths"—expressed in terms of being jointly agreed upon in specific communities being capable of demonstrating that certain epistemic things actually exist under certain conditions (see Hacking, 1983)—are mingling with social and cultural conditions making epistemic things hybrid assemblages including a variety of resources. In other words, to use a case from new drug development, a certain molecule has a certain structure and constitution but the possibilities for making the molecule the active substance in a new candidate drug depends on a series of scientific, managerial, ethical, and administrative processes and decisions, thereby making the molecule become part of a broader actor-network of resources. There are no molecules per se in the pharmaceutical industry but only assemblages of natural and social resources. Rather than representing a "relativist" position—a ready-made critique of realists aiming at discrediting any assumption deviating from their own—such a view is what Nietzsche once called "perspectivist"[6] and Law (2004) refers to as "perspectivalism". That is, a specific molecule (in our case) is evaluated on basis of different bases of knowledge and with different intentions. For the synthesis chemist, a molecule is a chemical entity; for the biologist or pharmacologist, the molecule is what needs to affect the target of the selected indication; for the marketing manager, the molecule is one entity in a broader set of packages that may open up new markets or defend already entrenched market shares. In a perspectivist framework, the molecule is never evaluated strictly detached from its setting but is always already located in contingent and situated regimes of knowledge and power; the molecule is partially natural, partially social and cultural, but always in motion, passed around in communities and organizational departments until it is (in the best of cases) finally stabilized and made immutable when it eventually becomes a new registered drug. Thus, the molecule and the various assemblages in which it takes part can never be regarded as being solely natural because it is always translated and examined in social communities, albeit scientifically trained and competent; nor can it be regarded as being fully social as long as it can demonstrate certain biochemical responses when being distributed in a biological organism. Such responses are largely but not wholly—to what degree remains a source of dispute among scientists—removed from social interest. Therefore, the perspectivist framework recognizes the natural constitution of epistemic objects while refusing to render them "mind-independent"; epistemic things are examined as being related to but not wholly determined by shifting planes of knowledge and interests whereof some are more social than others. A perspectivist epistemology is therefore in opposition to what Daston (1999) and later Feldman (2004) call "aperspectival objectivity", the belief that there are opportunities for, in Thomas Nagel's (1986) memorable phrase, a "view from nowhere". Daston (1999) carefully unveils the stock phrase of objectivity as not as unified and self-explanatory as its proponents suggest but in fact denoting a series of qualities and objectives:

> Our usage of the word 'objectivity' ... is hopelessly but revealingly confused. It refers at once to metaphysics, to methods, and to morals. We slide effortlessly from statements about 'the objective truth' of a scientific claim, to those about the 'objective procedures' that guarantee a finding, to those about the 'objective manner' that qualifies a researcher. Current usage allows us to apply the word as an approximate synonym for the empirical (or, more narrowly, the factual); for the scientific, in the sense of public, empirically reliable knowledge; for impartiality-unto-self-effacement and the cold-blooded restraints of the emotions; for the rational, in the sense of compelling assent from all rational minds, be they lodged in human, Martian, or angelic bodies. (Daston, 1999: 110)

Daston (1999) traces the idea of objectivity back to Cartesian thinking but it was not until the mid-nineteenth century that it gained its full legitimacy in scientific circles as what is representing the community of scientific experts and its shared knowledge and what is contrasted against the arts and its emphasis on individual contributions:

> Aperspectival objectivity was the ethos of the interchangeable and therefore featureless observer—unmarked by nationality, by sensory dullness or acuity, by training or tradition; by quirky apparatus, by colorful writing style, or by any other idiosyncrasy that might interfere with the communication, comparison, and accommodation of results. Scientists paid homage to this ideal [objectivity] by contrasting the individualism of the artist with the self-effacing cooperations of scientists, who no longer came in the singular—'l'art, c'est moi, la science, c'est nous', in Claude Bernard's epigram. (Daston, 1999: 118)

A perspectivist epistemology implies that subjective perspectives are recognized but are freed from their relativistic connotations—in terms of ethical and political relativism (Law, 2004), that is. Instead, subjectivity is recognized not as being arbitrary and poorly grounded but as being what is by definition and of necessity shared with others. Kramer (2002) eloquently defends such a non-relativistic view of subjectivity:

> The fear of subjectivity, is in any case based on the misconception that subjectivity itself is arbitrary, a kind of innate principle of eccentricity or deviation. Interpretative statements win an initial credibility precisely because they are subjective, that is, because they are culturally and socially conditioned, context-sensitive, and the product of education and dialogue. Subjectivity is regulated by the range of subject-positions available within a speech community. It is not to be understood as a condition of self-enclosed private existence, but as a condition of public relatedness—or series of positions—in a network of practices and representations. The world subjectivity feared by those who identify rationality with objectivity is not, to be sure, a mere phantasm, but it consists not in the inevitability of personal idiosyncrasy but in mistaken positional choices. No one can act outside of a subject position; the attempts to do so is one definition of delirium, psychosis, madness. (Kramer, 2002: 166–167)

The unwillingness to recognize subjective beliefs and biases is reflected in the way scientific work is represented in writing. Rheinberger (2003) notes out that after, say, 1900, the linguistic marker 'I' is excluded form scientific texts:

> Today, we find no 'I' anymore in these texts. Their grammatical structure suggests that the facts of the objects speak to the initiated laboratory worker or to a wider circle of readers. All along the above-mentioned authority gradient is a strict commitment to the passive voice, from which there is no escape. The supposed commitment to objectivity is built right into the language in which the scientist is allowed to speak to his or her fellows and to a wider audience Therefore, and in a certain sense, authorship as a warranty to speak appears to be, in scientific writing, always already crossed out. (Rheinberger, 2003: 311)

The only domain where subjectivity is permitted is "at the outer fringes" of a field, in "congressional openings and commemorations" and in scientific autobiographies. Here, Rheinberger (2003: 311) says, "the scientist may take the freedom to expose his or her personal view, something that has no place in the regular canon of scientific writing".

Recognizing subjectivity as an operative resource in a perspectivist epistemology underlines the central importance of what Mol (2002) and Law (2004) call *enactment*, the idea that epistemic objects, in our cases for instance individual molecules serving as the active components of compounds, are rendered coherent and unified within specific experimental systems. Law defines enactment accordingly:

> The claim that relations, and so realities and representations of realities (or more generally, absences and presences) are being endlessly or chronically brought into being in a continuing process of production and reproduction, and have no status, standing, or reality outside those processes. A near synonym for performance, the term is possibly preferable because performance has been widely used in ways that link it either to theatre, or more generally to human conduct. (Law, 2004: 159)

In our case, molecules are similarly enacted as being for instance promising or irrelevant pharmaceutical entities. In addition to the recognition of subjectivity, one of the principal ideas with the perspectivist epistemology is that it is the practising researcher that chose his or her favoured perspective. Cilliers (2005) points at such creative aspects of scientific analysis and defends it against allegations of relativism:

> 'Limited' knowledge is not equivalent to 'any' knowledge. If this were so, any modest claim, i.e. any claim with some provisionality or qualification attached to it, would be relativistic. The only alternative then would be an arrogant self-assurance. Such a self-assured position is deeply problematic since its complacency forecloses further investigation. Modest claims are not relativistic and, therefore, weak. They become an invitation to continue the process of generating understanding. (Cilliers, 2005: 260)

In the perspectivist epistemology, the researcher insists on the right of making statements: "From this particular perspective, chosen among a variety of competing and complementary perspectives, this object of analysis can be said to demonstrate such and such properties". As opposed to for instance Schmidt's (2001) accusation of "normative indifference", a perspectivist epistemology clearly specifies on what bases a theoretical argument is formulated. At the same time, the perspectivist epistemology does not assume—contrary to the realists' insistence on speaking on behalf of the things per se, regarding themselves as being spokesmen of immutable facts—that the specific analysis is a favoured or the ultimate one. Instead, the perspectivist epistemology regards scientific practice as a storytelling practice anchored in theoretical frameworks and established methodologies wherein many stories can be told and criticized. This stance suggests a pluralist view of scientific work and draws on what has been called the "disunity of science thesis" (Dupré, 1993; Galison, 1999; Keller, 2002).

In summary, studying new drug development activities in pharmaceutical industry implies that the researcher needs to recognize legitimate scientific evidence of biochemical effects of investigated substances. Therefore, new drug development is not wholly removed from "biological truths" (i.e., the ultimate matter of the biological organisms; the functioning of the biological organism; its responses to chemical substances; its absorptions and metabolism of the drug); nor is the new drug development process self-explanatory and enclosed as soon as the active molecule is detected. On the contrary, the molecule (as the central epistemic thing in the process) is passed around in different communities and departments, undergoes continuous translations and associations with various resources, and is examined from a variety of perspectives. One must not assume that a realist view of this heterogeneous and non-linear process is capable of capturing all the situational and contextual qualities of the process. Only through modulating between "the natural", "the social", and "the cultural" can one understand how new drugs are fabricated. Hence the perspectivist epistemology is adhered to in the study.

Data collection and analysis

The study reported in this book is based on a case study of AstraZeneca, a major British-Swedish pharmaceutical company. Case studies are a widely used methodology in management studies (for two standard accounts of the methodology, see Eisenhardt, 1989 and Yin, 1994). Case studies include number of complementary data collection methods such as interviewing, participant observations, and document studies. In the present study, interviews accounted for the bulk of the empirical material. While interviews have traditionally been viewed as a rather uncomplicated exchange of information between two or more interlocutors—often including the knowledgeable insider and the curious outsider researcher—the interview situation has been scrutinized in greater detail more recently. For instance, in a series of volumes edited by Gubrium and Holstein (2003), and Holstein and Gubrium (2003), the interview is portrayed as a complex social encounter resting on elusive epistemological grounds: "Treating interviewing as a social encounter in which knowledge is constructed means that the interview is more than a simple information-gathering operation; it's a site of, and occasion for, producing knowledge", Holstein and Gubrium (2003: 4) say. The interview is instead reconceptualized as "[a]n occasion for purposefully animated participants to construct versions of reality interactionally rather than merely purvey data" (Holstein and Gubrium, 2003: 14). In interviews, data and information is not merely being transmitted from one individual to another, but instead the encounter becomes a situation wherein knowledge and meaning is jointly produced. In addition, the interview situation "[t]ransforms the subject behind the respondent from a repository of information and opinions or a wellspring of emotions into a productive source of knowledge" (Holstein and Gubrium, 2003: 14). Rather than conceiving of interview utterances as being true accounts of unambiguous social realities, interviews are, in Rosenblatt's (2003) apt phrase, "at the border of fact and fiction". While some commentators (e.g., Denzin, 2003) are sceptical about the emerging "interview society" wherein the interview is regarded as a universally applicable method revealing individual intentions and beliefs, the interview remains one of the principal data collection methods in the social sciences. In Holstein and Gubrium's (2003) comprehensive anthology *Inside interviewing* there is a great number of recommendations on how to deal with a variety of aspects of interviewing, ranging from queer theory perspectives on interviewing to how to safeguard adequate transcriptions. Of specific interest are the forms of non-verbal communication that rarely are commented upon in interview-based studies. Raymond Gorden (1980: 335, cited in Poland, 2003: 273) identifies no less than four different types of nonverbal communication that the interviewer needs to notice:

- *Proxemic* communication is the use of interpersonal space to communicate attitudes;
- *chronemic* communication is the use of pacing of speech and length of silence in conversation;
- *kinestic* communication includes both body movements or postures; and
- *paralinguistic* communication includes all variations in volume, pitch, and quality of voice.

Although these forms of communication are little accounted for in this study, it is important that these variations on a given utterance may radically alter its meaning. Therefore, the transcripts that are presented to the reader cannot be seen as uncomplicated representations of actual utterances but are instead the researcher's interpretation of the interlocutor's intentions.

Notwithstanding all the epistemological intricacies and conditions restraining any claim to truth on basis of interview material, the choice of interview method is consistent with previous studies of science-based innovation, for instance Paul Rabinow's two research monographs (Rabinow and Dan-Cohen, 2005; Rabinow, 1996). In addition to the interviews, documents (e.g., annual reports) were examined and seminars where research findings were reported were held with employees in the focal company. In terms of data collection, a long-term relationship lasting over eight years and including a number of studies and research project with the company enabled for a more detailed understanding of the new drug development process. In the present study, 28 interviews were conducted in the company. Interview subjects were selected to represent the four different departments in the drug discovery organization. Half of the interviewees were male researchers. Interviews lasted for about one hour and were conducted by two persons, one academic researcher and one insider holding a role as Principal Scientist with extensive experience from pharmaceutical research and a Ph.D. in Management. The insider contributed greatly not only to select appropriate respondents across the Discovery research organization, but also through explaining and clarifying some of the more esoteric procedures and *modus operandi* in the new drug development process. All the interviews were tape-recorded and transcribed by the academic researcher. Finally, the interview excerpts were coded using a procedure reminding of what Strauss and Corbin (1998: 101, 123) refer to as an "open" and "axial" coding.

Summary and conclusion

In the last chapter, science-based innovation was conceived as a complex social practice embodying theoretical framework guiding actions and bridging communities of scientists, material resources such as laboratory equipment and technology and organic species such as cell lines and genetically modified laboratory animals, storytelling skills and rhetorical resources, and joint ideologies and beliefs on what science is and what scientists do. Science-based innovation is thus a tightly knitted texture of activities, events, and resources that is continually being transformed and translated in the course of action. In this chapter, new drug development in pharmaceutical industry has been examined as one discipline or domain wherein such assemblages of resources and practices are enrolled. There are to say the least considerable complexities involved in making a new molecule become a new registered drug. Not only scientific challenges but also juridical, ethical, and strategic and financial guidelines and objectives need to be carefully attended to in the process. Taken together, science-based innovation is an eminent example of what Charles Lindblom, discussing decision-making in public policy, once talked about as "the science of middling through"; it can never be fully anticipated and planned, yet is dependent on the thoughtful management capable of solving emerging problems and avoiding the worst threats to the new drug development process. The three remaining chapters will address three distinct but interrelated issues in the management of science-based innovation: the need for an element of play and risk-taking in all science-based innovation, the emotionality and demand for leadership practice in science-based innovation, and finally, effects from the design of and use of management control in innovation work. These three chapters do not seek to formulate any conclusive theoretical framework for the management of science-based innovation but point at a number of practical and managerial implications from science-based innovation.

Part II
Science-Based Innovation in Practice

5
Innovation Work as Play and Systematic Risk-Taking

Introduction

One of the standing concerns in the pharmaceutical industry is that major pharmaceutical companies are dedicating substantial time and resources to develop so called "me-too" drugs, that is, drugs that are modelled on a competitor's successful drug but sufficiently different to be patented (Busfield, 2006: 302). Busfield writes: "A study of approval by the US Food and Drug Administration (FDA) between 1989 and 2000 showed that approvals for new drugs consisted of relatively small proportion of all approvals, with only 35 of applications related to new chemical entities". Expressed differently, there is a concern in the industry and in society that pharmaceutical firms are primarily interested in short-term profits rather than developing more sustainable product portfolios (Angell, 2004). What is of great importance here is the willingness to expose oneself to risks in the pharmaceutical industry.

In this chapter, science-based innovation work will be examined in terms of being what is in essence open-ended, creative, and involving risk-taking. Rather than regarding science-based innovation as what can be administrated along predefined series of processes and activities, science-based innovation is understood as what is, by definition, involving residual factors such as luck, chance, and serendipity. At the same time, innovation is what needs to be controlled, managed, monitored and regulated. A concept that captures this two-sided nature of innovation—its reliance on predefined processes and activities and the need for experimental thinking and acting—is that of *playing*; playing is both organized around a set of rules, scripts, and practices, a predefined framework determining and regulating the activities, but also involves significant degrees of freedom for the individual to demonstrate skills, dexterity, and creativity within such a framework. Speaking of science-based innovation in terms of playing is not a wholly new idea. Anderson (1994) is claiming that the notion of play captures the energy and commitment that is demanded in innovation work. Anderson writes: "Work wears us out, even before we do it. Play energizes us, even after we're done. Play also gives direction and focus on our activities. In class the mind easily wanders. On the ball field, at the mall, or cruising singles' bars, the mind is incredibly focused" (Anderson, 1994: 81). Therefore, Anderson suggests, innovation work may be regarded as a form of playing. More recently, Dodgson, Gann and Salter (2005) argue that play is an important component in the innovation process mediating "thinking" and "doing", the conception and execution of new product and service innovations. "[T]he concept of 'play' enables the link between ideas and action. 'Play' is the medium between the 'thinking' and 'doing'", Dodgson, Gann and Salter (2005: 137–138) say. In this view, play is defined accordingly: "Activities associated with the selection of new ideas to ensure they are practical, economical, targeted, and marketable, including verifying, simulating, extrapolating, interpolating, preparing, testing, validating, transforming, integrating, exploring, and prioritizing" (Dodgson, Gann and Salter, 2005: 242). Dougherty and Takacs (2004) speak of play as what is making multi-functional new product development "interrelate heedfully" in their work. They here contrast *work* and *play* (2004: 576): "Research reports people perceive 'work' to be constrictive, structured, tedious, difficult and boring, while 'play' is seen as liberating, unstructured, refreshing and emotional, and suggests that the benefits of play can be achieved by framing activities, since relabeling tasks as play instead of work transformed people's perception, judgements and motivations". Dougherty and Takacs (2004) found that co-workers in innovative firms perceived innovation work as a form of playing based on *heedful interrelating* (Weick and Roberts, 1993), that is, the ability to "act carefully, critically, wilfully and purposefully with regard to the joint situation, rather than habitually". Moreover, play and heedful interrelating were co-dependent processes that constituted the innovative behaviour. Dougherty and Takacs (2004: 573) write:

> Play generates heedful interrelating, while heedful interrelating structures play: play and heedful interrelating complement each other to produce a sensible, manageable approach to structuring the

activities of innovation so that streams of new products are possible, even in established organizations with mature technologies.

Innovative firms were capable of forming multi-functional teams, perceiving innovation work as a form of play based on heedful interrelating, while non-innovative firms systematically failed to do so. Thus, play is a central category in Dougherty and Takacs's (2004) analysis. De Geus (1997), drawing on the psychologists D.W. Winnicott's (1971) *Playing and Reality*, argues that playing is an important vehicle for organization learning. Since all competitive companies need to continuously learn from its activities, de Geus argues, playing, *mutatis mutandis,* should be a part of the managerial agenda. De Geus (1997: 64) says that playing is a form of "experimenting with an object that in some way represents reality" and therefore enables new thinking. Quinn (2005) speaks of the concept of *flow*, first formulated by the psychologist Csikszentmihalyi, as a central experience in knowledge work. In Csikszentmihalyi's model, there are nine elements: "(1) a challenging activity with skills that are equal to challenge, (2) clear goals, (3) clear feedback, (4) concentration, (5) the merging of action and awareness, i.e., the 'activity becomes spontaneous, almost automatic' (Csikszentmihalyi, 1990: 53), (6) a sense of control, (7) the enjoyment of the activity for its own sake irrespective of rewards and punishments (an 'autotelic' experience), (8) a lack of concern for what others may think about the performer (the 'loss of self-consciousness'), and (9) time seems to speed up of slow down (the 'transformation of time')" (Quinn, 2005: 612). Quinn emphasizes the experience of flow in knowledge work:

[H]igh-performance experience is a real and relevant phenomenon in knowledge work. It exists, knowledge workers are aware of it, and they pay attention to variations in the degree to which they experience it, suggesting that we, as organizational scholars, could improve our understanding of performance by paying attention to subjective experience as well as objective measures and goals ... The degree to which people experience flow depends on the types of jobs and tasks they perform as well as on the clarity and difficulty of their goals and the feedback they extract from their tasks. (Quinn, 2005: 632)

Even though play and flow are not synonymous, flow and the sense of full control is what is central to successful playing; it is a sense of being in full control while conducting a specific task one is qualified and skilled for. For Quinn (2005), flow in knowledge work should thus be further explored.

In Anderson's (1994), Dodgson, Gann and Salter's (2005), Dougherty and Takacs's (2004), de Geus's (1997) and Quinn's (2005) discussions on the connections between play and innovation, play is used as a rather unspecified and general concept aimed at capturing the creative yet regulated activities in the innovation process. Play is then not given a proper theoretical analysis but is largely used in its everyday sense of the term. In this chapter, play is further elaborated upon as a concept capturing the human need for transgression, creativity, and competition under regulated conditions. The analysis of play draws on the writings of the French Social thinker Roger Caillois draws on the notion of the sacred and its role and function in modern, de-traditionalized, and "disenchanted" societies, and, more specifically, on his writing on the institution of playing in society. While Roger Caillois remains largely unexplored in the organization theory and management studies literature, he is at least partially recognized in the social sciences as one of the most important French "pre-postmodernist" writers (to use Singer's, 1992, formulation) besides writers such as Maurice Blanchot, Georges Bataille and Michel Leiris. Caillois is also a follower of Émile Durkheim and the anthropologist Marcel Mauss and was a member of the *Collège de Sociologie* in Paris in the 1930s, an association of researchers, philosophers and writers connected to Sorbonne, sharing a number of theoretical interests. Even though his work has been portrayed as being sketchy and transdisciplinary (Caillois, 2003), his writing on playing provides an interesting conceptual framework from which new drug develop-ment can be examined. Thus the goal of this chapter is to show that science-based innovation demands both clearly stated and jointly agreed upon rules but also a significant component of luck, chance, and risk-taking. The challenge for practising researcher is to develop his or her skills and scientific sleight-of-hand to be capable of exploit-ing opportunities emerging in the research process. Like all creative work, laboratory researchers have to pay attention to both details and see the broader picture wherein the specific research activity is located. Such a two-sided focus is representative of a playful relation to the work, bridging openness and closure, routine work and a recog-nition of the unexpected. Hopefully, such a view of innovation is capable of broadening the view of science-based innovation and under-lining the connection between "chance and necessity" in laboratory work.

The *Collège de Sociologie* and Caillois's theory of play

"[T]o declare it once and for all, Man plays only when he is in the full sense of the word a man, and *he is only wholly Man when he is playing*".

Friedrich Schiller (1795/2004: 80)

The *College de Sociologie* was founded by a number of French intellectuals that met regularly the end of the 1930s in Paris. Among its most prominent members counted Georges Bataille, Michel Leiris, Jean Wahl and Roger Caillois. Being influenced by, on the one hand, the recent interest in France for Hegel's philosophy, introduced and lectured on at Sorbonne by Alexandre Kojève, and on the other hand, the anthropology of Marcel Mauss with whom some of the members of the college had collaborated, the college aimed at identifying and examining the new modalities power, the sacred, and myth in modern society. Among the intellectual influences for the college was Durkheim's sociology of religion presented in his seminal *Elementary forms of religious life* (1995). Here Durkheim emphasized the distinction between the *sacred* and the *profane* as two distinct registers in all societies. Durkheim (1995: 36) writes: "[T]he sacred and the profane are always and everywhere conceived by the human intellect as separate genera, as two worlds with nothing in common". The distinction between the sacred and the profane has played a central role in contemporary social theory (see e.g., Agamben, 1998, pt. 2). The collegians wanted to examine how the sacred was reinvented and celebrated in modern, secular society. Genosko (2003) explains:

> Following Durkheim ... Caillois ... recognized [that] the two worlds of the mutually exclusive domains of the sacred and the profane do not mingle in unmediated ways, that is, the absence of collectively recognized rites of passage and acknowledged the risks of admixture. Caillois took great care to outline how the profane needs the sacred, and the regulation, through rites, of the process of consecration of the passage into the sacred from the profane; likewise, he also explained expiation in the process of desacralization in the passage from the sacred to the profane. (Genosko, 2003: 75)

Related to the notion of the sacred were also the notions of power and myth. These three concepts were central to the discussions in the college:

> The Collegians envisioned the sacred as a dynamic force propelling collective movements based in feelings that oscillate

between repulsion and attraction. Such outbursts can undermine as well as (re)construct the foundations of the social order. For these reasons, the Collège's predilection was to explore social formations—secret societies, religious orders, and political vanguard groups—often bypassed by traditional sociology. (Richman, 2003: 32)

The underlying source of critique was all forms of utilitarian thinking; rather than conceiving of modernity as the age wherein utilitarian and goal rational thinking finally dominate mankind, the collegians sought to investigate how the tendency to promote utilitarian ideologies is resisted or even undermined by acts of transgression, waste, excesses, or violent activities. Power, the sacred, and myth were institutions through which such non-utilitarian activities were manifested. "[T]he Collegians were united in their common explorations of myth, power, and the sacred as exemplary areas capable of undermining the hege-mony of utilitarian criteria", Richman argues (2003: 34). The most explicitly critical thinker of the utilitarian doctrine and ideology was Georges Bataille who spent his entire life thinking about means of transgression derived from the sacred. Pearce (2003) argues that Bataille is here a follower of Durkheim in terms of recognizing the dual nature of the sacred as what mutually institutes social practices but also undermines them through violent acts:

> [F]or both Durkheim and Bataille, the sacred invokes feelings of both attraction and repulsion ... but for Bataille it is also linked with instabil-ity, with violence and its violent containment; with the cruelty of sacrificing others and with the subsumption of individuals within total-izing group processes when they fearlessly confront death and willing to sacrifice themselves ... Further, while in contemporary societies sacral processes have become more obscure and suppressed, less obvi-ously religious, they are still present, as can be seen in the way men are attracted to sacrificial ceremonies and festivals. (Pearce, 2003: 3)

Another intellectual project launched by Bataille was his formulation of what he referred to as "the general economy" that overturned the conventional sense of the meaning of "economy" as *oikonomikos*, that is, a form of rational "householding" writ large. For Bataille, the con-ventional view of economy is that of what he calls "the restricted economy", the use of sparse resources in a rational manner. As opposed to the "restricted economy", Bataille conceives of a "general economy" based on waste of resources and squandering of what is in excess. Bataille argues on basis of historical and anthropological material that all societies institute mechanisms for wasting resources: "Georges Bataille ... [argues] that it is *precisely* what we waste, what we produce as excess, what makes us human", Linstead (2002: 669) concludes. Again, the general economy is a critique of utilitarian thinking. "Bataille's target is utility, in its root", Jean Baudrillard (1998: 192) writes *a propos* the general economy. For Bataille as well as for the other collegians, the general economy captures the human need for transgression that in turn is embedded in the sacred. In Hegarty's (2000) account, there are numerous instituted means for revolting against utilitarian thinking:

> The realm beyond this ['work, religion, utility (party) politics, laws, taboos, reproductive sex, truth, knowledge', i.e., legitimate institutions in modern bourgeoisie society] is that of excess: eroticism, death, festivals, transgression, drunkenness, laughter, the dissolution of truth and knowledge. This realm of excess is the general economy, but the general economy is also the process whereby the homogeneous realm interacts with excessive phenomena. (Hegarty, 2000: 33)

Overall, Roger Caillois shared Bataille's view of the role and function of the sacred in contemporary society but his work is less burdened by Bataille's Dionysian destructiveness and provocative rhetoric. While Bataille appears as a radical thinker turning social analysis into a descendence into the underworlds of the human psyche and practice, Caillois engaged in analyses of more conventional activities such as festivals and forms of gaming and playing. For instance, the festival is the institution in which society is renewing itself through the overturning of the predominant order of everyday life, thereby renewing itself and making it durable. Caillois (2001: 101) writes:

> Excess constantly accompanies the festival. It is not merely epiphenomenal to the excitement it engenders. It is necessary to the success of the ceremonies that are celebrated, shares their holy quality, and like them contributes to the renewal of nature or society. In reality, this seems to be the goal of the festival. Time passes and is spent. It causes one to age and die, it is that which *wears away*.

He continues:

> In fact, in its purest form, the festival must be defined as the paroxysm of society, purifying and renewing it simultaneously. The paroxysm

is not only its climax from a religious, but also from an economic point of view. It is the occasion for the circulation of wealth, of the most important trading, of prestige gained through the distribution of accumulated reserves. (Caillois, 2001: 125–126)

In other words, the festival is for Caillois a celebration of the sacred:

The sacred is a key element both in ordinary life and in the festivals found in 'primitive' societies (and to a much attenuated degree in contemporary societies), but it becomes of greater significance but also something different in such festivals. Ordinary life tends to be regular, busy, safe, and sclerotic. 'Time is wearing and exhausting' and there is a need for social regeneration. This is made possible by the 'popular frenzy' of the festival. It releases an active sacred energy, reverses the normal course of time and the forms of social order and is associated with widespread excesses and sacrileges, 'debauches of consumption, of the mouth or sex', and also 'debauches of expressions involving words or deeds'. (Caillois, 1988: 298)

Similarly to other analyses of carnivals and festivals (Bakhtin, 1968; Eco, 1986; Ladurie, 1982; Stallybrass and White, 1986), Caillois (2001, 1988) emphasizes the circular nature of life in society; the festival aimed at squandering and excess complements periods of normal accumulation. "It often takes several years to re-amass the amount of food and wealth ostentatiously consumed or spent, and even destroyed and wasted, for destruction and waste, as forms of excess, are at the very heart of the festival", Caillois (2001: 98) argues. Without the one institution, the other would not persist; everyday life would become tedious without carnival, and carnival would undermine social institutions if longer periods of stability and normality would be eliminated: "*Economy, accumulation,* and *moderation* define the rhythm of profane life; prodigality and excess define that of festival, the periodic and exhilarating interlude of sacred life that cuts in and restores youth and health" (Caillois, 1988: 298).

The modernization of society or the colonialization of remote territories is wielding destructive effects on the festival, Caillois (2001: 126) argues: "[W]hen these exhausting and ruinous festivals are abandoned, under the influence of colonialization, society loses its bonds and becomes divided". Consequently, the human society is losing one of its most important institutions wherein the line of demarcation between the sacred and the profane is reproduced and celebrated.

Caillois argues that more advanced social formations are intolerant to the festival because it is a disruptive event that disturbs the mechanisms of accumulation:

> With the rise of civilization, with the beginning of the division of labor, still more with the rise of the city and the state, festivals lose importance. They symbolize less and less the magnitude and total character that made the ancient effervescence a complete suspension of institutional interaction and a basic challenge to the universal order. A more complex society does not tolerate such a break in the continuity of its functioning. It insists upon the gradual abandonment of the alternation between phases of debility and paroxysm, of dispersion and concentration, of regulated and unrestrained activity, which is the rhythm of development at a time when collective life is less differentiated. (Caillois, 2001: 131)

Modern society is therefore by definition what is in opposition to the festival in the medieval or pre-modern sense of the term. Even though contemporary societies institute new forms of festivals, seemingly disruptive and excessive, they are in essence aimed at being productive events rather than merely squandering resources. In our society, festivals no longer play any decisive role in the reproduction of social formations. Festivals are instead ornamental and additional to the day-to-day accumulation as in the case of mass tourism. Similar to the other collegians, Caillois sought to identify the new manifestations of the sacred. One such mechanism is the practice of playing.

Play and the sacred

While festival or carnival is an all-encompassing activity, a transient total institution (Goffman, 1961) if you will, engaging all the members of a society, Caillois examines play and gaming as what serves a similar non-utilitarian function for the individual as the festival does for the collective. The members of the *Collège de Sociologie* thought that modern life offered few possibilities for transgression and other forms of escape from utilitarian thinking and therefore new means of escapism have to be invented. Richman (2003: 34) claims that myth is of increased importance for this reason: "Deprived of the possibility of contact with the sacred of transgression, unable to satisfy the need for loss of a violent sort, cut off from the tragic experience that relinquishes fate to chance and measures life in relations to death, the modern individual none-theless has recourse to myth". However, Caillois (2001) regards play an instituted practice providing a temporal escape from the hegemony of accumulation, goal-rationality, and utilitarian thinking. Walter Benjamin formulates a similar idea: "As life become more subject to administrative norms, people must learn to wait more. Games of chance possess the great charm of freeing people from having to wait" (Benjamin, 1999: 199, D10a, 2). Similar to the Dutch historian Johan Huizinga's (1949) analysis of play as what is not only *part* of culture but what is actually the *driving force* preceding any advanced culture, Caillois's emphasis on play as what is central to human existence is also supported by Winnicott's (1971) development psychology wherein play is a principal source of creativity. Caillois conceives of play and games as what is at the very center of human existence. Still, Caillois remains faithful to the critique of utilitari-anism of the *Collège de Sociologie* and defines play as what is in essence a waste, that is, that does not aim at fulfilling some external goal or objec-tive. Caillois writes: "Play is an occasion of pure waste: waste of time, energy, ingenuity, skill, and often of money for the purchase of gambling equipment or eventually to pay for the establishment" (Caillois, 2001: 5–6). In addition, play is a "free activity" that must be based on uncer-tainty: "Doubt must remain until the end, and hinges upon the denoue-ment" (Caillois, 2001: 7).

Caillois (2001: 12) identifies four ideal-types of games that exist in most societies: the first type is referred to as *agôn* and includes all sorts of games based on competition and bodily skills and control. *Agôn* is playing that emphasizes the players' physical, embodied performance. The second type of games is called *alea* (the Latin word for dice) and comprises all games including chance, that is, what cannot be imme-diately influenced by the players. While *agôn* is based on *skills*, *alea* is based on *luck*. "*Agôn* is the vindication of personal responsibility; *alea* is the negation of will, a surrender to destiny", Caillois (2001: 18) writes. Third, Caillois speaks of games of *mimicry*, that is, "simulation" of situations or individuals, historical or fictive. Mimicry is then closer related to the infantile child's training in what Mead (1934) called "taking the role of the other" than the more advanced rule-governed games of older children and adults. Finally, Caillois examines a group of games that he calls *ilinx* after the Greek word for vertigo. *Ilinx* include all sorts of games wherein the participants are exposed to phy-sical forces and movements that cause a sense of being released from the human body, for instance merry-go-rounds and roller-coasters are examples of *ilinx*. All these four ideal-types of games could be combined into hybrid combinations. For instance, *agôn* is often combined with some component of *alea* to introduce a component of uncertainty in what otherwise would be strictly a matter of skills. For instance, pinball games may be programmed to offer unexpected and randomly occurring events to surprise and challenge the player.

Caillois's theory of games is sociological in terms of conceptualizing games as being a substitute for the absence of real game-like situations in contemporary life. Instead of merely accepting a predictable life devoid of surprises and sensations, the player is inventing what may be called "means of excitement". Caillois explains:

> Play, whether *agôn* or *alea*, is ... an attempt at to substitute perfect situations for the normal confusion of contemporary life. In games, the role of merit or chance is clear and indisputable. It is also implied that all must play with exactly the same possibility of proving their superiority, or, on another scale, exactly the same chances of winning. In one-way or another, one escapes the real world and creates another. (Caillois, 2001: 19)

Playing thus substitutes for real life situations and opens up a domain wherein one can take risks and act more venturesome than one regularly does: "Play is not only the area of 'limited and provisional perfection'. It constitutes a kind of haven in which one is master of destiny. There, the player himself chooses his risks, which since they are determined in advance, cannot exceed what he has exactly agreed to put into play" (Caillois, 2001: 159). This does not suggest, however, that all players are merely indulging in escapist reverie; on the contrary, playing is paradoxically a non-utilitarian and non-rationalist activity—just like the festival—latently serving to reproduce a utilitarian and rationalist society through substituting real life situations with a world that is, in Caillois's formulation, "created". Caillois (2001) continues to make connections between different types of societies and cultures and games. Drawing on historical and anthropological material, Caillois distinguished between cultures favouring combinations of *agôn/alea* and cultures praising aggregated of *mimicry/ilinx:*

> [P]rimitive societies, which I prefer to call 'Dionysian', be they Australian, American, or African, are societies rules equally by masks and possessions, i.e., by *mimicry* and *ilinx*. Conversely, the Incas, Assyrians, Chinese, or Romans are orderly societies with offices, careers, codes, and ready-reckoners, with fixed and hierarchical

privileges in which *agôn* and *alea,* i.e., merit and hereditary, seems to be the chief complementary elements of the games of living. In contrast to the primitive societies, these are 'rational'. In the first type there are simulation and vertigo or pantomime and ecstasy which assure the intensity and, as a consequence, the cohesion of social life. In the second type, the social nexus consists of compromise, of an implied reckoning between hereditary, which is a kind of chance, and capacity, which presupposes evaluation and competition. (Caillois, 2001: 87)

In the primitive, Dionysian society, the ecstasy and transgression of the players is the main form of escaping from everyday life. In the more advanced, "rational" society, bodily control and calculation is privileged. Caillois thus suggests that different types of society institute different types of games. As a consequence, contradictory to Caillois's initial definition of games as what implies a waste, games cannot be regarded wholly detached from societal ideologies and objectives. In the "Dionysian society", rules and organization are eliminated in games, while in the "rational society" they are recognized as being of central importance: "Vertigo and simulation are in principle and by nature in rebellion against every type of code, rule and organization. Alea, on the contrary, like *agôn*, calls for calculation and regulation" (Caillois, 2001: 157). Herein lies also one of the most fascinating qualities of games: the simultaneous adherence to rules and the existence of basic liberties within such regime of rules: "Rules are inseparable from play as soon as the latter becomes institutionalized. From this moment on they become part of its nature. They transform it into an instrument of fecund and decisive culture. But a basic freedom is central to play in order to stimulate distraction and fantasy. This liberty is its indispensable motive power and is basic to the most complex and carefully organized forms of play" (Caillois, 2001: 27). Playing demands rule-following while simultaneously stretching the rules. As we will see regarding the case of new drug development, scientific work is substantially rule-governed, yet such rules must always be put into question in order to be overcome; the laboratory scientist is therefore engaged in a particular form of game wherein novelty is aimed for within what is already, at least partially, known.

In summary, Caillois's (2001) theory of play is aimed at identifying a series of instituted operations substituting for more violent and destructive forms of transgression and celebration of the sacred.

In modern society, deprived of archaic forms of celebration of the sacred, games stand out as an eminent practice of overcoming the repetitive nature of social life. For Caillois (2001), the underside of games is that of violence, today widely debated when for instance football hooliganism is bursting out in parts of Europe during championships and at individual matches attracting attention. Games may appear trivial or peripheral but they are, for Caillois (2001), still serving a very central function as the mechanisms that short-circuit the repetitive nature of everyday life; games liberate humans from what is predictable and open up a domain wherein social life is pursued by other means.

Playing and innovation

In the following, the notion of playing will be employed in the analysis of new drug discovery work in AstraZeneca. Rather than assuming that the discovery work is possible to predetermine and anticipate, the study suggests that all scientific laboratory work implies an element of chance and luck and, consequently, an adequate degree of risk-taking is needed.

Skills and chance in new drug discovery work

One of the senior scientists with an extensive background as researcher at the university, emphasized the impact of chance in all advanced scientific work aimed at discovering new substances. In addition, he thought that the opportunities for exploring unexpected findings would be rather limited in the new regime of management control, emphasizing the output of candidate drugs:

> Most of the greatest discoveries are random … the chances of exploiting serendipities are much lower now, absolutely. That is a dilemma because you cannot say that 'I'm off to play in the lab for a while. I don't really know what to do but the outcome may be something amazing'. That would be too 'anti-industrial' but it is a fact that it often works that way. (Manager, Medicinal chemistry)

Pharmaceutical industry is today forced to optimize its use of available resources to increase the output. Thus, identifying the mechanisms inherent to the very process of "scientific discovery" becomes a central managerial objective. However, to date, the attempts at eliminating the factor of chance have not been successful. The senior scientist continued: "To be successful here, you need to be competent and have a bit of luck, there's no doubt about it. We try to do away with this 'luck factor' but we will never succeed because it is all about luck as well". A senior integrative pharmacologist made this point clear: "Creativity as such, you cannot command; you cannot control it". Another scientist, a medical doctor working in the field of pharmacology in a project aimed at exploring inflammatory gastrointestinal diseases claimed that "all the interesting things that I've published have been serendipities". The factor of chance and even luck is therefore regarded a marginal but still significant factor contributing to the discovery process. One of the managers in the medical chemistry department pointed at the indeterminacy of scientific work and the ambiguities that needed to be taken into account when predicting and planning outcomes:

> After all, we are conducting research, that is, unknown things and we are supposed to do new things. Even if we may think that it will take us a year to go from here to there, it might be that nature is against us and we never reach that point because we cannot predict anything. If we would have been able to say that 'we need to make 25 syntheses and then we are finished', then we would have done those 25 or even just the single one we really want, but we cannot foresee where we end up. (Manager, Medicinal chemistry)

One of the Disease Areas Scientific Leaders pointed at the effects of a more process-based organization and emphasized that rather than working as an integrated project team, the division of labour demanded to maintain a state-of-the-art expertise also produced a fragmented project structure that influenced the innovation work negatively:

> A consequence of this more process-oriented research is that we have a lot of specialized groups, especially here in the discovery organization. We have people being experts on synthesizing recombinant proteins on large scale, experts on robotizing screening, HTS, experts on cloning genes, and God knows what. They work in many projects and participate in [the project] a certain phase and do their thing and then they're out of there. I think that is detrimental to the creative process. When we started, on a smaller scale, and when you asked someone 'what are you doing for the moment?' they said like 'I work on the X project'—and some people still answer like that—but a substantial amount of individuals do not identify with projects because they are so specialized. Off course, they can be creative in their domain of expertise but that is not really the same thing as a group of persons

working on a shared goal, stimulating and helping one another over a longer period of time. (DASL, Integrative pharmacology)

If scientific work could be predicted in greater detail, scientists would not have been forced to produce the massive amount of data that they regularly provide. The complexity of the undertaking of identifying new chemical substances that affected the target of choice does however imply that thousands of substances are "screened", i.e., examined through the use of advanced laboratory equipment capable of identifying predefined qualities in the substances. Still, the process of identifying promising substances needs to be approached in a somewhat playful manner. One of the synthesis chemists pointed out the importance of being able to exploit individual creativity and curiosity:

It is important to have a leader that allows you to be creative. It is really important. I think that in order to conduct research, you need to have a playful attitude. You need to take new routes and that it must be a bit quirky at times. People must be encouraged to present their ideas ... But at the same time, the leader needs to take charge when demanded. (Synthesis chemist)

She continued, pointing at the explorative nature of the work wherein a new substance was tested against the *in vitro* models employed by pharmacologists:

The most exciting is when you developed the idea regarding the substance yourself, and you have a firm belief in it when you submit it. Then you are really waiting for the results to come. You check your computer over and over. It's really exciting. (Synthesis chemist)

One of the scientists told a story of how thoughtful reflection, medical expertise, and luck intersected in one of the research project. The idea emerged when the scientist thought of exploring a new substance developed within "a completely different therapeutic area". Here, a "more or less finished molecule" was available. The molecule was not synthesized to be tested against the targets of the focal project, but still the scientist thought that there would be some interesting opportunities for new routes of thinking. The scientist said:

I was intrigued by this concept and then the question was what receptor should we use? I went down to the coffee shop and discussed the issue with the Disease Area Scientific Leader who was intrigued by the idea. Two weeks later, he happened to come across a publication, showing what receptor to use and now there is a project running. (Scientist, Integrative pharmacology)

In the stream of different ideas and hypothesis that researchers are navigating, specific ideas are at times brought forward because there happens to be a solution to scientific problems at the right moment in time. For instance, if the journal paper reporting the function of the receptor would have been missed by the Disease Area Scientific Leader, the molecule might have been abandoned and some other substance could have been selected. Scientific work under indeterminate and time pressured conditions includes an exposure to similar events and occurrences.

The ability to fully exploit one's scientific skills and *savoir-faire* was under the constant pressure of the demands of increased performance. Most of the interviewees in the pharmaceutical company were critical towards the increased emphasis on output, expressed in terms of the number of synthesized molecules per time unit for the chemists and number of candidate drugs per annum for the whole of the discovery organization (further discussed in Chapter 7). One of the chemists claimed that the lack of time for qualified scientific thinking posed a threat to the long-term innovativeness of the company:

> To be frank, I think it is tougher already ... There is a much stronger emphasis on performance: to deliver output and preferably much output. Even if we do discuss the importance of quality, I think we've lost what quality means on the way. Quality is also that the researchers are given the opportunity to be engaged in their projects and integrate various threads. I see that opportunity disappearing because they expect us to work in more projects. We 'speed up' everything in the laboratory, which of course is a good thing as such, that you don't need to dose the substances by hand when there are robots capable of doing it. But the risk is that rather than using the time released from the laboratory for letting the researchers engage in the projects, to serve as scientific experts, then we are given additional assignments, and are asked to deliver more data. However, it is also important to take care of data in the right manner. I think we are not really successful there now. (Researcher, Synthesis chemistry)

Even though top management of the site had declared they did not regard the implemented performance measures as an optimal choice or think of them as being by any means flawless, the latent function of the measures was to increase stress on the laboratory scientists. One of the managers in the chemistry department was critical of the new regime:

It is more complicated for all pharmaceutical companies ... The pressure to deliver results is substantial. Unfortunately, I think that they have defined objectives in terms of number of substances produced. They say that 'this is not a good performance measure, but it can actually be quantified and therefore we use it; however, we will not care very much about it since it is the quality that counts by the end of the day'. Those are certainly mixed messages and the laboratory scientists are stressed out ... the objectives are of course determining the actions and it does not add up! I don't think those are good objectives. (Manager, Synthesis chemistry)

Even though all of the scientists thought that it is important to deliver qualitative substances and tests, the one-sided emphasis on quantity was complicated to resist. Consequently, a substantial part of the interviewees argued that they felt their work were increasingly being determined by the ability to deliver a certain amount of substances on time, and that their scientific skills were reduced to the level of a matter of output.

In the discovery phase in the new drug development project, qualified and effective research appears to be a combination of a number of factors including scientific skills and experience and the time to fully engage in complex scientific undertakings. In addition, the researchers recognized the influence of chance and luck. The laboratory researchers were highly critical of the present regime wherein they did not have much time to invest in specific research questions, but needed to juggle two or three projects at the same time. In addition, the aggregate of interrelated leadership practices, management control activities, and organizational arrangements was not capable of eliminating the factor of chance that is, the interviewees claimed, inherent to all scientific work. The predominant management regime did not fully recognize or count on the residual factor of chance and luck but quite the contrary further structured and organized the drug discovery processes into smaller and more closely monitored units. For instance, the interviewees tended to complain that top management favoured what was called "front-loading" in the research project. Front-loading is a concept emanating originally from the car industry and is aiming to increase effectivity by pushing problems to the early stages in the research process. In the case of new drug development front-loading means trying to identify problems as early as possible and studies and tests should be located to the early phases of the development of a new compound. Front-loading involves a sense of doing more than necessary—instead of handling problems when they come. The risk involved with implementing front-loading on a large scale for the majority of projects is that it may generate efforts and resources that may lead to dead ends. Front-loading also involves a problematic abundance and divergent generation of data and information and decision problems on how to deal with it and decreases probability of off-shots (serendipities) and might jeopardize handling creative ideas.

When successfully eliminating compounds that do not meet quality demands prior to the development phase and especially the clinical trials, pharmaceutical companies can save significant resources. As an effect, frontloading means that new substances are examined more thoroughly and less chance for serendipities is provided. By and large, the new drug development activities in the discovery phase were becoming increasingly rule-governed, monitored and evaluated by external committees. Notwithstanding all these changes, the influence of chance cannot be wholly eliminated. Even largely determined and thoroughly designed scientific processes such as the discovery phase in a pharmaceutical company cannot reduce the exposure to non-utilitarian concepts such as luck. Therefore, Caillois's (2001) theory of playing as the combination of skills and luck can help shed further light on innovation processes.

Ultimately, new drug development work is embedded in the intrinsic motivation of highly skilled and specialized scientists, that is, variety of experts making individual contribution to the work. What motivates scientists to work as hard as they do is, as they emphatically point out, not primarily monetary rewards or career opportunities, but rather the excitements of uncovering new domains previously unknown. Seen in this perspective, the notion of "discovery" in new drug development is not a worn-out metaphor but is actually how synthesis chemists and pharmacologists perceive their work. The discovery process includes two major factors: first, the skills and know-how of the experienced laboratory scientists. This entire domain of interrelated practices, technologies, routines, inscription procedures, and so forth, constituting the laboratory researcher's sleight-of-hand and scientific *savoir-faire* corresponds to the mechanism of *agôn* in Caillois's theory; *agôn* is the totality of embodied and cognitive skills that are mobilized in the activity. Second, all advanced scientific procedures include moments of chance, unexpected outcomes, unpredicted events, surprising effects and so forth, in short a residual component that cannot be fully anticipated, managed, and predetermined. These rare moments of creative and unexpected outcomes are what all scientific practices must be able to exploit. Such moments are represented by what Caillois calls *alea*, the influence of chance in certain forms of playing. *Alea* is important to recognize as an integral component of scientific practice, not only because it underlines the ability to capture inconsistencies in the very research activity but also because it is an important cultural trait of laboratory work to make use of metaphors and tell stories that exploit the factor of chance in the work. The combination of *agôn* and *alea* is thus representing the need for maintaining a view of science that is recognizing both its dependence on scientific skills and know-how and the exposure to residual events. Scientific work therefore always unfolds like the games including both elements of skilful activities and luck and chance. This quality makes science exciting and serves as a central motivational factor for its practitioners. Science is neither possible to wholly determine through rationally evaluated and predefined procedures, nor is it a haphazard endeavour outside of control. Instead it is bringing together competence and chance into a productive relationship. Caillois's (2001) thinking provides a conceptual framework for understanding this relationship.

Next, one of the principal preconditions for playing in the *agôn/alea* regime, the notion of risk-taking, is examined as what restrains and delimits the skilful performance of laboratory scientists.

The importance of risk-taking

Traditionally, the managerial approach to balance open-ended search and activities monitored in greater detail in the firm was to allow for "individual research projects" aimed at identifying promising new targets and substances for future new drug development. One of the synthesis chemists reflected on the changes in policy during the last period of time:

> Back then [in the 1990s], about 15% of the total pharmacy resources were invested in what one may call 'explorative knowledge creation'. After the merger, they found out that we had the largest pharmaceutical organization in the world ... Then the boss—who is still the boss—said that from now on we should invest only about 5% in explorative work ... And then some of the managers are surprised

that the amount of patent applications has been lowered ... I would like to claim that they are the half of what they used to be the last couple of years. (Synthesis chemist)

For the laboratory researchers, the tendency in the pharmaceutical industry is to delimit and confine the time and resources dedicated to such "explorative knowledge creation" and to invest more resources in controlling and monitoring the process to finalize new candidate drugs that have been identified as being of central strategic importance. As a consequence, the laboratory researchers thought of their work as being gradually subsumed under a strict regime of managerial control mechanisms and techniques. The synthesis chemist was critical of this recent change in how the laboratory work was monitored:

> We are conducting a lot of 'template research' here. We have these spread sheets ... and then we tick the boxes, 'now we have done this', 'now we have done that', 'now we have done that'. But that isn't proper research. Research is by definition when you really do not know what is supposed to happen. Otherwise it is, for me, a development of a process or a product where you can predict and anticipate outcomes. Research implies that you are taking some risks; you don't know the outcome but you have your scientific intuition and try to build a scientific test of proof. (Synthesis chemist)

One Disease Area Scientific Leader agreed that the use of templates, guidelines, and other structuring models for the research work were heavily debated in the firm:

> We had quite a bit of discussions regarding the templatization and the process orientation. On the one hand, I can see a need for this in an organization this large; you cannot have a 'Wild west' so it is probably a good thing to standardize practices at the sites and so forth ... Then, on the other hand, I think there are too many templates and guidelines. I know that when we started to discuss this ... there were a lot of loud protests but I thought that we are wise enough to use these templates in a rational manner. I must admit that we have very much abandoned that today. (DASL, Integrative pharmacology)

"Ticking boxes" and answering to predefined standardized questionnaires may be helpful for management when monitoring the portfolio of research activities, but it does not help the laboratory researchers pursuing excellent research work. Beside the increased emphasis on formal documentation, some of the interviewees emphasized that they felt they were spreading themselves too thin over a number of different projects rather than being able to delve into one specific scientific problem. Another synthesis chemist argued: "We don't use the same vocabulary today: It feels like we're expected to do as much as possible in all conceivable targets and maybe we eventually find something. And we better do that fast. At any delay, then we abandon the activities because then we're not going to make it; someone else will get there before we do" (Synthesis chemist). Science-based innovation is not only riddled by scientific concerns and challenges but also needs to take into account the activities of other competing firms. In cases where top management thought of the comparative advantage of AstraZeneca as being limited vis-à-vis the competitors, projects were abandoned. In other words, the portfolio of projects was continuously modified, which produced a human resource management problem in terms of motivation because laboratory researchers who may have developed a certain degree of expertise in one particular field could in a nick of time be asked to drop their ongoing project and move on to another project. This predicament was widely known and discussed in the company and many of the interviewees were half-jokingly saying that in the pharmaceutical industry you may work your entire life without contributing to one single new registered drug if all your projects are being closed down. However, laboratory researchers were aware of these "rules of engagement" but were nevertheless emotionally affected every time their ongoing projects were stopped. One of the synthesis chemists said the degree of innovativeness is generally quite low because projects were aimed at producing "followers" to successful drugs, capable of fighting for "the billions of dollar on the market".

One of the standing concerns among the interviewees was the amount of risk-taking in AstraZeneca. In their view, it was important to balance projects that would safeguard a "product pipeline" that would satisfy financial analysts and hold on to the present market position and projects that were a bit more off the beaten track, enabling new scientific breakthroughs and the opening up of new therapeutic domains. One of the line managers in the integrative pharmacology department pointed at the use of the same chemical libraries in most pharmaceutical companies: "We are screening our libraries, the same libraries as in principle all other major companies screen. We are screening against the same enzyme or protein as many other companies do.

I am a bit concerned there is too little thinking going on right now". He continued: "All pharmaceutical companies work on almost the same targets. If you do a competitive intelligence analysis you notice that Pfizer work on the same targets as we do". One of the synthesis chemists claimed that large companies were less comparatively prone to take risks than smaller companies: "The large companies take proportionally smaller risks than the small companies ... You need to keep the organization units small, that is the only thing that works". He pointed at the amount of patents delivered by AstraZeneca in comparison with small biotechnical firms as an indication of the risk-averse strategy:

> There is less and less innovation in the major companies and more and more innovation outside of the major companies ... It differs between disciplines ... in my field, there are a great many companies working on nano particles. If you check how many patents they 'file', and how many we at AstraZeneca 'file', you can notice that a company of merely 50 co-workers may file substantially more patents that we do. You need to be careful when counting and so forth, but it is still an indication that they are more active in the innovative domains. (Synthesis chemist)

A synthesis chemist pointed at the need for exploring new domains as an integral part of the innovation work: "I believe creativity is essential today. But to be able to produce an innovation, then you need to give the permission to move into new terrains. This may be a failure but it may also produce something unexpected, something no one has yet explored". In order to increase innovativeness, the synthesis chemist suggests that researchers should be given more time for basic research and enhance the contact over disciplinary boundaries, for instance between chemists and pharmacologists and biologists. One of the integrative pharmacologists emphasized the need for thoughtful analysis of the empirical material: "The things we are doing here are so complicated that no one can predict beforehand that 'this is the thing'. It is really complicated". Another synthesis chemist answered the question whether her work was complicated with references to the "discovery work": "Of course it's complicated. We are trying to find something no one else has yet found and try to cure something, of course that is hard". This sense of being able to suddenly find the unexpected and the new is also what motivates the researcher; in addition, "curiosity" motivates the researcher: "We see connections and causalities that no one has seen before. I think that is the answer; it is as easy as that" (Integrative pharmacologists). However, even though research is of necessity unpredictable, it is still supported by clear objectives and leadership practice. One of the molecular pharmacologists was critical of top management's inability to take risks in terms of moving faster from elementary biological systems such as cell lines to more complex biological systems:

> We ask for evidence for these observations in humans ... in lower systems, like in a mouse or a cell line. [managers ask] 'Do you observe the same thing there?'. No, of course we do not generally do that, thus we should continue working on it. That must be a wrong attitude ... I think we are much more comfortable working down low in simple systems, making observations on a cell line, and then slowly working all the way up to mouse, or pig or a primate. (Researcher, Molecular Pharmacology)

He claimed that observations in more complex systems often lead to situations where risky decisions have to be made:

> It is an uncomfortable situation: you enter the material that is relevant for the patient's illness. You make your observation there and ask: 'What is the next step?' ... Next step contains a substantial increase in risk. (Researcher, Molecular Pharmacology)

For one of the line managers, the inability to take risks may not be wholly dependent on top management's risk aversion but may also be a matter of explaining and evaluating the potential risks involved in particular research activities: "I think the risk-taking is too small, at least in our company. Or it may be that we do not have the right researchers capable of explaining to the others that this is something we should go for. We may have too poor a pedagogy in the early phases" (Line manager, Integrative pharmacology). One of the integrative pharmacologists stressed the broader financial and institutional setting and its influence on pharmaceutical companies as an important explanatory factor when understanding the low degree of risk-taking:

> The large institutional owners have not demonstrated the same confidence in that 'you're fixing this, right?'. Instead, our performance is compared to others' performance: 'Now, the pipeline looks

good, and now it doesn't'. Of course, then you expect top management to take action all the time and then you disturb the work pace
and the willingness to take risks on the lower levels ... the ability to
take risks is a key quality; you cannot actually 'play safe' all the
time. (Integrative pharmacologists)

In addition, some of the interviewees pointed at the inertia of a large
and multinational and successful company, confident in the viability
of previous practices. One of the Disease Areas Scientific Leaders remarked
wryly on how newcomers' ideas were received in the company: "'Come
on in, have some new ideas, do things differently, and as long as you
conduct them in the same way as we've done for the last twenty years,
that's fine'. I've been struggling for two and a half years to make these
organizations do things differently. There's an unbelievable inertia"
(DASL, Integrative pharmacology). By and large, laboratory researchers
deplored the general tendency in pharmaceutical industry to invest
only limited time and financial resources in projects that would potentially provide new therapeutic effects. In their reasoning, the major
pharmaceutical multinationals were too preoccupied with defending
their market positions and to satisfying the actors of the financial
markets to fully capture the possibilities of more risk-taking endeavours. The interviewees instead hoped for the small and medium-sized
biotechnology firms as arenas where new scientific breakthroughs
would be managed.

Taken together, the laboratory researchers emphasized that scientific work in the life sciences, in the pharmaceutical industry, the disciplines of medicinal chemistry, pharmacology, toxicology, and some
other relevant scientific domains, could never be fully managed as a
rational machinery whose outcomes could be fully predicted and anticipated. Instead, scientific work is characterized by non-linearity, disruptive changes, serendipity, and a certain influence of chance and
luck. As opposed to this somewhat fuzzy and indeterminate process,
the management system, constituted by a variety of monitoring mechanisms and routines and standard operating procedures, represent an
ambition to establish a well-ordered and highly transparent innovation
system in the pharmaceutical company. One the one hand, a world of
laboratory research practices affirmative of the ontological and epistemological fluidity of knowledge; one the other hand, a system
aiming at making what is inherently unpredictable appear controlled
and determinate. Balancing these two views remains one of the key
challenges for pharmaceutical companies. One of the interviewees

summarized a recipe for successful new drug development: "Luck in combination with a bit of self-confidence and skilled co-workers". (Line manger, DMPK)

Science-based innovation as play and risk-taking

Much of the innovation literature is assuming that functionalist and rationalist analytical models are capable of identifying and formulating one best way of innovating. Such mechanistic models of innovation may serve as useful maps over the different components and sub-systems of innovation systems but they fail to capture the indeterminate or elusive facets of innovation. In the words of Hellström (2004), innovation is a "social practice", a complex aggregate combining a variety of heterogeneous resources and skills. Scientific work in new drug development in the discovery phase is one such highly specific and specialized aggregate including technological, managerial and human resources. Today, new drug development has developed into an increasingly regulated practice introducing new technologies (e.g., high throughput screening, robotization of laboratory work) and scientific knowledge (e.g., proteomics, genetics, genomics). Using Thrift's (2005) concept, one may speak of the "routinization" or even "bureaucratization" of innovation in these "mega-machines" (see Mumford, 1934) of innovation. However, the Enlightenment dream of a wholly transparent and all-encompassing innovation machinery based on scientific principles and procedures remains a utopia, a hope for eliminating all inconsistencies and human factors from the process of innovation. Rather than reducing the influence of human behaviour and thinking in innovation work, the analysis of new drug development pursued in this chapter takes an opposing position: it not only recognizes human behaviour but makes it a central factor in innovation work. Rather than conceiving of scientific work as the highest and most accomplished human activity, the jewel in the crown of modernity, one may think of science as a regulated, highly specialized and theoretically and technologically advanced social practice embedded in the human demand for playing. This does not suggest that scientific practice and its accomplishments are not respected. Quite the contrary. Science is perhaps the most sophisticated and advanced form of organized play developed by mankind. Science and science-based innovation are derived from the same set of principles and generic forms of social interaction as any kind of schoolyard games children engage in. The mechanisms are all there: the presence of semi-fixed rules; the need for skilful performance; the exposure to chance and other unexpected events; the competition between individuals, and so forth. Science is playing pursued by other means.

Even though Caillois's (2001) theory of games is formulated as an anthropological and cultural historical exposé over a series of societies, Caillois's underlying theoretical project must not be neglected. Caillois sought to identify, similarly to the other participants of the *Collège de Sociologie*, the means of transgression in modern, de-traditionalized society. For Caillois, playing is a form of waste, a mode of existence refusing to adapt to utilitarian principles and rationalist form of being. It would be complicated to claim that scientific work in pharmaceutical industry obeys the same principles, but it is important to recognize that most of the laboratory scientists did not regard their scientific work as being solely a means to accomplish predefined ends. For them, scientific work has a value per se, detached from any external objectives. Similarly to children playing a game, scientists do not locate the rationale for their work *outside of the very practice* but actually regard the practice *as such* a form of accomplishment. Scientists spend most of their time conducting research that does not pay off immediately; a scientific contribution is a rare event that cannot serve as a source of motivation during work periods with little or no progress. In other words, to treat science-based innovation or innovation work as what needs to be defined and theorized in terms of its output is to reduce the human contribution to such practices to an instrumental means-ends relationship. Scientists do not innovate because they want to accomplish predefined goals but because they are engaged in a complex intellectual activity they appreciate and regard as meaningful. Appreciation and meaning in science-based innovation is closely entangled with mechanisms of playing.

Summary and conclusion

In the philosophy of science formulated by Karl Popper (1963, 1959), at times labelled *falsificationalism* because Popper emphasizes the process corroborating scientific hypothesis—making them "valid for the time being" through empirical tests—rather than verifying them once and for all, all scientific work is based on the process of formulating conjectures and the testing of such conjectures against data. In this view, the output from scientific work is knowledge not making any broader claims than to remain valid and legitimate until one proves that so is no longer the case. Popper's principal point, directed against the logical positivists and their emphasis on verification, is that the demand for verification implies that bold hypotheses are never formulated when all hypotheses have to be proved. Popper thus cuts the Gordian knot of verification through overturning the legitimation of scientific hypotheses; to prove things (i.e., hypotheses) "not-to-be-wrong" is more useful than prove things "to-be-right", Popper says. The point that Popper emphasizes, important when speaking of new drug development, is that risk-taking and the ability to formulate bold and thought-provoking hypotheses is a scientific prerogative and virtue. Only through assuming that one may think in new terms new ideas are advanced. Seen in this view, science-based innovation is what is inherently dependent on the ability of laboratory researchers and managers to invest time, effort, and prestige in formulating research projects and objectives that are potentially solving therapeutic needs while simultaneously generating adequate incomes for the company. For Popper, scientific work is always of necessity involving risk and chance; that is why one must not operate solely on basis of small and more easily verified hypotheses but must on the contrary formulate scientific problems that include chance and the indeterminate.

In this chapter we have discussed science-based innovation as a form of playing, that is, a regulated, monitored and controlled social practice that also includes opportunities for individual skills and competencies and the ability to explore what was previously unknown. Such a view represents a non-functionalist or non-instrumental, or, better still, non-linear model of innovation that seeks to capture what is of necessity in-between what is already known. Play is a useful analytical concept that bridges dualities such as open/closed, known/unknown, chance/necessity. In addition, all playing involves some kind of risk-taking, that is, the recognition that one cannot always already know what to expect when engaging in science-based innovation work; some connections and associations remain unpredictable and therefore one must not assume that a series of complex events can be anticipated and predefined. However, it is important to recognize that scientific ideologies may be hostile to the concept of play, seeking to maintain a hard surface of rationality and reason as the solely legitimate resources in scientific work. Playing is here a concept too endowed with frivolous qualities that cannot be compatible with the façade of authority and solemnity that (certain) scientists privilege and think of as a virtue of science. But such a façade is, one may argue, primarily ornamental and as soon as one gets into the laboratory and the mangle of practice one notices—we learn from the studies of laboratory practice—that what from afar appears as structured, uncontested, and detached from social interests and politics in fact remains in a state of becoming. Such processes of becoming are what are aimed at capturing with the concept of playing.

6
Leadership and Emotional Management in Science-Based Innovation Work

Introduction

One of the most intriguing aspects of the predominant scientific ideology is the emphasis on emotional detachment from the object of study and from the results and findings produced. While other work is either explicitly based on the ability to perform what has been called emotional work (Hochschild, 1983), for instance various groups of service workers and professionals such as medical doctors or lawyers, or is regarded a human resource to be nourished and emphasized under the label of motivation, scientific work is in many respects portrayed as a social practice wherein too much emotionality is not of necessity a good thing for neither the process, nor the outcome. The tradition of modest witnessing, the ability to provide tempered and analytical accounts of what is observed, is clearly taking an argument against a too emotional relationship with the object of study. Underlying this disregard for emotionality is the long-standing Western tradition wherein *ratio*, human reason, is contrasted against the more fluid and ambiguous human affects. In the Cartesian tradition of thinking, mind and body remain separated and the emotional capacities are located in the body as opposed to the cognitive capacities of the mind. Over the years, the Cartesian doctrine has been subject to criticism from a number of theoretical camps including philosophers, feminist theorists, and physicians, pointing at the reductionist features in the Cartesian work (Gatens, 1996). For instance, Lutz (1996) writes:

> As both an analytic and an everyday concept in the West, emotion, like the female, has typically been viewed as something natural rather than cultural, irrational rather than rational, chaotic rather

than ordered, subjective rather than universal, physical rather than mental or intellectual, unintended and uncontrollable, and hence often dangerous. This network of associations sets emotion in disadvantage contrast to more valued personal processes, particularly to cognition and rational thought, and the female in deficient relation to her male other. (Lutz, 1996: 151)

While emotionality is a potential danger in scientific work, that is, a human faculty too "impure" and ambiguous (see Douglas, 1966, on the associations between impurity and danger) to fully qualify as a legitimate resource in scientific work, it is also somewhat paradoxically commonplace to think of scientists and researchers as being dedicated and committed to their work. Few professions are so closely associated with a life-long engagement in a particular and narrow field of interest as scientists. Therefore, the scientific ideology demonstrates a Janus-faced view of emotionality; on the one hand it is condemned or at least not fully recognized as a useful and legitimate resource in scientific work, while on the other hand it is a form of commitment that serves as the *primus motor* for scientific progress and the scientific system as such. Emotionality is therefore an "absent-present" concept in scientific work that is simultaneously recognized and excluded. This ambivalent relationship to emotionality is representative of the concern that science cannot become "subjective"; it must always in its every instant remain a collective enterprise. When the practising scientist speaks, he or she lets science speak through his or her mouth (see Heidegger, 1971).

Contrary to the predominant view, perhaps less clearly articulated today than in the heydays of positivist epistemologies, this chapter will critically discuss the impact of emotionality and the insistence on leadership as a mechanism that regulates and controls the emotional qualities of scientific practice. It is important to notice that, in our discussion, leadership is an *effect* from the emotional work in scientific practice. Scientific work is based on coordination, specialization, expertise and the ability to integrate components into wholes, and, the other way around, break down overarching problems into strings of separate research assignments. Such a coordinated activity demands authority and mechanisms that guide the undertakings on the local level. On the macrolevel, scientific work may be regarded a self-organizing process (Knorr Cetina, 1995) where there is no center of control and coordination but where scientific work and results are channelled into different institutions such as university departments, conferences, journals, and professional associations. There is no Pope of the Church of Science but merely a capillary network of activities and means of communication and arenas where such activities are presented, evaluated and discussed. Seen in this view, leadership in scientific work is not leadership in the conventional sense of the term. Instead, it is a process essentially addressing the emotional content of the work. In a society increasingly preoccupied with leadership and management practice such a view of leadership may appear counter-intuitive. But when operating as a practising scientist in a corporation, one inhabits a terrain abundant with intersecting managerial and strategic objectives and scientific interests, and therefore leaders help handling the practical and emotional consequences derived from such "conflicting interests".

Emotionality in non-emotional work

When it comes to classic organization theory and management studies there is a long tradition of making emotions what is *not* at the very centre of operations. If emotions are discussed in any length, they are primarily what are controlled, not outlived or explored and exploited. Similar to the scientific ideologies, emotions are present but rarely recognized. In the process of bureaucratization in American companies, the focus shifted, Bendix (1956) argues, from the employees to the managers. While pre-bureaucratic and proto-bureaucratic firms relied on the co-workers' skills and professionalism in the day-to-day work, the bureaucratic organization form lifted the burden of responsibility from the individual co-worker to the manager. Managers became responsible for output. In order to safeguard output, new managerial activities were invented. Emotional and social concerns became one such domain of interest in the new managerial regime (Bendix, 1956: 440). Employees were no longer simply expected to conduct their work but they were also increasingly demanded to demonstrate commitment and emotional engagement in their work. This was particularly accentuated among white-collar workers, the new cadre of administrators that preoccupied sociologists of the 1950s such as Charles Wright Mills (1951) and William H. Whyte (1956). Mills (1963: 271–272) points at the difference between blue and white collar workers: "If there are not too many plant psychologists or personnel experts around, the factory worker is free to frown as he [*sic*] works. But not so the white-collar employee. She [*sic*] must put her personality into it. She must smile when it is time to smile". The bureaucratization of the corporation and the substantial growth of firms in the post-World War II period served as a field of emergence for a new regime of management more interested in the emotional aspects of work. Already the famous Hawthorne studies, the largest single case study in organization theory to date and the *pièce de résistance* of the Human Relations School led by Elton Mayo, showed that workers were demonstrating emotional responses to interventions rather than strictly obeying rational choice principles.

Contrary to Bendix's (1956) association between emotions and bureaucracy, Brewis and Linstead (2000) argue that bureaucratic principles in fact served to exclude emotions. Brewis and Linstead (2000: 23) write that "Weber's conceptualization of bureaucracy makes emotion its central organizing principle, given that it is constructed specifically to banish sentiment, passion, favouritism, coercion, violence, indiscipline, unpredictability and their resultant disorder from the operations of the organization". This is a position more generally adhered to in the organization theory literature; bureaucracies suppress, marginalize or exclude rather than affirm emotions. Mumby and Putnam (1992) talk of this suppression of emotions as *bounded emotionality*. In organization theory, it is feminist organization theorists that have presented the most comprehensive critique of the lack of or exploitation of emotionality in organizations and firms. Arlie Hochschild's *The Managed Heart* (1983) is a seminal work wherein Hochschild studied airline flight stewardesses and how they at times were expected to exploit their emotions and conduct embodied performances (e.g., smiling at customers) while in other cases they were demanded to suppress emotions such as irritation, anger, or contempt in cases where clients were behaving badly. In *The Managed Heart*, Hochschild presents a series of concepts such as "emotional labour" and "surface acting" that have constituted the vocabulary of emotional management theory (Sturdy, 2003; Brown, 1997; Fineman, 1996). Several studies have pointed out that women are more exposed to stereotypical and embodied expectations in their work. Martin, Knopoff and Beckman (1998: 433) write: "Women are more likely than men to engage in self-disclosure, express a wider range of emotions, and seek ways to acknowledge the inseparability of work and personal lives without letting work concerns take priority over family needs" (see also Meyerson, 1998). Martin, Knopoff and Beckman (1998) also underline that it is primarily *some* emotions that are legitimate in organizations while others are regarded too ambiguous or fuzzy to "make a contribution": "Some emotions, such as anger and competitiveness, are generally condoned in bureaucratic organizations, while others such as sadness, fear, some forms of sexual attraction, and vulnerability are taboo" (Martin, Knopoff and Beckman, 1998: 434). Rosabeth Moss Kanter shows in her classic study *Men and Women of the Corporation* (1977) that women as a group are in fact often regarded as being more closely associated with their emotions while men are perceived as being more "emotionally detached" vis-à-vis the object of discussion. In addition, such beliefs have been used, Kanter says, to exclude women from certain positions: "If women have been directed into the 'emotional' end of management, they have also been excluded from the centers of power in management for the same reason. Perhaps the most pervasive stereotype of women in organizations is that they are 'too emotional', whereas men hold the monopoly on rational thought" (Kanter, 1977: 25). Thus, women are regarded as "too emotional" to be fully capable of dealing with certain issues; in addition, "female emotions" are regarded less legitimate or "useful" than "male emotions" or emotional responses. In addition, when female managers are unwilling or unable to demonstrate "female emotions", they are regarded "unfeminine" or "manly" and are discredited for this purpose. Emotionality thus locates women in what Bateson (1972) calls a "double-bind situation": No matter what they do or say, it is held against them.

Emotional management has been studied in a number of organizational settings: as a means of easing concerns in times of radical change (Huy, 2002, 1999; Carr, 2001), as a factor in organization learning (Vince, 2002), as a resource in consultancy work (Wellington and Bryson, 2001; Lundberg and Young, 2001), service work (Korczynski, 2003; Sutton, 1991), law firms and among law professionals (Harris, 2002; Lively, 2000), health care work (Theodosius, 2006), or call center work (Deery, Iversen and Walsh, 2002). A specific kind of emotions is mobilized through the use of humour. Several studies show that emotional events or strains are mediated through the use of humour in organizations (Westwood and Rhodes, 2007; Terrion and Ashforth, 2002; Grugulis, 2002; Collinson, 2002; Hatch, 1997). For instance, Sanders, in her study of sex workers in UK points at a number of functions of humour:

> First, humour is a strategy of 'emotional work' employed as both a business technique and a psychological distancing strategy to manage the emotions of selling sex. Second, joking relations foster friendship, sorority and group membership. Third, jesting is a means of communicating different types of information within the

group and with outsiders as well as re-interpreting life's hardship and their risk of prostitution. (Sanders, 2004: 281)

Emotions are responses to ambiguous, puzzling or otherwise complicated or unfamiliar social situations (Harré and Parrott, 1996) and humour is a mechanism making such emotions meaningful and a means for collectively sharing emotions. However, one must not ignore the subconscious aspects of emotions; they can never be wholly known to us but instead emotions may reveal to us what we actually think or believe (Theodosius, 2006). Theodosius (2006) emphasizes the relational and subconscious qualities of emotionality:

> Our emotions and feelings not just arise in isolation with ourselves, they are directly elicited in response to the relationships we have with others. Between people, emotions states collide, bouncing and feeding off one another, creating a further emotional state born out of that interaction. Thus, in the very simple example of the nurse giving sympathy she also receives gratitude in return and further responds to this—a conscious and socially informed encounter. There are also a whole plethora of feelings and emotions unconsciously involved in any given interaction. (Theodosius, 2006: 900)

A common assumption is that the movement from embodied work in e.g., the manufacturing industry to service industries and knowledge-intensive work implies a larger emotional content of the work. Since human beings are social beings, dependent on their ability to jointly constitute meaning in their everyday life, it is more likely that the emotional *content* of the work has changed rather than increased in scope. While for instance manufacturing work implies certain emotional responses (e.g., the ability to deal with monotonous operations, Cavendish, 1982; Burawoy, 1979), work in call centers, in fast food restaurants, and elsewhere in the new work places provided by the "post-industrial society" leads to other demands and expectations on the part of the employees. However, the more social interaction a work assignment demands, the more "emotional work" is invested on part of the worker (Sutton, 1991). From symbolic interactionists and ethnomethodologists such as Harold Garfinkel (1967) we learn that human beings are interacting with other human beings without barely noticing that is the case. When such social interactions deviate from the norm, human beings are responding emotionally. Therefore, exposure to brief and continuous social interactions implies a substantial emotional work effort. Using George Simmel's (1971) term, analysing life in the modern metropolis, one may say that one becomes *blasé*—unable to respond to social stimuli. In the case of science-based innovation work, a specific set of emotional resources is utilized. Formally, the virtues of patience, commitment, concern for details, and so forth are praised as important qualities of a researcher in scientific communities. Informally, the ability to promote one's ideas, follow one's own beliefs, and engage in activities that might help promoting what is on one's agenda may be helpful to remain competitive in the community. The individual's ability to reconcile what Hochschild (1983) calls *surface acting* (official objectives) and *deep acting* (personal objectives and interests) is one of the emotional skills of the practising researcher. Under all circumstances, science-based innovation work is a specific form of emotional work, putting the individual under the pressure to conform with certain standard behaviours and beliefs and expecting him or her to engage in a long-term activity riddled by ambiguities and uncertainties. In the next section, we will explore such ambiguities and uncertainties in greater detail.

Leadership

Managers versus leaders

One important distinction in organization theory is that between *management* and *leadership* (Grint, 2005). The term management is not easily captured in one, single, unified definition. We employ the concept of *management* to denote all sorts of processes that are aimed at administrating, monitoring, controlling, governing, and steering a certain practice or activities in an organization (Styhre, 2003). According to Griseri (2002), management is a hybrid concept comprising different processes, events, and qualities.

The second notion, leadership, is equally complex. For the sake of simplicity, we here adhere to Fred Fiedler's definition wherein the *leader* is defined as follows: "The individual in the group given the task of directing and coordinating task-relevant group activities or who, in the absence of a designated leader, carries the primary responsibility for performing these functions in the group" (Fiedler, 1968: 8). The leader can thus be formally assigned or operate without such mandate. Katz and Kahn (1966: 334) define *leadership* rather broadly as "any act of influence on a matter of organizational relevance". Research on leadership is a long-standing tradition in organization theory and management studies. Carlsson (1951) conducted one of the first detailed empirical studies of how leaders actually spend their work time.

Carlsson found that the working day of the leader is disruptive and fragmented and composed of a series of brief encounters, meetings and exchanges with co-workers and stakeholder's external to the firm. Mintzberg's (1973) study of leaders, very much modelled on Carlsson's research, made similar conclusions about the disruptive nature of leadership work. More recently Tengblad (2002) has shown that leadership work follows similar trajectories, even though the time the amount CEOs spend on travelling has increased significantly since Carlsson's (1951) study. Kotter (1982) summarizes his findings from research on "successful General Managers" (GMs) in the following 12 points:

1. They spend most of their time working with others.
2. The people they spend time with include many in addition to their direct subordinates and boss. GMs regularly go around the formal chain of command.
3. The breadth of topics they discuss is extremely wide.
4. In these conversations, GMs typically ask a lot of questions.
5. During these conversations, the GMs rarely seem to make 'big' decisions.
6. These conversations usually contain a considerable amount of joking and kidding and concern non-work issues.
7. In not a small number of these conversations, the substantive issues discussed are relatively unimportant to the business or organization.
8. In these encounters, the executives rarely give orders in a traditional sense. That is, they seldom 'tell' people what to do.
9. Nevertheless, GMs frequently engage in attempts to influence others. However, instead of telling people what to do, they ask, request, cajole, persuade, and intimidate.
10. In allocating their time with others, GMs often reach to other's initiatives. Much of the GM's day is unplanned.
11. Most of the time with others is spent in short, disjointed conversations. Discussions of a single question or issue rarely last for more than ten minutes.
12. They work long hours. The average person I have studied works under 60 hours per week. Not many work fewer than 55 hours per week. (Kotter, 1982: 158–159. The points have been shortened)

The everyday work life of the practising General Manager consists of brief and seemingly informal encounters with a great number of individuals. In Kotter's account, GMs rarely tell people what to do but rather help them making adequate decisions through "asking, requesting, cajoling, persuading, and intimidating". Expressed differently, leadership practice includes aligning individual practices with predominant institutions, that is, to understand the broader social processes that actors need to take into account. Philip Selznick's *Leadership in Administration* (1957) proposed a view of leadership closely associated with the institutionalization of certain activities and behaviors in the organization: "Leadership is a kind of work done to meet the needs of a social institution" (Selznick, 1957: 22). As a consequence, leadership is embedded in social processes: "Leadership is not equivalent to office-holding or legal prestige or an authority or decision making ... understanding leadership requires understanding of a broader social process" (Selznick, 1957: 24). Selznick concludes: "The idea developed in this essay is that leadership is not equally necessary in all large-scale organizations, or in any one at all the time, and that it becomes dispensable as the natural process of institutionalization becomes eliminated or controlled". (Selznick, 1957: 25) Rather than treating leadership as what is the *primus motor* of the organization, Selznick regards leadership as what is determined by pre-existing institutions and but also what is shaped by the new institutions enacted by leaders. In summary, leadership work is constituted by brief encounters with co-workers wherein instituted beliefs and practices and actual undertakings are continuously compared and co-aligned. Leadership work is therefore highly symbolic and serves, at the bottom line, to make sense out of complex social realities.

The 'new leadership genre'

In his review of the leadership literature, Bryman (1992) identifies four "traditions of research" in the leadership research (see Table 6.1).

The trait approach examines how physical factors (e.g., height, physique, constitution), ability characteristics such as intelligence, scholarship, rhetorical skills, and a wide range of personality features influence leadership work. The style approach, the second tradition dominating in the 1950s and 1960s, is more concerned with what leaders *do* than what they *are*; leadership behaviour and practice is here examined as a precursor for organizational effectiveness (Bryman, 1992). In the 1968s, Fred Fiedler (1968) formulates what he calls the "contingency model of leadership", suggesting that leadership styles and practices always need to be adapting to changes in the

Table 6.1   Trends in leadership theory and research (Adapted from Bryman, 1992: 1)

Period	Approach	Core theme
Up to late 19940s	Trait approach	Leadership ability is innate
Late 1940s to late 1960s	Style approach	Leadership effectiveness is to do with how the leader behaves
Late 1960s to early 1980s	Contingency approach	It all depends; effective leadership is affected by the situation
Since early 1980s	New leadership approach (Includes charismatic leadership)	Leaders need vision

environment. Very much in line with Selznick's (1957) emphasis on institutional factors in leadership work, Fiedler argues that leadership needs to be situational and context-specific. The contingency theory approach identified a number of leadership approaches: *instrumental* or *directive* leadership, a task-oriented leadership model emphasizing objectives and individual's roles; *supportive* leadership, a relation-oriented position emphasizing the well-being of the employees; *participative* leadership, a consultative approach in which the subordinates are involved in decision-making processes; and *achievement-oriented* leadership, focusing on output and performance (Bryman, 1992: 12). For Bryman (1992), the period after 1980 has entailed a "new leadership approach" wherein concepts such as charisma play a central role for the understanding of leadership work. The identification of different traditions in leadership research does not suggest that a certain tradition is abandoned over a night or become once and for all obsolete. For instance, Bryman (1992: 3) points out that trait approach continued to attract attention well into the 1970s. In a recent paper, Conger (2004) suggests that "normative models" of leadership, e.g., charismatic leadership, emotional intelligence-based leadership, and transformational leadership are representing "unitary" approaches to leadership failing to capture the situational nature of leadership. Conger (2004: 138) argues: "We have been losing an appreciation for the fact that leadership approaches do indeed depend upon the *situation*". For Conger (2004), a key issue for future leadership research is then to return to a contingency model of leadership capable of capturing the "behavioral repertoires" employed by leaders when shifting their leadership styles under "changing circumstances". Seen in this view, Fielder's (1968) contingency model of leadership is apparently still relevant for leadership researchers.

In a review of the leadership research in the period 1995–2004, Yammarino *et al.* (2005) identified 17 different perspectives on leadership. One of the most frequently used theoretical framework in the recent research is the distinction between *transactional* and *transformational* leadership (Bryman, 1996). Yammarino *et al.* (2005) speak of transformational leadership as being part of the 'new leadership genre'. Transactional leadership denotes the day-to-day management of activities and transformational leadership is the entrepreneurial, forward-directed and essentially dynamic component in leadership work. Yammarino *et al.* (2005) write:

> Different from transactional leadership (defined as an exchange process to motivate follower compliance with a leader's requests and organizational role requirements), transformational leadership involves an underlying influence process that motivates followers by encouraging to transcend their self-interests fir the sake of the organization and goal accomplishment. Followers, through transformational leadership, are motivated to do more than originally expected and feel trust, loyalty, and admiration toward the leader. (Yammarino *et al.*, 2005: 897)

In the literature, it is generally the transformational style of leadership that is being investigated and praised as what is contributing to organization change. In the contemporary research on leadership, there is also an interest for the influence of what Max Weber (1992) calls *charisma*, authority based on the ability to influence others through one's personality, charm or rhetorical skills and eloquence. In this strand of research, the notion of charisma and its function for the constitution of an entrepreneurial self is tightly knitted together with broader social changes increasingly emphasizing symbolic management and performance-based interaction (Flynn and Staw, 2003; Ball and Carter, 2002; Weierter, 2001; Steyrer, 1998; Conger and Kanungo, 1987). In their review of the literature, Yammarino *et al.* (2005) address charismatic leadership accordingly:

> Like transformational leadership, charismatic leadership is part of the 'new leadership genre' ... charismatic leadership is generally

defined in terms of the leader's influence over followers and the nature of the leader-follower relationship. Key leader behaviors include articulating an appealing vision, communicating high performance expectations, displaying self-confidence, role modeling exemplary behavior, expressing confidence in follower's ability to achieve goals, and emphasizing ideological aspects of work and collective identity ... Other key aspects of charismatic leader behavior are articulating an innovative strategic vision, displaying unconventional or creative behaviors, taking personal risks, and showing sensitivity to follower needs and environmental constraints, opportunities, and threats. (Yammarino *et al.*, 2005: 896)

Even though transformational leadership and charismatic leadership share a number of characteristics, there is, Yammarino *et al.* (2005: 897) argue, a difference between the two concepts: "A leader may be charismatic without being transformational in that little or no influence to change is exerted ... While charismatic leadership is a key, perhaps the key, component of transformational leadership, charisma is a necessary but not sufficient element of transformational leadership". For Conger and Kanungo (1987), charisma is an "attributional phenomenon" wherein the co-workers ascribe charismatic qualities to individuals taking on a leadership role in a group:

When members of a group work together to attain group objectives, observations of the influence process within the group help them determine their status. One who exerts maximum influence over other members is perceived as a leader. The role is consensually validated when followers recognize and identify the leader on the basis of the interaction with him or her. Charismatic leadership is no exception from this process. Like other kinds of leadership, charisma must be viewed as an attribution made by followers who observe certain behaviors on the part of the leader within organizational contexts. (Conger and Kanungo, 1987: 639)

For Conger and Kanungo (1987), charismatic leadership is derived from *leadership behaviour* rather than rank and position in organizations. Since charisma is not fixed in positions or roles, it is, as Weber claimed, a form of authority that is "essentially unstable and transitory" (Conger and Kanungo, 1987: 644). For instance, Bryman points at a number of historical case where followers or detractors engage in what Bryman (1992: 67) calls "*post mortem* charismatization or *de*charismatization", inscribing extraordinary qualities into political figures like Abraham Lincoln or Evita Péron. For instance, Hobsbawm and Ranger (1983) point out German authorities failed to establish Kaiser Willhelm I of Germany as a paternal figure for the new nation. Instead it was Bismarck that took Willhem's place in history as "the great man" who united Germany:

> The German Empire did not succeed in its efforts to turn the emperor William I into a popularly accepted founding father of a united Germany, nor in turning his birthday into a genuine national anniversary. (Who, by the way, now remembers the attempts to call, him 'William the Great'?). Official encouragement did secure the building of 327 monuments to him by 1902, but within one year of Bismarck's death in 1898, 470 municipalities had decided to erect 'Bismarck columns'. (Hobsbawm and Ranger, 1983: 264)

A closely related field of research is exploring the dramaturgical and embodied aspects of leadership, for instance how leaders are making public performances and using various insignia and symbols to promote their ideas (Harvey, 2001; Ropo and Parviainen, 2001). Balkundi and Kilduff (2005) advocate a social network analysis view of leadership emphasizing the leader's use of social relations in the organization to make effective use of resources. Balkundi and Kilduff (2005) identify three different "networks" that the leader should influence and draw on:

> [A] leader occupies a strategic position in three social network structures relevant to organizational behavior; the ego network, comprising the individual's immediately connected to the leader; the complete organizational network, comprising not just direct connections but also the leaders' indirect connections to everyone in the organization; and the interorganizational network of relationships important to the leader's work outside the focal organization. (Balkundi and Kilduff, 2005: 949)

In a social network analysis, leader effectiveness involves "building social capital" (Balkundi and Kilduff, 2005: 953) that benefits the organizations and individuals. Alimo-Metcalfe and Alban-Metcalfe (2005) propose a "new paradigm" for leadership practice based on what they refer to as "a nearby approach" to leadership in contrast with a "heroic" or "distant" approach, very much in line with what Yammarino *et al.*

(2005) talk about in terms of a "new leadership genre". Alimo-Metcalfe and Alban-Metcalfe's (2005) new paradigm is based on transformational leadership and what they call a "servant leadership" emphasizing the development of individuals in an organizational context. For both Balkundi and Kilduff (2005) and Alimo-Metcalfe and Alban-Metcalfe (2005), leadership is a social practice that must accommodate a wide range of social, cultural, and behavioural aspects.

In addition to the normative leadership literature, a more critical stream of research on leadership is formulated. First, the so-called critical management studies tradition has examined the underlying ideologies of the leadership discourse, pointing at the frail epistemological grounds for the portraying of leaders as being superior to their co-workers in terms of know-how, efficiency and ethical standing (Alvesson and Svenningsson, 2003; Alvesson, 1996, 1992). In this view, leadership is a social practice that tends to become romanticized and veiled by ideology. In addition, issues of power are inherent to the leadership discourse and must be recognized in leadership studies. In a harsh critique of the leadership concept, Gemmill and Oakley (1992) speak of leadership as a "social myth" based on what Georg Lukács (1971) calls "reification" of social relations:

> Reification is a social process which converts an abstraction or mental construct into a supposedly real entity. Through reification the social construction of leadership is mystified and accorded an objective existence. It is a social fiction that represents a form of what Fromm labels 'false consciousness' which refers to the content of the conscious mind that is fictious and has been introjected or assimilated without awareness through cultural programming. With reification, social progress is viewed as 'caused' by or 'determined' by a leader, a cadre of leaders or 'leadership'. It is assumed by researchers and practitioners that because there is a word ('leader' or 'leadership') there must be an independent objective reality it describes and denotes. Reification functions to trap such labeled individuals within a mode of existence that serves to meet various unconscious emotional needs of members of an organization and of a society. (Gemmill and Oakley, 1992: 114)

For Gemmill and Oakley (1992), leadership is a social practice based on manipulation and domination, mobilizing a set of concepts, techniques, mythologies, and other resources reinforcing and reproducing a perceived need for "leadership". In another critical paper, Pye (2005), advocating Karl Weick's notion of sensemaking as being central to leadership practice, cites Chester Barnard saying that "leadership has been the subject of an extraordinary amount of dogmatically stated nonsense" (Barnard, 1948: 81. Cited in Pye, 2005: 32). In Pye's (2005: 46) view, much of the leadership research has been preoccupied with "solving the wrong problems precisely". Barker (2001: 81) is equally critical of the leadership literature: "Most books with the word *Leadership* in the title are either self-help books, promoting self-efficacy labeled as leadership, or pop-management books that agree with Yukl and Van Fleet [1982] that leadership and management is the same thing". Another critical tradition engaging with leadership is the feminist orientation, both pointing at the theoretical underpinnings of the leadership discourse (Calás and Smircich, 1991) and providing empirical studies. What is of interest for feminist researchers, *inter alia*, is the relative underrepresentation of female leaders such as CEOs, board members, professors, and so forth (Helfat, Harris and Wolfson, 2006; Dreher, 2003). Some feminist leadership researchers even claim the very idea of leadership is a masculine construct, refusing to acknowledge any female experiences or competencies:

> Maleness and masculinity are the templates for leadership. Within the confines of technological rationality, leadership has been constructed on the basis of male experience, but this experience has been universalized, and women have been labeled as deficient leaders. By definition, they lack what they can never attain. Men are the norm, women the deviant, the different, the lesser. (Oseen, 1997: 175)

Both the critical management studies tradition of research and the feminist reception of leadership research point at underlying assumptions and beliefs about leadership and what role it is supposed to serve in organizations and society at large. A third form of critique of leadership is formulated by Wood (2005) who, drawing on the process philosophy of Alfred North Whitehead, speaks of "the fallacy of misplaced concreteness" in leadership studies. Rather than being a "clear-cut, definite figure", leadership is a *social practice*; as a social practice, leadership must be examined as a *relational* concept, emerging in the actual activities and interactions performed by various actors. Leadership is thus not simply located in the "immediate individuality" of leaders but must be understood as a process of becoming. Wood (2005: 1116) continues: "[L]eadership is fundamentally a process and a process is not an object, but a tending toward novelty, innovation, and emergence". Wood (2005) suggests that rather than conceiving of leadership as what is centered on individual's actions or personal traits, one can speak of leadership in terms of what Whitehead (1978) refers to as an "event", a point wherein various forces and intensities are intersecting. Wood (2005: 1117) concludes: "Exploring leadership as an event implies a certain movement and a methodological focus of relations, connexions, dependencies and reciprocities, over time: a set of advantageous circumstances becoming identical with the 'objective' subject of leadership". Wood thus advocates a radical change of perspective in leadership studies. Rather than thinking in terms of objects and entities, the researcher must apprehend the processes, events, and becomings—"a tending toward novelty, innovation, and emergence"—in leadership practice. Barker (2001: 472) formulates a similar idea: "Leadership, as we experience it, is a continuous social process. But industrial leadership studies are usually conducted by isolating single events or bounded series of events as though this event has a definable beginning and end, and by analyzing as though this element is subject to cause-effect relationships". Barker (2001), critical of the lack of adequate definitions in much leadership literature, emphasizes that leadership is not the sum of individual leader's actions, or, worse still, actions *derived* from the characteristics of "great leaders" such as Franklin D. Roosevelt or Mahatma Gandhi. Instead, leadership is to be examined as a *systems property*, a component in a complex and partially chaotic social system; leadership is then not about control, full knowledge of the system, or is reversible—it is rather an *outcome* from the reciprocal or recursive relations between actors and structure and is therefore an emergent property of the organization. "Process and structure is the vessel of leadership; chaos and complexity are not problems to be solved, they are the engines of evolution, adaptation, and renewal", Barker (2001: 489) says. Barker (2001: 491. Emphasis in the original) therefore defines leadership accordingly, as "*a process of transformative change where the ethics of individuals are integrated into the more of a community as a means of evolutionary social development*".

The critical view of leadership is important because it defamiliarizes the taken-for-granted views of leadership, that is, the romantic, heroic, and, as feminist organization theorists may argue, masculine image of leadership (Acker, 2006; McDowell, 1997). Contrary to such conventional views of leadership, critical views of leadership emphasize other properties of leadership and point at its broader organizational, social and cultural implications. In summary, in his review of the "new

Table 6.2 Themes in new leadership literature (Adapted from Bryman, 1992: 111)

Less emphasis needed on	Greater emphasis needed on
Planning	Vision/Mission
Allocating responsibility	Infusing vision
Controlling and problem-solving	Motivating and inspiring
Creating routine and equilibrium	Creating change and innovation
Power retention	Empowerment of others
Creating compliance	Creating commitment
Emphasizing contractual obligations	Stimulating extra effort
Detachment and rationality on the part of the leader	Interest in others and intuition on the part of the leader
Reactive approaches to the environment	Proactive approach to the environment

leadership genre", Bryman (1992) identifies a number of "old" and "new" themes addressed in the literature (see Table 6.2).

The new leadership literature is then anchored in an epistemological tradition conceiving of what is novel, new and innovative as being of great interest; it presents a movement from "old" leadership practice to its "new" forms.

Leadership in creative and innovative milieus

Alvesson (2004), studying knowledge-intensive firms (KIFs) argues that leadership in KIFs differs from other forms of organizations because the co-workers are professionals capable of executing their tasks on their own: "Management in most KIFs is strongly affected by the nature of the tasks and qualifications of the employees, both tending to weaken the significance and positional power of top management" (Alvesson, 2004: 122). Alvesson (2004: 137) continues: "Apart from certain stages such as the foundation and early expansion of a firm and during crises calling for conflict-ridden changes, leadership is probably a less important aspect of KIFs than of many other organizations". Even though there is a point in emphasizing the ability of professional knowledge workers to execute the work independently, it is, as has been argued, still a need for coordinating the multiplicity of activities in a large organization and for making decisions regarding the trade-off between the short-terms goals and the long-term strategies of the organization. Therefore, it is not assumed here that leadership makes a difference solely during "conflict-ridden changes" but also in the day-to-day work. However, it is important to recognize that leadership in science-based firms may imply other practices than in other forms of organizations.

Managers in new drug development activities in pharmaceutical companies are not easily put into the conventional categories. In practice, leadership is more complicated and ambiguous. Research in the industry suggests an image of the manager not as an administrator but as a person whose primary interests are science and research. Traditional management practices and managerial concerns come, at best, second. In the case of AstraZeneca, this is supported by the fact that line and project managers have high academic credentials—often doctoral degrees in the biomedical sciences. Several studies testify to scepticism and unwillingness to discuss traditional management practice in life science industries (e.g., Llewellyn, 2001; Kitchener, 2000; Parker, 2000). For example, in a study of a health care company, Llewellyn (2001: 604) found a tendency to keep managerial issues at arms' length: "Any clinician taking up a management position—even with the medical establishment—risks loss of respect and clinical visibility". Compared to the role of science and research, management concerns have a relatively lower status within the industry (Kalling and Styhre, 2003). Finally, Llewellyn's thesis uses a somewhat extended definition of management in new drug development. Managers control and govern the daily work but also act as scientists, that is, support, guide, and protect projects and their ideas. Contrary to such a sceptical view, McAuley, Duberly and Cohen (2000) found that researchers in a public research organization in the UK demonstrated a lively understanding of the challenges and problems facing top management. Rather than assuming that managerial direction would be detrimental to their activities and interests, the research scientists thought that management shared their basic objectives—the ambition to pursue "good science".

Studies of leadership in innovative organizations

Creative and innovative milieus are perhaps the most complicated social organizations to lead and manage. A number of studies address the leadership of creative and innovative individuals (for an extensive overview of the field, see Mumford *et al.*, 2002; Humphrey, 2002; Sundgren and Styhre, 2006). Shalley and Gilson (2004: 36), addressing the connections between leadership and creativity, speak of creativity in the following terms: "Creativity relevant skills can be defined as the ability to think creatively, generate alternatives, engage in divergent thinking, or suspend judgement. These skills are necessary because creativity requires a cognitive-perceptual style that involves the collection and application of diverse information, an accurate memory, use of effective heuristics, and the ability and inclination to engage in deep concentration for long periods of time". In their analysis, Shalley and Gilson (2004) identify a number of social and contextual factors pertaining to the leadership of creative organizations. They distinguish between (1) *individual-level factors*, (2) *job-level factors* such as "job characteristics", "role expectations and goals", the access to "sufficient resources", "rewards", "supervisory support", "external evaluation of work", (3) *team or work group factors*, including "the social context" (i.e., how tightly coupled individuals are in their work) and "group composition", and (4) *organizational-level factors*, such as "organizational climate" and "human resource practices". In Shalley and Gilson's (2004) account, leadership practice in creative organizations is a most complex undertaking including a great number of aspects and considerations. Basadur (2004) emphasizes that "creative leadership" is a matter of making people collaborate and communicate with one another. Basadur (2004) therefore proposes a four stage model including the phases (1) generating ideas, (2) conceptualizing them in an adequate manner, (3) optimizing ideas through selecting the best solutions and alternatives, and (4) implementing the ideas in the organization. For Basadur, creative leadership is the balancing of the "apprehension of knowledge" through *thinking* and *experimenting*, and the utilization of knowledge through *creating* and *evaluating* options. In all these different activities, Basadur emphasizes the need for leaders to facilitate the process and delegate responsibilities rather than trying to apprehend the whole complexity of the matter:

> A creative leader indices others to focus on the process and process skills on meeting their challenges. They become consultants or facilitators in the process of solving the challenges rather than giving orders or doing the work themselves. Having transferred ownership, they then help others to achieve their own goals. These creative leadership skills hardly fit with the traditional management style that most organizations employ, but they can be learned. (Basadur, 2004)

In a study based on both qualitative and quantitative methods, Amabile *et al.* (2004) identify 14 leadership practices supporting creative activities.

In the qualitative analysis of two project teams, they found that the three most important practices were *Monitoring, Clarifying Roles and Objectives*, and *Consulting*.[7] The conventional separation between task oriented and relationship-oriented leader is here abandoned and effective leadership practice includes both the ability to "initiate structure" and showing consideration for the subordinates' feelings, interests, and social relations. Pirola-Merlo *et al.* (2002) found that leadership practice affects team climate that in turn influences team performance in terms of creativity. Team climate thus plays an intermediary role in between leadership and performance. Finally, Cardinal (2001) found in her research in the pharmaceutical industry that specific goals were *negatively* related to innovation, while broader output expectations were positively related to innovation. Moreover, Cardinal (2001) reports that the use of rewards was positively related to both drug enhancement and new drug introductions. Tangible goals and extrinsic motivation thus makes a difference in terms of innovativeness.

In summary, leading creative work is based on the ability to make heterogeneous groups collaborate and being able to establish clear goals and objectives and to monitor the progress while simultaneously caring for the co-workers socio-psychological work conditions. Using Weick and Roberts's (1993: 374) concept of *heedful interrelating*, it may be argued that leadership in creative environments is based on the ability of the leader to "act with attentiveness, alertness, and care". Heedful interrelating is a central competence for organizations operating with tight couplings and complex interrelations, for instance in new product development teams, operators in environments dealing with risky activities such as nuclear plants control rooms, or teams of surgeons and nurses (Edmondson, 2003). Heedful interrelating is of central importance because it enables thoughtful and effective communication and continuous sharing of information in the course of action. When heed declines, performances become "[h]eedless, careless, unmindful, thoughtless, unconcerned, indifferent. Heedless performance suggests a failure of intelligence rather than a failure of knowledge. It is a failure to see, to take note of, to be attentive to" (Weick and Roberts, 1993: 362). More recently, Druskat and Pescosolido (2002) used the concept of heedful interrelating in a study of team-based work and Dougherty and Takacs (2004) examined heedfulness in innovation work. Druskat and Pescosolido (2002: 293) summarize the argument:

[H]eed is not behavior; rather it refers to the way in which behaviors are enacted. Interpersonal interactions assembled with heed are attentive, purposeful, conscientious and considerate. They increase team effectiveness by improving members' ability to work together effectively (Cohen, 1994). Without the enactment of heed, inter- personal interactions and relationships are paid little regard.

Heedful interrelating is then an important social competence in complex and tightly coupled organizational activities. It is important to notice that heedful interrelating is not a "leadership practice" such as those listed by Amabile *et al.* (2004); arguably, it is not even a practice per se. Instead it is a *relationship* between two or more individuals based on mutual understanding and attention. Perhaps one can speak of "heedful leadership" in this context, conceived of as a set of leadership practices and activities embedded in an attentive, purposeful and considerate relation between leaders and co-workers.

Leadership in science-based innovation work

Emotionality in new drug development work

During the last 15 years period, the demands for higher productivity in the new drug development process in pharmaceutical industry have been accentuated. This new focus derives from a number of institu- tional changes. First, the costs of medicines and therapy have increased in the Western world. Today, authorities and institutions such as hos- pitals are no longer willing to dedicate increasing parts of their budgets to drugs. On the contrary, cheaper "me-too drugs" imitations of suc- cessful original drugs, are introduced and in many cases selected by the authorities. Second, the demands on transparency, predictability and safety in the new drug development process have increased. Drugs need to have fewer side-effects and need to be based on solid clinical studies before being accepted for registration. Numerous interviewees told stories how common off-the-shelf drugs such as Aspirin would not have been accepted for registration in the new harder regime of clinical control. Since the bulk of the resources are actually spent in the clinical phases and not in the discovery and development phases, the costs for developing drugs are rising sharply when new demands for additional studies with greater precision and accuracy are enacted. As a con- sequence, all areas of new drug development are subject to cost cutting and rationalization. A third factor that some of the interviewees pointed at was that some of the ongoing projects examined more bio- logically complex disease areas including more alternatives for selected targets and indications, thereby being more complicated to empirically study and involving alternative or competing theoretical explanations. For instance, a range of neurological drug research projects was included in this category. By and large, in AstraZeneca the co-workers in the discovery activities experienced a more closely monitored and controlled management regime that simultaneously has to increase transparency and deal with increasingly complex research activities. For some of the co-workers with significant organization tenure, this recent situation represented a break with the past. The co-workers declared that they in various ways responded emotionally to the changes and the increased control of the laboratory work activities. During the last period of time, benchmarking studies and internal comparisons between sites put new pressure on the co-workers to "deliver more with less". One of the interviewees argued that this whole discussion was poorly managed by the organizations, causing a stressful situation for some of the co-workers:

> '*It's bad*', sort of [performance, top management claims]. But there is no information on how to solve this and then there are numerous persons that cannot influence the process being worried: 'Don't they control the situation?'. That is a leadership fallacy: if you point at a problem you also need to point out how to handle the problem. You cannot pass that on to the co-workers with little mandate or resources to influence the situation ... Benchmarking is fine to know what to focus on but we also need a plan for how to proceed. (Integrative pharmacologist)

The motivation factor was brought into the discussion in most of the interviews, both in terms of being a central factor explaining scientific performance and in terms of being a factor strongly affected by the organizational changes. One of the synthesis chemists speaks of the changes in motivation among his peers: "Parts of the 'effectivisation' has de-motivated some of the synthesis chemists. They feel they are under pressure to continuously deliver ... They don't think they have the mandate to join different constellations and learn to understand the biological side" (Researcher, Synthesis chemistry). He also claimed that the "internal networking" has declined; "it used to happen more naturally", he concluded. Rather than being propelled by joint interests and collaborations between disciplines, the synthesis chemists argued, the new source for motivation in the innovation work was higher pay: "The whole company has become a bit Americanized: we're supposed to be stimulated by money" (Researcher, Synthesis chemistry). Since all new drug development is based on the integration of the domains of chemistry and biological organisms, de-limiting the domain of expertise in one of the two domains radically reduces the opportunities for seeing the full picture. One of the researchers in the integrative pharmacology department pointed at the need for such a broad picture: "To be able to deliver a candidate drug, then you need to know the background for the assignment, not just sit down and say that 'let's test these 10,000 substances and hope for the best'. I prefer to have a background to work on and test" (Researcher, Integrative pharmacology). Besides the need for an integrative view of the substance and its impact on the biological organism, some of the interviewees pointed at the need for formulating clear objectives and goals for each phase of the project, because working solely on a long-term perspective makes the final output an abstract goal. One of the group leaders argued:

> It is quite important to achieve the goals of each part ... We may in fact work an entire career without experiencing any launch of a new drug; it may actually be the case for most of us. That is quite a depressing thought if you think about it. (Group leader, Integrative pharmacology)

The crux with science-based innovation is that even though it may be organized and managed like any other organizational procedure or process, it still demands, some of the interviewees argued, that some of the co-workers are willing to fully commit themselves to the project. Scientific breakthroughs are not a matter of administrative competence but of skilful scientific expertise, hard work, systematic routines, and to some extent luck (see Chapter 5). One of the group leaders argued:

> You may of course come here to do your Nine-to-Five routine. A lot of us do that—maybe too many. But not everyone mustn't be 'Nine-to-Fivers' but some of us must be dedicated so that we can do those 'leaps' and find new things ... It is the extraordinary accomplishments that enable those leaps. (Group leader, Integrative pharmacology)

Speaking of personal motivation, commonly divided into *extrinsic motivation* (e.g., pay, bonuses, and rewards) and *intrinsic motivation* (e.g., credit and recognition from peers, a sense of self-fulfilment, a sense of accomplishment, etc.), the interviewees demonstrated a somewhat ambiguous relationships to the pay. On the one hand, they jointly agreed that the pay was not the single most important source of motivation; on the other hand, some of the interviewees argued that they would appreciate to have some formal recognition of "hard work". A synthesis chemist pointed in somewhat melancholic terms at the limited impact of the salary: "For me personally, the salary is not a fact of motivation. It is nice to have a good salary but you are getting used to it. After three months you are used to it and if you want to get more, you are unhappy again" (Researcher, Synthesis chemistry). The other view is captured by one of the researchers in the domain of molecular pharmacology who claimed that "there is no real recognition for hard work". He continued: "The frightening part is, you will kind of get rid of the few rewards that existed ... In the future you are not going to be recognized for being innovative" (Researcher, Molecular pharmacology). In general, rather than speaking of motivation in terms of pay, the interviewees argued that a sense of participation and mutual recognition was of greater importance for motivation. A synthesis chemist lamented the lack of formal and informal meeting points between domains of expertise: "There is not much contact [between departments]: you do the synthesis, you submit it ... go on with the next synthesis, and once in a month you receive information in the project meeting. I believe many chemists are a bit frustrated" (Researcher, Synthesis chemistry). Such a reduction of the project to a series of activities and operations is devastating for both the quality of the project goal and for the motivation, the interviewees claimed. Since motivation is underlying to any creative work, it should not be underrated. The lack of time to fully commit to one assignment was another concern for the co-workers. One of the DMPK researchers said: "When you are engaged in the project and are given the chance to participate and fully understand the project, you feel more motivated and stimulated and then you become more creative". Since many of the researchers spread their time and energy over three of four parallel projects, many interviewees expressed their frustration over the lack of full commitment to one single activity. A synthesis chemist used the metaphor of the assembly line to capture this sense of fragmented work:

> Personally, I would not appreciate if the laboratory work was like assembly line work ... if I cannot be personally engaged and come up with new ideas ... then I just work to produce this substance ... To find a substance or a good drug you need to 'brainstorm'; you pinch a few ideas here, and few ideas there. (Researcher, Medicinal Chemistry)

A molecular pharmacologist pointed at the same tendency in his domain of expertise:

> To be very creative, you need a bit of time and close working with some really enthusiastic groups. That is important to recreate here. I feel we ... become too much process-driven and the groups have people who are not really connected to each other but doing too many different projects. (Researcher, Molecular pharmacology)

Besides the lack of commitment to one single assignment and the absence of time for reflection, some of the experts in the organization pointed at a rather different motivation problem. In some cases, experts were given explorative work assignments where for instance the potentials of a new technology such as genomics were be evaluated. In the recent wave of new biotechnology and pharmacological tools and techniques, the major pharmaceutical companies have to adopt these new techniques. In some cases, these experts did not feel their managers were either capable of seeing the full implications of the new tools and techniques, or were willing to emphasize the need for a change in the work procedures in their reporting to top management. Consequently, the experts felt they were sidelined and that their expertise was little used or attended to, at the same time as their work were regarded as being valuable for the firm and therefore could not be terminated. In other words, they had a sense of being in limbo, unable to influence the processes, yet not being given additional assignments. One of the researchers in molecular pharmacology outlined this situation:

> I have great degrees of freedom to do that [promote his ideas]. My closest manager allows me to do that. You may think that sounds good but I actually avoid doing that because it is a problem when you are entitled to do what nobody cares about whatsoever. An important part is to 'promote' the results. It implies a massive campaign where you convince the company that this is interesting and of great importance. (Researcher, Molecular pharmacology)

Experienced from numerous attempts at promoting a new tool or a new view of a particular process but failing to attract the right political support in the organization, the researcher is today disgruntled about his manager's inability to put down his foot and make a decision regarding the use of certain new technologies. One must not only be a skilled and experienced researcher to attain recognition but one also needs to have the political skills to get the ideas implemented in the organization. The researchers did not appreciate such "politics"; scientific results should instead be able to "speak for themselves". One of the Disease Area Scientific Leaders, the leading medical expert within a disease area, pointed at a similar experience:

> The ideas are not absorbed by the system ... You may have numerous good ideas, but since there is little motivation to change, there will be no positive feedback to the co-workers so they struggle and struggle to get recognition for their ideas ... It is not transparent who is responsible for different things, and there are no clear systems for how to exploit the co-workers' creativity. (Disease Area Scientific Leader, Integrative Pharmacology)

In summary, the interviewees pointed at a number of emotional-laden aspects of their work: The need for motivation in all creative scientific work, the need for a sense of coherence and participation, the demands for being recognized for one's ideas. While scientific work is heavily governed by instituted routines and standard operating procedures, the system of laboratory equipment and machinery, peer-review systems and other forms of institutionalized control, it is still dependent on the creative and committed individual or, more likely, the groups of individuals. Researchers know that all of their work is piecemeal, collective, and socially embedded rather than being grand, individual, and removed from interests and context, and therefore leadership is influencing the quality of the output from the research process. As was discussed in the introduction of this chapter, the demand for leadership is an effect of the emotional-laden nature of scientific work. Researchers need to be given instructions not because they are not skilled enough to conduct research on their own but because they have to collaborate with others in their day-to-day work and therefore cannot see the whole picture. Similar to the philharmonic orchestra being able to perform without the direction of the conductor, musicians still tend to agree that the conductor plays a central role in enhancing the performance of the orchestra. In this case, leadership is a matter of making what already works on its own attaining an additional impetus that further enhances the performance.

The impact of leadership

The researchers at AstraZeneca criticized their leaders for both their transactional and transformational leadership, that is both the everyday leadership work and the ability to motivate and inspire the co-workers in their research. One of the domains where the researchers would have appreciated more clarity was in the day-to-day decision-making. One of the group leaders in the Department of Integrative Pharmacology pointed at the changes during the last 20 years:

> The hierarchical system that has been constructed is dependent on the size of the firm ... We used to say that we have a flat organization but I am not sure about that. However, there were not that many tiers. Now you notice that it takes longer time to get a decision. You notice the administrative, the bureaucratic, the hierarchical [systems] that have been developed. (Group leader, Integrative pharmacology)

The researchers with longer organization tenure tended to fall into nostalgic reveries regarding how things used to be in the past when there were just a few hundred employees, all communication were face-to-face, and the whole company worked on a few shared projects. For the newcomers, the intransparency of the decision-making became major concern. A Disease Areas Scientific Leader in the Integrative Pharmacology department argued:

> There is a weak line of command concerning decision-making. There are ambiguities ... regarding who have the responsibility and mandate to make decisions. Everybody really wants to run back to their bosses and ask if they should do this or not, and that makes the time run away. Then you feel that the only thing you do is to repeat what's been said for the last half a year in presentations at different meetings. You need to get all the managers into the same boat so they dare making the decision. (Disease Area Scientific Leader)

One of the chemists spoke of decision-making in similar terms:

> I miss clear decision-making. They declare something and then it's on our desks but we get no further instructions and then we are supposed to manage the whole thing without knowing what the objectives are. Even if we appreciate working on our own, you need to know what to achieve in greater detail and how to achieve that objective. (Chemist, DMPK department)

Another researcher at the DMPK department also brought the issue of decision-making into discussion: "It's really hard making certain things happen. There are never any decisions made, I think". A molecular pharmacologist argued that "they [managers] listen but they don't act", while a co-worker at the integrative pharmacology department said that her manager "has an 'open door policy' but [he] is never there". Another researcher, a molecular pharmacologist deplored the lack of long-term perspective: "There is no long-term perspective. A manager is assigned a position, makes some changes, moves on, and leaves something that is not really working". One of the interviewees emphasized the need for recognizing individual work and claimed that it did not demand much effort from the managers to accomplish a sense of recognition: "I think we need pay attention to people; many times, when the work is done we do not fully know who did what. Nothing special really: to mention someone's name or that you are invited to present your work. That is about what it takes" (Researcher, Integrative pharmacologist).

Because of the large risks and sums of money involved in all decision-making in the pharmaceutical industry, decisions tended to move up the organizational tiers to the top management group. Although this is a plausible explanation and highly understandable response to the predicaments of pharmaceutical companies, it may be, as some researchers claimed, an indication of the lack of risk-taking in large, multinational pharmaceutical companies. A manager in the DMPK department emphasized this strategy of "playing safe" as a challenge for the company and the industry in general:

> There is so much money involved that one does not dare being first on the market because the authorities are skeptical towards new ways of thinking, a new 'class' of pharmaceuticals. You have to fight fiercely to get something approved. If you join the next wave then the market is prepared a bit for these new medicines. It hard work being first ... Then you rather play the safe cards first. (Researcher, DMPK)

He continued: "The increased competition has raised new demands ... that every single product should finance itself. Preferably one should not have any products on the market not generating a profit. Then they are rather dropped in an earlier stage. One indication of the lack of risk-taking was suggested by a researcher in the Molecular Pharmacology department, saying that the managers demonstrated a poor ability to close down projects that proved to be less promising than expected or being unable to stand the competition over resources from other projects. "It is as important to close projects as it is to continue them. That is vital", he claimed.

In addition to decision-making, leaders were criticized for not being able to provide sufficient direction and adequate visions for the activities. A group leader deplored the lack of "visibility" of the top managers in the organization and pointed again at the relatively large size of the corporation:

> Our managers are not really visible. For instance, our head of the department—I think I've talked to him twice since I started here ... He does not have the time. We are 250 persons or something and how should he be capable of talking to each and everyone and develop a relationship with them? It is really hard. (Group leader, Medicinal Chemistry)

Such lack of visibility is accentuated when the pharmaceutical industry is experiencing one of its most turbulent periods of change comprising new regulatory demands, new demands for financial performance, a wave of mergers and acquisitions, and a substantial scientific and technological transformation in terms of the use of biotechnologies such as genomics and proteomics. In AstraZeneca, this comprehensive change implied a stronger focus on productivity and efficiency which further underlined the demands for leadership support. A researcher at the molecular pharmacology department deplored the absence of direction from the leaders in the firm:

> When we have the most inefficient pharma company today, I think that the most important thing they [top management] have to do is to give us a clear direction on what kind of target we should be looking at, how much risk we should take on this target, and how much validation we should be doing with this. That kind of things would be nice rather than just telling me 'that you're inefficient'. They should be able to have an overview to see 'where are we inefficient'; Tell me where are we inefficient? Are we equally inefficient? Are we inefficient in some aspect? Can we change that? (Researcher, Molecular pharmacology)

Leadership also includes a long-term focus of the activities, often expressed in the terms of the "vision" or "strategic intent" of the firm. One of the line managers asked for a clearer stance regarding how the new situation is to be handled:

> Regarding the leadership ... I am not fully impressed, I must say. I don't think they are seeing the consequences from the complexity

of making drugs ... They try to eliminate some of the steps in the chain to make things easier for us. I think that is the right way to go. There have been too many decision-makers and too little mandate in the projects. (Line manger, DMPK)

What was needed, the line managers argued, was a clear long-term vision that could unite and create a sense of coherence and direction among the co-workers of AstraZeneca. The line manager pointed at the benefits of such an action: "If a department manager announces a vision: That would produce an impact. If he or she dares to say 'we'll do this' and 'we won't do this'. Many managers keep a low profile today ... I think there is a fear, a fear of being wrong". One of the group leaders called for a similar vision being capable of bridging the various objectives. She said that the leader should "create a vision, a sense of excitements and curiosity but with clearly specified goals. One needs to find the balance between the difficulties and the ways of solving them so they do not appear insurmountable" (Group leader, Medicinal Chemistry). Today, research projects continued as previously and there were, some researchers argued, with little if any concerns regarding how to anticipate future challenges.

The final and perhaps most difficult and demanding challenge for all leaders in scientific milieus was to serve as a source of inspiration for the researchers. Even though scientists are aware that scientific contribution is an outcome from joint efforts, there is still a significant space for stories of "great scientists" and "great achievements". In addition, charismatic leadership is another resource in scientific work that is greatly appreciated by those working together with inspirational persons. For instance, one of the researchers in the DMPK department claimed that "you need to be motivated and stimulated by your manager ... A poor leader can really make you lose your motivation". One of the researchers in the molecular pharmacology department expressed this idea in rather harsh terms:

Our managers are so boring it's getting a kind of occupational health problem. If we at least could reflect society as a whole and have at least a few charismatic persons. I am not asking for everything; you can be scientifically competent and ambitious, or you can be a charismatic person—a strong person making people enthusiastic, or intimidating them, or whatever, but there is no such thing now. (Researcher, Molecular Pharmacology)

In this account, working together with an inspirational leader is not always of necessity a pleasant experience; on the contrary, it implies expectations on making one's best in order to accomplish new and pre-viously unseen things. This concern for managers being incapable of motivating the co-workers was discussed by some of the researchers. A senior researcher agreed that "today, I believe there is an overrepresen-tation of rather square persons being good at administration" among the managers (Researcher, Integrative pharmacologist) and another researcher speculated about the streamlining of the operations and absence of or diminishing spaces for mavericks [Swedish, *vildhjärnorna*] in the company. She was musing over possible explanations:

> I think it starts already at the university; there used to be some 'weirdoes' but they have no space there either because the doctoral students are passed through the system in short time these days. The whole of the system is based on delimiting the opportunities for deviance. (Project Manager, DMPK)

The need for having a manager that has documented expertise in field but is still capable of motivating the co-workers was addressed by many researchers. One younger female co-worker stated: "I expect to have someone I can look up to, a role model. Someone prioritizing time to think and to read and to discuss with others. I have not seen that the last few years" (Integrative pharmacologist). A synthesis chemist claimed that "creative managers" need to defend the department against "new directives" from top management taking time from "the creative processes" and to take care of the co-workers; she actually called for more "leaders" than "managers", and especially leaders capable of "coaching" the co-workers. In her view, that was not really the case today: "We work *despite* our organization, not because of it", she contended. A senior researcher also emphasized the courage to argue against top management when needed:

> What is needed is a management team at the department standing up and objecting [against top management directives]: 'No way, that is wrong, we don't believe in that and we won't do it'. We have that here but that is not the case everywhere. It is about being a bit experienced and having some cool persons in the team who dare stand up for what they believe in and not just go with the stream. (Researcher, Integrative pharmacologist)

Working with leading researchers means that one is given a sense of using one's own competencies and of contributing to qualified research.

For many but not all of the interviewees, this aspect of leadership work was virtually absent and they felt a bit abandoned by top management. Above all, leadership—in its historical, actual, or potential form—denoted a series of emotional responses and accounts. Scientific work is an emotional-laden work, an emotional work, and leadership is one of the mechanisms that regulates and determines the activities. When organizations and firms fail to provide such mechanisms the responses are likely to be emotional in terms of harsh critique, disappointments, or even cynicism (Kosmala and Herrbach, 2006; Fleming and Spicer, 2003). In other words, there is a proximal relation between emotions and leadership.

Summary and conclusion

In this chapter, emotionality has been associated with scientific activities such as innovation work. Scientific ideologies prescribe that scientific work must not be "interested" in terms of being negatively affected by subjective assumptions, norms or belief. The tradition of modest witnessing is then in opposition to emotionality, by tradition rendered as what is in conflict with human reason and therefore a fickle ground for scientific endeavours. Moreover, leadership is claimed to be an effect of the emotional work in all science-based innovation. Since scientists are given the prerogative to conduct research in accordance with a set of managerial objectives and long-term strategic intents, they cannot know what findings and results that are regarded as being of relevance for the company but only for a scientific discipline per se. For instance, a synthesis chemist may argue that he or she has made an interesting observation but that he or she cannot know if the result is accepted for further exploration. This lack of detailed direction means that the scientific work is surrounded by ambiguities regarding the connection between scientific practices and managerial objectives. Leaders in science-based innovation work serve as an intermediary function in between the domain of laboratory work and that of what Mintzberg (1983) calls the "strategic apex" of the firm, that is, top management. For instance, transparent decision-making, visibility, and direction are demanded by the laboratory researchers to undertake their work effectively. Moreover, more abstract expectations regarding inspiration and motivation are articulated. Here leaders transcend their intermediary role and serve as scientific champions that could help the laboratory researchers develop their skills and competencies further. Leaders ease the anxiety of operating in a domain characterized by uncertainty and are expected to play the role of the cartographer envisaging the field of operations and pointing out the direction. In summary, science-based innovation is not devoid of emotional content but emotionality is on the contrary one of the central resources in all advanced science-based and knowledge-intensive work.

7
Management Control in Science-Based Innovation Work

Introduction

While the last two chapters addressed the more soft or subjective aspects of scientific work and science-based innovation, that of management cognition and the play and risk-taking element in all scientific endeavours, and the influence of emotions and leadership in laboratory work, this chapter will return to the "hard core" of management practice, namely management control. While what Thrift (2005: 6) calls the "cultural circuit of capitalism", the totality of "business schools, management consultants, management gurus and the media", tends to portray contemporary knowledge-intensive organizations as some kind of bazaars where knowledgeable individuals meet and freely exchange know-how and experiences, such a market metaphor is not very representative of the day-to-day work of knowledge workers, perhaps with the exception of specific regions such as the Boston region or Silicon Valley where there is an abundance of job opportunities and possibilities for collaborations (see Owen-Smith and Powell, 2004; Powell, 1998; Powell, Koput and Smith-Doerr, 1996). In general, it is questionable whether the mobility of and autonomy of knowledge workers is as high as suggested in the some of the literature. Instead, many knowledge workers, especially in smaller economies such as Scandinavia, tend to pursue their career in a few large organizations. When market opportunities are weak, transaction cost theory suggests, hierarchies tend to evolve. In general, knowledge workers are not excluded from managerial control and influence. Instead, knowledge workers are monitored and governed by specific, at least partially new but rarely radically different regimes of control and regulation. In this chapter, the literature on management control will be examined and criticized for not addressing the management control of knowledge workers such as laboratory researchers in greater detail.

Management control in knowledge-intensive firms

The very notion of management is inextricably entangled with the idea of control (Jacques, 1996; Griseri, 2002; Boje, Gephart and Thatchenkery, 1996). Management is the systematic knowledge of how to lead, administrate and control organized activities. In the recent discussion on knowledge intensive firms and post-industrial organizations, the notion of management control is revisited. In a critical review of the literature, Mir, Mir and Upadhyaya (2003) distinguish between two schools:

> While the notion of organizational control has been theorized from a variety of divergent perspectives, we may think of the various theories as being loosely grouped under the following two heads: (a) the 'mainstream' narratives, which posit control mechanisms as being the drivers of normatively desired organizational goals, and (b) the 'radical' perspective, which seeks to view control either as a process of whimsical reality creation by dominant groups, which then gets paraded as the normative truth, or as an alienating mechanism designed to render organizational constituents vulnerable to domination. (Mir, Mir and Upadhyaya, 2003: 57)

The mainstream school conceives of control as a rational means for achieving organizational goals and assumes that control systems per se are rather uncomplicated. In a seminal work representative of the "mainstream narrative", Tannenbaum (1968: 5) defines control as "[a]ny process in which a person or group of persons or organization of person determines, that is, institutionally affects, the behavior of another person, group, or organization". Tannenbaum (1968: 3) explicated this position: "It is the function of control to bring about conformance to organizational requirement of the ultimate purposes of the organization. The coordination and order created out of the diverse interests and potentially diffuse behavior or members are largely a function of control". In a more recent publication, Feldman (1989: 86) defines control in similar terms: "Control is defined as the exercise of authority through a hierarchical structure that limits or channels behaviour". Such "mainstream" view of control has been put into question by the "radical" critique suggesting that management control is either (1) a thinly veiled will to power of privileged and influential groups in organizations and in society, or that (2) control is a chimera because social reality and organizational processes cannot be subject to full control. Kärreman and Alvesson (2004: 152), advocating the former position, argue: "Management control typically includes an apparatus for specifying, monitoring, and evaluating individual and collective action. Management control is predominantly an activity carried out by a powerful social group that orchestrates and exercises definitional and executive authority over other social groups within an organization". Gabriel (2002: 141), representing the latter view, says that "managers may harbour the illusion of control, but such control is, at best, precarious, fragile and iconic". In an earlier publication Gabriel (1999: 194) criticizes much of the management control literature for overemphasizing the importance of control: "That our lives are controlled by diverse forces operating both on us and through us cannot be doubted. That our lives can be reduced to these forces in a totalitarian gloom runs against what history has to tell us". Therefore, Gabriel suggests that the "importance of control may have been exaggerated" and that organizations "contain areas which are unmanaged and unmanageable". Von Krogh, Ichijo and Nonaka (2000: 4)—otherwise to be located in the mainstream camp—express similar concerns: "In fact, the term management implies control of processes that may be inherently uncontrollable or, at the least, stifled by heavy-handed direction". In more specific terms, Power (2004: 778) criticizes performance measurements for being incapable of capturing complex organizational activities and processes: "We might say that performance measurement systems are technologies of representation which are, by virtue of their necessary reductionism, inherently defective from birth and carry the seeds of their own demise. They provide transitory managerial rationalities, myths of control, for an essentially unmanageable world". Even though management control systems are in fact incapable of providing any conclusive control mechanisms, they serve the function of demonstrating "symbolic management". For instance, Cavanaugh and Prasad (1994) argue that drug testing, increasingly popular in the U.S. in the 1990s, did little to detect and eliminate drug users from American workplaces but still the use of the drug testing procedures testified to management's ambition to deal with the problem, real or imaginary, in a rational and systematic manner. The use of drug testing thus becomes a form of symbolic management, a performative act demonstrating management's commitment to certain values and norms. Taken together, management control remains a contested topic, both in terms of its actual ability to capture organizational activities and resources and influence action, but also in terms of its political implications and the unequal exposure to management control in organizations.

Forms of control

Kelemen (2001) contrasts "bureaucratic control" and "post-bureaucratic control":

> Bureaucratic control refers to the internalization of rational rules and routines by organizational selves. Discipline is a form post-bureaucratic control which draws significantly on all these previous forms of control and yet it is, to a certain extent, different in that it appears not to control but to offer a high degree of individual autonomy at work. (Kelemen, 2001: 2)

She continues, pointing at the interest for the subjectivity of the individual in the so-called post-bureaucratic organization:

> Subjectivity ... becomes a resource to be exploited by the organization: individuals are invited to know themselves with respect to what is expected of them and with respect to the others, assess their position and eventually improve it in order to align themselves with preferred rationality. But to do so, individuals must be provided with appropriate tools and technologies. (Kelemen, 2001: 18)

Iedema (2003) uses the notion of a *post-bureaucratic ethos* to capture the new emphasis on disciplinary forms of control and what Du Gay (1996) calls "auto-surveillance": "[T]he post-bureaucratic ethos asks no less than a 'frameshift' with respect to work, other, meaning, and self ... Put in discourse terms, post-bureaucratic workers are asked to conceive of work and self as socially constructed, performatively maintained, and organizationally anchored" (Iedema, 2003: 131). Maravelias (2003) uses the notion of "trust-based control" and Rose (1990) speaks of various "soft" modes of control as the "governing of the soul". The co-workers of the post-bureaucratic organization are increasingly asked to identify with the organization and its objectives. The literature on management control testifies to a variety of forms of what Perrow (1986) called *unobtrusive control*, Barley and Kunda (1992) named *normative control*, and Barker (1993: 408) addressed as *concertive control*, that is, control that "[g]rows out of a substantial consensus about values, high-level coordination, and a degree of self-management by members or workers in an organization". Barker (1993: 412) contrasts bureaucratic modes of control and the "concertive system": "Under bureaucratic control, employees might ensure that they come to work on time because the employee handbook prescribed it and the supervisor had the legal right to demands it, but in the concertive system, employees might come to work on time because their peers now have the authority to demand the workers' willing compliance". The distinction between bureaucratic and post-bureaucratic management control is of relevance for knowledge intensive firms (KIFs).

Several authors suggest that a new regime of managerial control has been developed in KIFs (Starbuck, 1992; Donaldson, 2001; McKinlay, 2000; Robertson and Swan, 2003; Ditillo, 2004). While traditional organizations are controlled and monitored through a variety of organizational arrangements such as job-descriptions, standard operating procedures, verbally enacted routines, written manuals and standardized reports, KIFs have developed new means of maintaining control. Supposedly "soft" management techniques such as the manipulation of organization culture (Parker, 2000; Ezzy, 2000; Willmott, 1993), the employees' identification with the company, the emphasis on intrinsic motivation and new forms of subjectivities anchored in the company objectives and modes of functioning, are some examples of how the knowledge intensive organizations are managed (Alvesson and Willmott, 2002; Wray-Bliss, 2002; Wajcman and Martin, 2002; Humphreys and Brown, 2002; Grey and Garsten, 2001; Schultz, Hatch and Larsen, 2000; Hill, Martin and Harris, 2000; Covaleski *et al.*, 1998; Newton, 1998; Sturdy, 1998; Garsten and Grey, 1997). However, some recent studies of management control in KIFs suggest that there is a tendency to combine bureaucratic and post-bureaucratic modes of control. Kärreman and Alvesson (2004) say that what they refer to as *socio-ideological control*, soft forms of control achieved through identification and professionalism, and *technocratic control* in terms of direct measurement and evaluation of individual output, are operating in tandem in the major consultancy firm they studied. Kärreman and Alvesson (2004: 152) define these two terms: "[W]e will use the label socio-ideological control for attempts to control worker beliefs and technocratic control for attempts to directly control worker behavior ... In the technocratic type, management works primarily with plans, arrangements, and systems focusing behavior and/or measurable outputs". Similarly, Robertson and Swan (2004) argue that the UK based consultancy firm they studied over a twenty years period moved from being an adhocracy based on "entrepreneurial governance" to a "soft bureaucracy" where more conventional means of control are employed. Moreover, Clegg and Courpasson (2004) examine management control in project organizations and identify three forms of control: *Reputational control, calculative control,* and *professional control.* For Clegg and Courpasson (2004), the growth in use of in project management models does however not imply that conventional or "bureaucratic" means of control are abandoned. Contrary to the findings in these empirical studies, several writers have argued that "knowledge-workers" are of necessity incapable of being managed in ways similar to low or semi-skilled workers. Florida writes:

> To some degree, Karl Marx had it partly right when he foresaw that workers would someday control the means of production. This is now beginning to happen, although not as Marx thought it would, with the proletariat rising to take over factories. Rather, more workers than ever control the means of production because it is inside their heads; they *are* the means of production. (Florida, 2002: 37)

A similar view is represented by Alvesson (2004), speaking of knowledge-intensive firms in general:

> The basic idea of management, as conventionally understood, that of a separation between the planning and execution of tasks, is hardly at all a key feature of KIFs. KIFs in this sense by definition are non-managerial: the more it makes sense to talk about knowledge-intensive activity, the less it becomes relevant to employ a (conventional) management model of thinking. (Alvesson, 2004: 121)

Rather than employing conventional forms of control, Alvesson (2004) argues, KIFs are primarily using normative form of control:

> KIFs tend to be characterized by stronger inputs of normative control than is common in most other organizations. Some KIFs do rely heavily on technocratic form of control—soft rules and procedures as well as measurements by performance indicators—but these are included in, and fuel, normative control by operating in a non-mechanical way, influencing the idea, expectations, and subjectivities of people. (Alvesson, 2004: 137)

A third position in between what Gabriel (1999) calls "the totalitarian gloom" (Farrell and Morris, 2003; Ackroyd, 1996; Raelin, 1985) and the more affirmative view of management control (e.g., Tannenbaum,

1968) is the literature suggesting that professional groups are in fact either positive towards managerial control and direction or are capable of defending their traditional ways of working against managerial initiatives. McAuley, Duberly and Cohen (2000) say that research scientists in a public organization displayed a lively understanding of the challenges and problems facing top management. Rather than assuming that managerial direction and control would be detrimental to their activities and interests, research scientists thought that management shared their basic objectives—the ambition to pursue "good science". Bolton (2004) reports a longitudinal study of nurses' work in a gynaecology unit in a British National Health Services (NHS) hospital implementing a "reform program" emphasizing empowerment, "responsible autonomy" and viewing the patients as customers. Bolton found that the nurses were capable of maintaining an autonomous position vis-à-vis the new managerial objectives and practices, especially regarding how "bedside care" is to be delivered. Mueller, Harvey and Howorth (2003) argue in the same vein that the Board of Directors in another in NHS hospital in London were able to defend the professional culture against managerialist influences. Mueller, Harvey and Howorth (2003) even argue that the dichotomy professionalism-managerialism is too a simplistic model to be practically and theoretically useful. Even more positive towards the idea of management control, Rosenthal (2004) argues that front-line service workers could use systems of management control to defend their interests and therefore regard management control practices as a resource in their work. Rosenthal (2004: 605) criticizes, like Gabriel (1999) a too strong emphasis on management control: "Too strong a fascination with the management's attempts to 'colonialize from within' may obscure the lived experience of employees in service organizations". Similarly, Kärreman and Alvesson (2004) found that the dress code enacted by a major consultancy firm was regarded as source of identity for especially the junior consultants. In summary, in this body of literature, management control is not of necessity always regarded a major threat to autonomy and meaningful work but were in some cases a sense-giving system of rules and regulations (see Gioia and Chittipeddi, 1991; Hill and Levenhagen, 1995) guiding and directing co-workers in organizations. Moreover, a number of researchers have pointed at the correlation between creativity and innovativeness and forms of systematic management control (Turner and Makhija, 2006; Gilson, Shalley and Ruddy, 2005; Feldman, 1989).

Management control as selection and mathematization

The discovery phase in new drug development relies in the effective integration of two principal scientific domains: synthesis chemistry or medicinal chemistry and pharmacology. Synthesis chemists are responsible for providing new molecules that can affect a selected target, in many cases a protein, in the biological organism. The molecule is here a fabricated chemical entity that is constructed in a laboratory setting. The concept of pharmacology includes a wide domain of practices, tools, and models that test the newly synthesized molecule against the selected target in either *in vitro* models (in cells), *in silico* models (in computer-generated milieus simulating the organism) or *in vivo* models (in laboratory animals such as rats or mice) to verify its effects. New drug development process is therefore dependent on the ability to make the domain of chemistry and pharmacology become integrated and establish screening procedures wherein new molecules are effectively tested.

Speaking in theoretical terms, a molecule in new drug development is what Rheinberger (1997) calls an *epistemic thing*, that is, an agreed upon scientific entity that is produced in the process of scientific work and thus serves as the shared ground—a "boundary object" (Star and Griesemer, 1989)—for the scientists (see Chapter 3). An epistemic thing is not what is once and for all fixed. On the contrary, it is what is moulded in the scientific practice (see Pickering, 1995), through critical analysis and the development of a field (Rheinberger, 1997: 226). Following Rheinberger's (1997) perspective on scientific work, epistemic things are not fruitfully conceptualized as fixed and unified entities that are "discovered", but instead they emerge as material and social assemblages jointly constituted through scientific procedures. Knorr Cetina (2001) goes even further and says that "epistemic objects" (*sic*) by definition in fact do not have a clear and fixed quality, but are always "lacking completeness":

> From a theoretical point of view, the defining characteristic of an epistemic object is this changing, unfolding character – its lack of objectivity and completeness of being, and its non-identity with itself. The *lack in completeness of being* is crucial: objects of knowledge in many fields have material instantiations, but they must simultaneously be conceived of as unfolding structures of absences: as a thing that continually 'explode' and 'mutate' into something else, and that are as much defined by what they are not (but will, at

some point have become) than by what they are (Knorr Cetina, 2001: 182).

Speaking of new drug development activities—officially labelled as the "discovery phase" in the focal company—the molecules serve epistemic things/objects. They are first synthesized on basis of a hypothesis regarding the selected target and thereafter tested in a variety of pharmacological models. The molecule is then, if it is evaluated in positive terms, modified, and then the process continues until the molecule is tested in integrated *in vivo* models. The molecule is then the outcome from a series of scientific procedures and encounters between different scientific domains and disciplines. Since the very process of constituting epistemic things is complex and complicated and not always fully transparent process, embedded in the practices of the laboratory scientists and at times not even devoid of ambiguities for the scientists themselves, there is a need—from a managerial perspective—for making what is "invisible" or fuzzy become stabilized and open for inspection. Lynch (1988) speaks (as discussed in see Chapter Three) of *selection* and *mathematization* as the two principal components in endering epistemic things stable and visible. Selection denotes the act where certain processes or output entities are selected as being representative of scientific excellence, performance, effectiveness or any favoured performance measure. Mathematization means that the selected process or output entities are formulated as *quanta*, as a numerical, that can be easily used in quantitative analysis. Mathematics is the tool *par préférence* for this transformation from what is essentially invisible, fuzzy and elusive into what is accessible for inspection and evaluation. Mathematics is often regarded the "queen of sciences", a prestigious human accomplishment applicable in all sorts of scientific domains; a modern science without proper mathematics is simple inconceivable. However, when examining mathematics in terms of epistemology there are several writers pointing at the social components of mathematics (Tiles, 1991; Mackenzie, 1999; Livingston, 1986). Rather than thinking of mathematics as a self-enclosed and wholly deductive system of representation devoid of human interests and politics, mathematics is today increasingly regarded a set of conventions and agreements. For instance, Husserl (1970) writes:

> Mathematics and mathematical science, as a garb of ideas, or the garb of symbols of the symbolic mathematical theories encompasses everything which, for scientists and the educated generally, *represents* the

life-world, *dresses it up* as 'objectively actual and true' nature. It is through the garb of ideas that we take for *true being* what is actually a method—a method which is designed for the purpose of progressively improving, *in infinitum*, through 'scientific predictions', those rough predictions which are the only ones originally possible within the sphere of what is actually experienced and experience able in the life world. (Husserl, 1970: 51–52)

Husserl's discussion of mathematics must be seen as what is in many ways in contrast to the Western canon where mathematics has a privileged position. For Plato, mathematics represented a "value-free" form of knowledge (Badiou, 2004: 29) and ever since mathematics "[h]as been the locus of images of reason in western culture" (Tiles, 1991: 2–3). Tiles continues: "Mathematics is the paradigmatically rational discipline, sometimes serving as the source of images of reason, at other times subject to constraints by images derived from other sources." However, the formulation of a non-Euclidean mathematics in the nineteenth century and the rise of modern mathematics undermined the idea that mathematics had some intrinsic ontological relationship with the outside world. For instance, the eminent French mathematicians Henri Poincaré spoke of mathematics as a "convention":

Mathematical axioms are neither a priori synthetic judgments nor experimental facts. They are conventions. Our choice, among all the possible conventions, is guided by experimental facts; but it remains free and is limited only by the necessity of avoiding any contradictions (Henri Poincaré, cited in Bourdieu, 2004: 79).

Tasić (2001) cites another eminent French mathematician:

French mathematician Jean Dieudonné wrote: 'If I wished to sum up in one sentence the way in which ideas unfolded during this period [1800–1930], I would say that its essence was a progressive abandonment of the concept of "evident truth", first in geometry, and then in the rest of mathematics' ... Mathematics was making its own 'linguistic turn'. With the inertia of a luxury ocean liner, it was veering toward the discrete, formal-computational approach that reflected a growing concern with language. (Tasić, 2001: 31)

The philosopher Imre Lakatos (1970) has shown that mathematical proofs, the most central procedure for advancing mathematics (Livingston,

1986), is always a matter of recognizing that there are a number of inconsistencies that cannot be fully accounted for. MacKenzie (1999: 18) clarifies:

> Mathematics, Lakatos concluded, should not be seen as a simple accumulation of clear-cut truths for which unquestionable proofs exist. Even mathematical concepts are 'stretchable', and this is not a flaw: concepts 'grow'. Mathematics is a creative process in which conjectures and proofs are subjected to criticism and improvement. (MacKenzie, 1999: 18)

In summary, during the last century, mathematics was increasingly regarded an analytical tool only loosely coupled with underlying realities. Still, mathematics and all sorts of knowledge expressed in numericals enjoy a certain status. As Bourdieu (2004: 48) points out, the mathematization of sciences implies an exclusion of certain groups and creates a sense of exclusiveness: "Mathematization first produces an effect of exclusion from the field of discussion ... With Newton (I would add Leibniz), the mathematization of physics tended increasingly, from the mid-eighteenth century, to set up a very strong social separation between professionals and amateurs, insiders and outsiders". One cannot underrate the aura of objectivity surrounding mathematics. As Porter (1995: 3) points out, "'objectivity' arouses the passions as few other words can". Its articulation is often seen as a warrant for "basic justice, honest government, and true knowledge". Speaking of accounting and its "trust in numbers", Porter warns that concepts such as objectivity must not be regarded as being uncomplicated or detached from social interests and ideologies. Instead, objectivity remains, Porter (1995: 7) argues, a chimera, an unattainable ideal: "This ideal of mechanical objectivity, knowledge based completely on explicit rules, is never fully attainable. Even with regard to purely scientific matters, the importance of tacit knowledge is widely recognized ... The public rhetoric of scientific expertise, however, studiously ignores such aspects of science". Objectivity here means "the rule of law" and not "the rule of men"; personal interests are here subordinated to formally enacted standards. Therefore, Porter (1995: 89) suggests that it is time to de-familiarize the concept of objectivity—expressed in terms of formalized theory—as the yardstick for anything scientific and to recognize its organizational features. In terms of mathematization and accounting, Porter (1995) argues that one must not dismiss accounting and statistics as being a mundane routine activity that does not deserve any detailed analysis because such an attitude reinforces the influence of such practices: "We must be wary of dismissing it [accounting] as routine and unoriginal. The reputation of accountancy and statistics for greyness helps to maintain their authority. Considered as a social phenomenon, accounting is a much more powerful and problematical than scholars and journalists generally realize" (Porter, 1995: 51). In summary, then, Porter insists that one needs to be suspicious of the concept of objectivity and the various social practices that invoke the term (e.g., accounting) because there is no such thing as a "proper objectivity" devoid of social interests and politics.

Another social effect of mathematics that Husserl (1970) points at is that groups capable of interpreting and formulating ideas in mathematical terms tend to put the cart in front of the horse: Mathematics, that is, a method or a heuristic, tends to become a goal in itself since it is removed and safeguarded from common sense thinking and critical reviews. "Merely fact-minded science makes fact-minded people", Husserl (1970: 6) says. The use of *quanta* is a social practice that in itself needs to be evaluated.

Performance control in AstraZeneca

The abundance of information

The pharmaceutical industry is today increasingly dependent on the financial markets favouring short-term financial performance. This causes a conflict of time perspective since the entire new drug development process can take up to a decade from the first target validations to a new registered drug. Moreover, monitoring authorities such as the Food and Drug Administration (FDA) in the USA has imposed more regulatory demands throughout the process. The demand for providing a number of new drugs annually has made the pharmaceutical companies develop and apply a number of advanced scientific technologies screening a large number of potential molecules. Out of maybe 10,000 screened molecules, only a few will eventually qualify as a new registered drug. One of the most significant effects from this screening strategy is a massive production of information. Storing and analysing such amounts of information put the researchers in the discovery organization under substantial pressure. One of the DMPK scientists pointed at the problems associated with the identification of the best molecule among thousands of screened entities:

At times, you believe that there is too much information. There is always that risk. In the development projects, you synthesize like

3,000 substances ... a real good substance may easily disappear then ... I think we've seen that tendency, that you miss something. It would have been great if we could reduce output and think more. (Researcher, DMPK)

Similar concerns were addressed by one of the synthesis chemists:

For me, personally, I cannot fully understand how to handle the information generated from thousands of substances ... after all, it is a certain feeling you have to follow. (Researcher, Synthesis chemistry)

The continuous production of test results that demanded thoughtful analysis and reflection implied that the reseachers had a sense of always shovelling against the tide. Many experienced a kind of information overload which allowed minimal time to engage in the detailed analyses they believed were in many cases necessary. One of the pharmacologists described this situation:

The co-workers are overloaded with work assignments and they do not have the time to reflect; in many cases, they do not have the time to sit down and see what the results stand for ... to see a pattern in a series of experiments. You rarely have the time to put these pieces together. (Integrative Pharmacologists)

Another pharmacologist thought that the entire field of the "new biology" consisting of new area of "omics"-techniques (e.g., genomics, proteomics, pharmacogenomics) was representing a paradigm shift in the pharmaceutical industry. To date, AstraZeneca has not fully adopted the "new biology techniques" and therefore many of the co-workers and especially the managers failed to see the full potential of the new opportunities. The pharmacologists argued:

I think there is a great fatigue. We have so much muscles, so much technology, access to so much information. This dream they discussed when they segmented the human genome came true: The immense access to information. The thing is, there are always a shortage of resources ... sooner or later, you reach a point where somebody need to take a look, conduct an analysis, and make a decision. AstraZeneca here in Mölndal has no tradition in this field. The managers are not trained in this spirit ... This new 'era' in the biology—I am thinking of genomics and genetics where you can obtain much information and the technique I work with myself where you can evaluate the genetic code of a cell—creates incredible amounts of information. In addition, there is information provided by the research community, available in data bases on the internet ... I don't think we are used to and prepared to receive all this information, and I think that people celebrate when they realize that this new deal also implies disappointments like any other previous technology. I think people are relieved when they hear that HTS has not generated any new significant drugs on the market. I think people are relieved when they hear that genetics has not produced any new forms of treatment. (Molecular Pharmacologist)

Not only were the scientists exposed to a massive amount of information produced in-house; they were also to some extent expected to follow a series of academic journals in relevant fields to be capable of keeping track of the scientific advancement. Some of the scientific experts in AstraZeneca did not see the time during the workday to sit down and read journal papers. One of the synthesis chemists argued:

The problem is for me is to combine the work and all the literature reading that belongs to the project ... I don't see the time during the day to do my literature reading ... Then I print it out and take it home and read it at home. It's difficult balancing: there's so many papers, so many journals you can read ... to keep up with the standards of science. It is impossible to do this all the time. You have always in your mind. "You should read more, you should read more" ... I talk to a lot of people—friends and colleagues—and they all say the same.

The massive amount of information available had implications for decision-making in the company. Top management relied on a number of scientific committees and scientific boards consisting of leading medical experts to provide advice for what substances to prioritize. In order to share information between various projects, project leaders and senior scientists were asked to present results and the latest findings for committees and boards monitoring the work. One of the senior scientists spoke of his research as "power point research", suggesting that research was from the outset formulated in terms suiting the power point presentation format. In general, the knowledge sharing between the projects and the line managers was regarded a complex matter. Some of the senior scientists thought that the line managers did not have the expertise to fully understand the scientific complexities facing the project co-workers. As a consequence, decision-making was perceived as slow and fuzzy to the project team workers.

Management control as output control

The new drug development process is, in essence, aimed at identifying the right target, understanding its mechanism, and finding the right molecule to interact with that target. The continuous production of data and information implies two series of management practices. First, the logistics of the data and information had to be taken care of; storage of information and systems for making data available were implemented. Second, adequate performance measures were to be formulated.

Regarding the data logistics, some of the interviewees thought that there was an overemphasis in the company on storing all kinds of information. The ambition to make all sorts of data available in databases accessible to relevant co-workers was good in theory but overlooked the actual work pressure of the co-workers. One of the pharmacologists expressed his highly critical view of such databases:

> We emphasize the logistics, to document data and make it available for everyone. I think it's ridiculous! It is of course a good thing to being able to share data and make it visible in the company, but it is much more important that there is an end-user receiving it. You do something for a reason and the person who posed the question needs to be the end-user for only that person is capable of seeing the full value of the analysis. If there is no such person, you mustn't think that AstraZeneca co-workers are 'browsing around' in some computer database someplace saying 'well, here's somebody who did an interesting thing six years ago' and bring that research forward. That's silly. I think we focus the wrong things: investing such amounts of time to categorize and make data available when there is not such end-user. (Pharmacologist)

Being himself disappointed with the inability of top management to understand or see the potential of the *in vitro* analysis methods he had developed over a number of years, the pharmacologist insisted on identifying clear end-users prior to implementing new technological systems or information technologies. In his view, there is no properly functioning "internal market" for "unspecified" data and information.

The second management practice addressed the formulation and implementation of adequate performance measures in the new drug development process. In the present performance measurement regime, top management had enacted an output-based model emphasizing the number of molecules delivered per time unit. The interviewees were sceptical towards the idea that one could define how many new candidate drugs that needed to be delivered annually and thereafter break down that figure into the amount of substances that needed to be delivered from each department or even each individual as in the case of synthesis chemists. One of the senior scientists explained:

> They have calculated how many new drugs that need to be introduced every year and then you apply some basic mathematics and calculate what the consequences are for us. This means there will be less time for 'explorative studies' ... innovations and so forth ... Our laboratory engineers will be fully engaged in screening [substances] ... I think there will be much less tolerance for these 'on the side' projects.

Prioritizing the delivery of new NCE exclusively implies that the room for serendipity and other forms of exploratory initiatives will be eliminated. While the consequences for the company are complicated to predict, it means that the scientists are given less time to explore what they regard as being interesting opportunities. Even though the interviewees understood the rationale for the breakdown structure of the performance measure and accepted the company objectives to maintain a high level of new registered drugs, they still thought the validity of the performance measure was low. Similarly to any rationalization of manufacturing operations, it is not the co-workers that are given the time being released, but instead more assignments are added to the workload. "Speeding up" did therefore not mean that there was more time for analysis or reflection. Instead, more projects are initiated.

Some of the interviewees thought that regardless of the debate concerning the quality of the molecules and the substances, the performance measure "number of synthesized molecule compounds per time unit" was an invalid proxy for high performance. One of the synthesis chemists was critical of the performance measures:

> But what does this number tell you? I can set up twenty reactions every day and write that eighteen reactions did not work. But management cannot read all the procedure, they just see the numbers. I am afraid it is going this direction, that everyone [now thinks] that

they judge me by the number of reactions that I do, so why not setting up this also ... then I have one reaction more.

He continued, pointing at project management skills and the role of scientific advisor in his department:

It is not the number of compounds, the number of reactions [that matters] ... [but] also the contribution to the discussion: How do you help your colleagues? How do you push your project forward? ... But it's difficult to measure: How do you measure that?.

One of the DMPK scientists pointed at the direct effects from the performance measures in terms of reporting molecules that may need additional analysis: "You'd rather deliver in December 2004 than in February 2005 because then you can report it 'the right year' ... but it may be that it would have been better to wait for two months and do a few tests and maybe be able to say that 'no, this does not qualify'". For him, an increased reliance on the production on a certain amount of substances posed a threat to the long terms performance of the company:

[A threat may be] the pressure to deliver more and more substances in different stages; we need more pre-CDs and CDs because that is a good way of measuring effectiveness ... You may lose a bit of quality if you increase the number of substances. I am not sure you are capable of delivering more registered drugs just because you increase the amount of produced compounds in the early stages. You need to be really careful in delivering substances that are qualitative, that you have worked on for a while and that you think are capable of standing the test so that the clinical studies more or less confirm what you already thought you knew. Preferably, there should be no 'Oops! insights', at least not any negative ones. I think that is the case at times when we are forced to deliver substances; we are not fully convinced the substance will make it but we have a deadline and then we will deliver the substance on time. (Researcher, DMPK)

Another researcher at the DMPK department argued that the time released from the automatization of the laboratory work should, be used for scientific analysis and reflection rather than producing additional data:

We are doing things at a higher speed in the laboratory, and that is fine because you do not have to do everything by hand now when we can use robots and everything. But the risk is that the time saved is not used for creative thinking on scientific matters. Instead, we are asked to conduct more tests and produce more data. It is very important to take care of data in an adequate manner. I don't think we have really succeeded in that. (Researcher, DMPK)

In general, the scientists in the new drug discovery organization were all very dedicated to their work and they tended to regard the one-dimensional performance measures as being an approach trivializing their complex assignment and their expertise. One the other hand, they could see the need for maintaining some sort of output control in the company to safeguard long-term competitiveness. However, they claimed that the inability of the agents of the financial markets to understand and fairly evaluate the challenges in new drug development was a key concern for the industry. Some of the interviewees thought that fickle movement of the stock price poorly reflected the solid scientific work conducted and expertise of the company. The scientific domain had thus been to some extent "hi-jacked" by financial objectives and did no longer operate in accordance with its own favoured performance indicators. "There is more talk about efficiency than quality", a project manager at the DMPK department remarked. One of the pharmacologists lamented this movement toward more clear-cut financially derived performance measurements:

It is almost a taboo to put into question all these 'numbers': 'Number of substances', 'number of CDs' [candidate drugs], because all of the time, they show, using statistical models, that there is a need for a specific number of substances to deliver a new drug. 15 years ago, people would have been laughing if they [top management] had presented such figures. You did not work that way back then. I think we need to get away from all this, the 'numbers', because in a long-term perspective, I think it is destructive.

In summary, the continuous production of data and information demands not only a large apparatus of logistics and storage of information, but it also enabled performance measures. Identifying such performance measures that can be widely agreed upon has however proven to be far from trivial. Implemented measures were generally regarded as having low validity and one-sidedly emphasizing quantitative output. Consequently, the researchers were highly critical of the performance measures and pointed at its negative long-term consequences for the company's competitive advantage. In addition, they emphasized that the performance measures did not encourage more detailed scientific analyses. Scientific work is then no longer sheltered from detailed monitoring or strict numerical performance indicators. It may be argued that scientific innovation becomes "routinized" when it is increasingly anchored in a series of predefined and fixed or semi-fixed performance indicators. For the practising scientists, this means a loss of some of the principal scientific liberties, namely those of, "in the service of mankind", being able to explore interesting findings in greater detail and pursue objectives that are not obeying any "extra-scientific" objectives (i.e., financial concerns). Therefore, the selection or and mathematization of certain scientific procedures—in this case the identification of number of synthesized molecules per time unit—stands in stark contrast against the scientific ideology. For the scientists, a new regime of managerial control not being overtly concerned about scientific liberties and the institutions of the *ancien régime* is emerging. What is interesting here is that this regime of managerial control is not solely aiming at regulating through "soft" techniques and forms of identification but through the implementation of performance indicators exploiting facts and figures.

Management control in science-based innovation

The predominant image of work in knowledge-intensive organizations suggests that the "knowledge worker" is a self-monitoring and enterprising agent, basically outside of the full control of management (see e.g., Florida, 2002: 37). Such knowledge workers are primarily influenced through a variety of unobtrusive or socio-ideological forms of control including strong company cultures, identification with the company, the emphasis on intrinsic motivation, and other "soft" forms of control and governance. The underlying rationale for such unobtrusive or socio-ideological forms of control is that the epistemological qualities of the primary organization resource in the knowledge-intensive organization, that is, forms of knowledge, know-how and expertise, make knowledge complicated to manage and control. Rather than managing knowledge per se, managerial practices tend to be centred on the knowledge worker. Following Kelemen (2001), control must of necessity become *indirect* in the knowledge-intensive organization (Roberts, 2005; Sewell, 2005). However, several studies suggest (e.g., Kärreman and Alvesson, 2004) that soft forms of control are complemented by "hard end-point" of performance measurement that evaluates the effectiveness of individuals, work teams, or departments. In an industry like the pharmaceutical industry, relying on the ability to demonstrate scientifically based facts and figures, various quanta and statistical methods play a key role; the pharmaceutical industry is simply inconceivable without its mathematical procedures and routines.

The study of AstraZeneca shows that even though the scientists themselves, many of them eminent academic researchers holding chairs in prestigious Swedish Universities such as Karolinska Institutet or Uppsala University, regarded the output measures as being only loosely coupled with output and having the latent function of eliminating proper scientific analysis, they were not able to fully resist the new regime of managerial control. Speaking in theoretical terms, the identification of performance measures has been examined in terms of the *selection* and *mathematization* of relevant operations. However, rather than conceiving of such selection and mathematization procedures as being solely representative of some managerial interests formulated "from above", detached and separated from the laboratory researchers' professional ideologies and beliefs, the study suggests that socio-ideological control and technocratic control are entangled and complicated to separate for equally the researchers themselves and for outsider researchers. While the selection of performance indicators is aimed at providing valid and widely agreed upon performance indicators, the mathematization of the selected indicator is aimed at creating reliable measures. Such performance indicators must be then anchored in the predominant scientific ideology of the organization. Even though the laboratory researchers were sceptical about the validity of the performance measures, they also expressed an understanding for the rationale for the goal-breakdown structure advocated by top management. Similar to McAuley, Duberly and Cohen's (2000) study of researchers in a public organization in the UK, the laboratory researchers displayed an understanding of the challenges and problems facing top management. Therefore, the use of mathematically grounded management control systems is both representing socio-ideological and a technocratic means of managerial control.

The study is thus consistent with a number of studies of management control in KIFs suggesting that such organizations employ a combination of "old" and "new" forms of control; rather than relying on solely normative, socio-ideological, or other forms of unobtrusive forms of control, KIFs mobilize an assemblage of management control practices. However, contrary to the dichotomy suggested by Kärreman and Alvesson (2004), speaking of "socio-ideological" and "technocratic" means of control as two essentially separated domains wherein one form of control is subtle and ambiguous and the other is carefully expressed in hard end-points and distinct categories and measures, it is suggested that the line of demarcation between ideology and technology (as in the term "technocratic") is too permeable and fluid to make sense in empirical studies. Following writers like Gaston Bachelard, technology is an embodiment of human thinking. Since mathematics is a form of technology or a social practice relying on a technical regime of representation, the boundary between the ideological and the technological is ambiguous. For laboratory scientists, the use of procedures of selection and mathematization are activities embedded in ideologies (and more specifically, *scientific* ideologies) per se in terms of being closely connected to the training and secondary socialization of laboratory scientists (see e.g., Becker *et al.*, 1961). In the case of the laboratory researchers, the socio-ideological forms of control "spilled over" into the technocratic forms of control, i.e., the professional beliefs, assumptions and practices were drawn on in the design of technocratic control. Similarly, in other organizational or professional cultures, it may be conversely said that technocratic forms of control are becoming a part of the socio-ideological control. For instance, highly competitive professional groups such as salesmen may embrace detailed technocratic control since it enables a continuous and ongoing comparison of performance between individuals or work teams and therefore such technocratic systems of control may influence the company culture, a supposedly "soft" form of control. It must not be assumed that the "soft" and the "hard" means of control are representing two divergent lines. Instead, they are intersecting and mutually affecting one another in complex ways. In summary, the regimes of management control in AstraZeneca were not composed of clearly separated means of control; management control is instead an assemblage of a variety of heterogeneous practices, beliefs, ideologies, and so forth, in many cases complicated to separate for equally insiders (in this case, laboratory researchers) and outsiders (i.e., researchers and consultants). As a consequence, the research on management control in KIFs and other forms of organizations needs to be more sensitive to local and contextual factors affecting the reception of management control practices. Expressed differently, no management control practice is inherently "good" or "bad" in itself, but helps accomplishing or hindering organizational objectives and goals though its alignment with various resources in organizations. Thus one may, similarly to the findings reported by Gabriel (1999), Rosenthal (2004) and McAuley, Duberly and Cohen (2000), take a more affirmative view of management control as what is not always already of necessity detrimental to the autonomy of professional groups but what may even be regarded a resource for the employees to exploit in their day-to-day work.

Summary and conclusion

In the emerging literature on knowledge-intensive organizations, the notion of management control has been examined as a central process for managing and monitoring knowledge workers. Several studies point at the combination of soft and hard end-points forms of control in KIFs. What is of particular interest is Kärreman and Alvesson's (2004) distinction between socio-ideological and technocratic control, separating the soft and the more immutable forms of control. The study of AstraZeneca suggests that such a distinction is complicated to make because the technocratic forms of control, formulated in terms of performance ratios such as the number of syntheses conducted per time unit (normally months), is based on a process of selection and mathematization that is closely connected to the laboratory researchers' socio-ideological beliefs and assumptions. In other words, the technocratic means of control is entangled with the ideologies of the group of researchers. The education, training and secondary socialization emphasizes the use of mathematics as the principal regime of representation in scientific work—qualified and competent laboratory researchers are capable of mastering mathematics. Thus, the use of selection and mathematization in management control is at the same time a socio-ideological and a technocratic means of management control. Therefore rather than regarding the social-cultural and technocratic form of management control as being clearly separated systems, management control systems are to be examined as assemblages comprising different means of control, neither wholly separated nor wholly integrated but intersecting in many ways.

Part III
Reflections

8
Thinking of Science-Based Innovation

Introduction

In this book, the specific form of innovation work that is here called science-based innovation has been examined. Such innovations have their roots in the modest witnessing of pioneering scholars such as Copernicus, Galilei and Boyle, and over the years and in the course of time, scientific knowledge and scientific procedures have been developed into veritable machineries for innovation; one actually speaks of innovations—like managers and co-workers in the pharmaceutical industry actually do—derived from scientific expertise and procedures in terms of being distributed in pipelines. Such a leap from modest witnessing to pipeline thinking is not a linear or uncomplicated trajectory. In a famous scene in Stanley Kubrick's *2001*, a bone is in a split second—collapsing a period of over 2 million years into one single moment—transformed into a space shuttle, thus locating oceans of time of the evolution from hominids to man's development of advanced space technology in one single point of time. Even though the cinematographic medium allows us to perceive complicated evolutionary changes this way, in actual history there are no such smooth and seamless transitions. Yet, the scientific procedures in pharmaceutical companies, feeding the pipelines with new chemical entities and new candidate drugs, are the outcome from the gradual establishment of scientific practices and procedures beginning with modest witnessing and other early attempts at establishing a proper scientific *modus operandi*. However, one of the principal mistakes when examining science-based innovation is to believe that a machinery is a self-enclosed and self-perpetuating system *per automata* continuing to produce a steady output. Although the machinery is a handy metaphor capturing the functional organization of a system effectively integrating a great number of components and mechanisms, it is a deceiving metaphor in terms of overrating its ability to operate without input from the environment and proper maintenance. Although scientific disciplines may be self-regulating on the macro level—it is after all for instance physicists themselves deciding what physics is and what physicists should preferably do—on the meso and micro levels, there is always controversy, debates, arguments, etc. over where to go and for what purpose. When scientists become enrolled in innovation work under the pressure of financial performance and the expectations to exploit identified market opportunities, scientific activities are no longer safely demarcated from non-scientific concerns. Science-based innovation is undertaken in an open field characterized by heterogeneity. Machinery, laboratory equipment, researchers, managers, laboratory animals, market analyses, annual reports statements, accounting procedures, and a long series of resources are mixed and folded into one another in the everyday work. Being able to sort out and understand the relationship between these heterogeneous resources is helpful when examining science-based innovation.

Much of the knowledge management and innovation management literature is too unspecific and too generic to fully capture the central features of science-based innovation. Further, the social studies of science literature—otherwise an excellent source for insightful analyses of scientific work—is too little connected to managerial concerns to provide more clear directions on how to manage science-based innovation. Thus, science-based innovation in organizations needs to be further studied and explored in greater detail. In this book, three aspects of science-based innovation have been discussed, namely the influence of playing and risk-taking in innovation work, leadership and emotionality, and the effects of management control. The metaphor of playing has traditionally been little recognized in the knowledge management and innovation literature, but is here used as a root metaphor for the driving force in all humans experimental activities conducted. Leadership and emotionality are at times discussed in terms of being, if not irrelevant for knowledge-intensive work in today's companies, in many cases only marginally influencing self-motivating knowledge workers such as researchers. Here, leadership and emotionality have been examined in terms of being the most important resources for successful innovation work. Management control is, at least in its most conventional technocratic forms, associated with vanishing organization practices hopelessly bound up with a mass production regime. Contrary to such a view, management control takes many shapes and forms but the conventional output form of control is far from anti-quated. On the contrary, it is in use and is still regarded as being necessary for safeguarding an adequate output in AstraZeneca. Therefore, taking new perspectives on knowledge-intensive work may imply that complementary or even competing perspectives are enabled; the new regime of knowledge-intensive firms and knowledge-intensive work does not of necessity represents a radical break with past management practices. Instead, there may be parallel lines of continuity, disruptive changes, and new emerging patterns constituting a new texture of organized activities that are at times deviant from previous forms and at times converging towards them. This final chapter aims at discussing the implications from the analyses for knowledge management theory and the innovation management literature.

Science-based innovation: implications for the knowledge management and innovation management literature

Much of the knowledge management literature is bound up with what Robert Chia (1996b) calls "being-realism" portraying reality as an entity-based, immutable order not capable of apprehending a social reality that is fluid, fluxing and changing (Schultze, 2000). John Law's (1994: 14) declaration, directed towards sociologists, is also adequate for knowledge management writers: "[S]ociologists, like many others, tend to prefer to deal in nouns rather than verbs. They slip into assuming that social structure is an object, like the scaffolding round a building, that will stay in place once it has been erected". For Law (1994: 139), what is social is "[n]ever purely social" but is always *materially heterogeneous* and includes "talk, bodies, texts, machines, architectures". The two implications are that social reality is fluid and changing rather than stable and fixed and that social reality is heterogeneous and composite rather than unified and homogeneous. Speaking with Robert Chia, a "becoming-realism" is thus better suitable than a "being-realism" when understanding how social activities are constituted and evolve over time. One of the principal problems with the (mainstream) knowledge management literature is that it is primarily preoccupied with examining things and conditions in terms of being stable and predictable entities. A knowledge management theory embedded in a becoming-realism epistemology may operate along new routes of investigation. Calling for such a reformulation of knowledge management theory means to overturn some of the assumptions regarding the quality of the human resource commonly referred to as knowledge. In the following, some of these qualities will be examined in greater detail.

First, all engagement with knowledge-based activities implies a certain degree of ambiguity and elusiveness. John Dewey (1988: 17) spoke of mankind's "quest for certainty" as a primordial human condition: "Perfect certainty is what man wants. It cannot be found by practical doing or making; these take effect in an uncertain future, and involve peril, the risk of misadventure, frustration and failure. Knowledge, on the other hand, is thought to be concerned with a region of being which is fixed in itself". Knowledge is here what is capable of doing away with beliefs and guessing and instead becomes what is always already certain and fixed, ready to apply to cases and not contested. Dewey (1988: 20) says: "We *believe* in the absence of knowledge or complete assurance. Hence the quest for certainty has always been an effort to transcend belief". Knowledge is here an effect of mankind's inability to endure uncertainty and its willingness for rendering certain things stable and immutable. Chaos and stability, knowledge and non-knowledge (beliefs, hearsay, and so forth) coexist in close proximity; at times a thin red line of demarcation only separates the two. For instance, the so-called placebo effect in medical therapy is one such case haunting the guardians of the boundary between knowledge and non-knowledge and beliefs (Collins and Pinch, 2005). Speaking in terms of laboratory practices and scientific activities, similar ideas have been expressed. Rheinberger (1997: 27) writes: "A researcher ... does not, as a rule, deal with isolated experiments in relation to a theory, but rather with a whole experimental arrangement designed to produce knowledge that is not yet at his disposal. What is even more important, the experimental scientist deals with systems of experiments that usually are not well defined and do not provide clear answers". Concepts like *elaboration, experimentation, conjectures,* and *trails* and *studies* underline the influence and presence of ambiguity and emergence in scientific practice. Science-based innovation is therefore the handling of a situation wherein many things cannot be fully known, anticipated, and estimated prior to actual laboratory experiments and scientific negotiations. Ambiguities are an essential component in any scientific program.

Second, all scientific procedures and practices, the totality of laboratory routines and mechanisms for joint evaluation and justifications, are dependent on historically emergent conditions. Numerous historians of science emphasize that what is deemed to be scientific is not an arbitrary labelling but is what is in fact embedded in centuries of sediments of discussions and problem-solving. Starbuck (2004: 1239) points at the historical contingencies of scientific practice: "Scientific rationality is an extreme ideal type that has been constructed through centuries of discussions by philosophers and scientists implanted in researchers through education and socialization". But Starbuck also warns that scientific practices may be deceiving: "We seek scientific rationality because it pleases our minds, but what gives our minds please may not give us insight or useful knowledge". For instance, Robert Boyle's insistence on "modest witnessing" was not uncontroversial or immediately received by Boyle's contemporaries, but over the centuries this particular idea, that science should be evaluated by the *primus inter pares*, has been modified, retranslated, and instituted in many ways and in many forms. This scientific practice and, consequently, science-based innovation is not what is possible to fully understand merely through an analysis of synchronic practices but only through combining synchronic and diachronic approaches. In Foucault's phrase, one may here speak of "the history of the present".

Third, all scientific undertakings are of necessity collective endeavours because every contribution must be small and specialized. Contrary to mythology and common sense belief, all scientific contributions are in fact the outcome from collaborations and exchanges of ideas and research results. There is no such thing as an autonomous and isolated researcher (Knorr Cetina, 1995). Bourdieu (2004: 72) writes: "Knowledge is based not on the subjective self-evidence of an isolated individual but on collective experience, regulated by norms of communication and argumentation". Seen in this view, all scientific knowledge is constituted through its circulation in certain communities (Latour, 1987); the collective evaluation of research findings is the perhaps most central feature of the research work.

This leaves us with a practice comprising social and material components, that is of necessity riddled by ambiguities and uncertainties, that evolves along historical routes, and that is in its essence a collective undertaking. Seen in this way, the widely used metaphor of the "pipeline" of science-based innovations, for instance in the production of new drugs in the pharmaceutical industry, is not capable of accommodating all the social, cultural, material, and institutional complexities and interrelationships underlying to any science-based innovation endeavour. Even though science-based innovation can be managed and influenced in various ways, it is never solely a matter of eliminating analytical skills, individual creativity, and residual factors such as luck or chance altogether. Therefore, the metaphor of the pipeline is an appealing one, suggesting that someplace—in the "back office", Goffman (1959) would say—there is an entire apparatus continuously feeding scientific work into the pipeline that can be conveniently tapped into the market. Such a metaphor may make sense from a marketing perspective but has limited analytical value; it obscures rather than clarifies. Instead, speaking of science-based innovation as an assemblage, a unified whole that comprises many parts and that can unfold infinitely, offers some analytical advantages. For Stengers (1997: 204) an assemblage in scientific work is a complex including "objects/representations/practice". These components can never be explained isolated from one another because they are irreducible to themselves; they only make sense and attain their meaning and function within the *assemblage*. In addition, specific assemblages are connected to one another in complicated ways: "The location of a particular assemblage never constitutes an ultimate or complete explanation; assemblages are connected together in multiple ways and create communications between what is classically distinguished as different levels of explanations" (Stengers, 1997: 204). Lanzara and Patriotta (2001) explain how knowledge in organizations emerge as assemblages:

> Rather than a discrete commodity, organizational knowledge could be better pictured as an 'assemblage' subject to continuous transformations and reconfigurations. It is an assemblage precisely because it is the outcome of controversy and *bricolage*, resilient as a whole but subject to local disputed, experiments, and resembling ... An assemblage is neither a unity nor a totality, but a multiplicity, a collection of heterogeneous materials that are mutually but loosely interrelated. In other words, the notion stresses the importance of relations over the elementary parts, i.e., what goes on 'between' the part (Cooper, 1998, p. 112). In this regard, what makes knowledge distinctive is not the discrete collection of commodities, but the nature of the assemblage and, we should add, the making of the assemblage in time. An assemblage is an evolving artifact and it is unique because it springs out of unique history. In summary, the notion of assemblage emphasizes the pasted-up, path-dependent nature of knowledge systems and reinforces the definition of knowledge as a phenomenon in the making, which eventually make sense in the retrospect. (Lanzara and Patriotta, 2001: 964)

In this perspective, organization knowledge and, more specifically, what is here called science-based innovation are to be examined on an aggregated level; components of the assemblage must be examined as such, as being part of multiplicities capable of unfolding and enfolding in many directions. As a consequence, the management of science-based innovation is not subject to linear cause-effect relationships but any attempt at influencing the assemblage may produce unanticipated outcomes. The management of science-based innovation is thus the management of a complex, non-linear system—a system that adapts to changes inside and outside to the firm in various ways. Speaking of the knowledge management literature, there is relatively little recognition of the challenges involved in managing knowledge-intensive firms wherein scientific work predominates. A more detailed and thorough account of science-based innovation work would further broaden the knowledge management literature.

Discovery and fabrication in science-based innovation

One of the persistent themes in the popular literature on science is the emphasis on regarding scientific output in terms of "discoveries", that is, the insistence on treating contributions from scientific work as *"objets trouvés"* rather than fabrications. In common sense thinking, the world is already in place in its full complexity and the practising scientist is entering such a world to uncover and reveal what is always already there. In such a view, the metaphor of "discovery", a concept laden with extensive ontological and epistemological connotations, makes sense. Thus seen, scientific work is modelled on a colonialist vocabulary of discovery and conquest (see e.g., Mir, Mir and Upadhyaya, 2003). The world of this scientific work is not solely apprehended and rendered intelligible, it is in fact dominated and controlled. Modern thinking is shaped by such projects of domination and control, and the scientific tradition is then no different from many other accomplishments of European origin. As opposed to the metaphor of discovery stands the idea of scientific work as a form of social practice, a tinkering, a fabrication of facts under determinate conditions. Rheinberger (1997: 133) here speaks of *conjunctures*[8] rather than discoveries: "Junctures, or *conjunctures*, as I prefer to say, come along with unprecedented events and may lead to major rearrangements and recombinations between given partial spaces of representation of an experimental system. Likewise, I prefer the notion of 'unprecedented events' to the often used notion of 'discovery'. The latter part is of a positivist lexicon that I have sought to avoid throughout this book" (see also Law, 1994: 48). Speaking of scientific work as what is making discoveries is trivializing the intricate systems of joint "fact-making" that stabilizes science and gives its specific characteristics and idiosyncrasies. For instance, studies of laboratory work show that social interaction within and outside of the laboratory is a central activity in any scientific work. Thus knowledge must not be taken for granted *en bloc* and it cannot be assumed that it is always in place: "Knowledge is mostly thought of as coming and circulating in canned packages. The facticity of knowledge—its 'matter-of-factness'—is taken for granted while little attention is paid to the highly interactive and contentious nature of knowledge making", Lanzara and Patriotta (2001: 944) argue.

If science-based innovation is conceived of as an assemblage, a unity with many parts capable of unfolding in various directions, the metaphor of discovery becomes deceiving because it does in fact take knowledge "for granted". Contrary to such a closed systems-view of knowledge, the fabrication metaphor underlines the uncertainties and ambiguities throughout the entire research process. Speaking with Popper (1959, 1963), research findings are in fact never more than corroborated, standing the tests of being "not-false" for the time being. Only at a few occasions in the history of science have research results been immediately acknowledged as a scientific breakthrough. In most cases, however, scientific work evolves as accounted for by Rheinberger (1997) and Pickering (1995), that is, as the gradual mutual adjustment between "[m]achines, instruments, conceptual structures, disciplined practices, social actors and their relations, and so forth" (Pickering, 1995: 70). Similarly, Robert Cooper (2005) is speaking of *relationality* as a central concept when understanding social practice and the objects produced (see Chapter 1):

> The participation of relationality means that the subject *parti*cipates as a constitutive part of the 'movement' of being and composition just as the other parts *part*icipate in the subject. The scientist, for example, is never an objective observer of the world but is constituted as a subject who participates in the particular study of a particular part of the world using a particular methodology and technology. The scientist *re-lates* his or her acts of research and in turn is *re-lated* by them. In other words, the scientist as a participator in research does not simply act *on* an object of research but is also constituted in turn by the particular object and methods used. Participation in this example means that the scientist exists in the interior of the activity of research not outside it as an external

and independent observer. (Cooper, 2005: 1699. Emphases in the original)

This view of scientific work, as a form of factory inextricably bound up with the relations forged in the process, is also a *horizontal* rather than a *vertical* model of science; science is—to use the vocabulary of Deleuze and Guattari (1988)—*rhizomatic*, located on a single plane where heterogeneous resources are continuously intersecting and interacting, creating new relations and producing new entities such as concepts, epistemic things, machinery or laboratory techniques (Patton, 2001: 1094). In such a view, the metaphor of discovery is, again, not a very accurate or meaningful image of scientific work.

Apprehending science-based innovation: the value of alternative thinking

Ways of thinking: masters and puzzlers

Science-based innovation has been envisaged as a complicated and complex social practice evolving as an assemblage. One of the implications from such a view of scientific work and science-based innovation is that the methodological approach to the study of scientific work and knowledge-intensive organizations must be critically examined. A principal concern when studying knowledge-intensive firms is that knowledge and know-how tend to be regarded as *any other* organizational resource rather than being a *specific* organization resource. The capacity of conceiving and apprehending what is complex, ambiguous, and unfolding is of great help when thinking of knowledge as an organization resource (see e.g., Chia, 1996a, 1996b, 1998; Tsoukas and Hatch, 2001). Friedrich von Hayek (1978) is talking about "two types of minds", radically different from one another and operating along divergent routes. The first type of thinkers are referred to as "the masters of subjects": "It is the kind of mind who can retain the particular things he has read or heard, often the particular words in which an idea has been expressed, and retain in for a long time" (Hayek, 1978: 51). The second and more complicated type of thinkers Hayek calls the "puzzlers". Puzzlers are people whose work "seem clearly to rely in some measures on a process of wordless thought, something of existence of which is occasionally denial but which at least bilingual persons seem to me often to possess" (Hayek, 1978: 53–54). Puzzlers are endowed with the capacity to see connections between entities, events or processes but they are not of necessity in possession of a vocabulary that can describe such connections: "To see certain connections distinctively does not mean for them that they know how to describe them in words" (Hayek, 1978: 54). As a consequence, the puzzlers are struggling to appropriate a language and a vocabulary that enables proper accounts of what the puzzlers have cognitively apprehended. Hayek writes: "Their constant difficulties, which in rare instances may be rewarded by a new insight, are due to the fact that they cannot avail themselves of the established verbal formulae or arguments which lead others smoothly and quickly to the results" (Hayek, 1978: 53). The puzzler's reliance on language is worthy of some further discussion. The epistemological position that language is what enables and shapes cognition, most famously expressed in the (early) Wittgenstein's (philosophical) claim that "The limits of my language mean the limits of my world" (Wittgenstein, 1922: §5.6. Emphasis omitted), is challenged by the Russian psychologist Lev Vygotsky's (1986) empirically grounded psychology. For Vygotsky, contrary to the Wittgensteinian view, thought and language are parallel processes, not always of necessity intersecting in every instant. Vygostsky writes: "Thought and word are not connected by a primary bond. A connection originates, changes, and grows in the course of the evolution of thinking and speech. It would be wrong, however, to regard thought and speech as two unrelated processes, either parallel or crossing at certain points and mechanically influencing one another" (Vygotsky, 1986: 210–211). For Vygotsky, the use of language is initially for the infant one tool for cognition among others such as perception and tactile skills (e.g., the use of hands or the mouth to examine artifacts). Here, the child's cognition is entangled with his or her *perception,* his or her *visual field.* However, as the intellect develops, the child—contrary to for instance primates—is able to transcend perception and disconnect the intellect from perception.[9] Vygotsky (1978: 32) exemplifies with the differences between small children and older children's account of a picture: "[T]he way small children describe pictures limits his description to separate objects within the picture. Older children describe actions and indicate the complex relations among the separate objects within the picture". Small children say what they see; older children make use of the pictures as a resource in their thinking, in their narrative created on basis of pictures. Vygotsky concludes: "*[T]he most significant moment in the course of intellectual development, which gives birth to the purely human forms of practical and abstract intelligence, occurs when speech and practical activity, two previously completely independent lines of development, converge*" (Vygotsky, 1978: 24. Emphasis in the original).

For Vygotsky, the implications are substantial; for instance, the mind is what is multiple and composed of many different cognitive capacities and skills:

> [T]he mind is not a complex network of *general* capabilities such as observation, attention, memory, judgment, and so forth, but a set of specific capabilities, each of which is, to some extent, independent of the others and is developed independently. Learning is more than the acquisition of the ability to think: it is the acquisition of many specialized abilities for thinking about a variety of things. Learning does not alter our overall ability to focus attention but rather develops various abilities to focus attention on a variety of things. (Vygotsky, 1978: 83)

This leads us to a concept so central for the puzzler, the notion of *imagination*. For Vygotsky, imagination is a central capacity for the advanced intellect and a key psychological process:

> Imagination is a new psychological process of the child; it is not present in the consciousness of the very young child, is totally absent in animals, and represents a specifically human form of conscious activity. Like all functions of consciousness, it originally arises from action. The old adage that child's play is imagination must be reversed: we can say that imagination in adolescents and school children is play without action. (Vygotsky, 1978: 93)

Puzzlers are thinkers that actively recognize the loosely coupled relations between language and thinking. The process to connect the ensemble of signs constituting a language with other intellectual capabilities such as perception and tactile skills is in Vygotsky's view a naturally occurring process that all humans go through in their development. But there is also a cultural factor to consider. Imagination is not always of necessity a praised skill; numerous children have been accused of lying by little understanding adults when they occasionally have let their imagination roam freely. Thus, in a society like ours, imagination is employed legitimately in a few instituted domains (e.g., in "creative works" such as in the arts, research, and design). In addition, the masters of subject type of mind are generally credited in contemporary society; they do not always bother to put things into questions and they demonstrate excellent abilities for recalling facts and details. However, the puzzlers are thinkers that are able to allow for a productive temporal disconnection between thinking and language; their language is not always already determining what is thought: they rather develop a useful and adequate vocabulary *en route*. The puzzlers know that, as Vygotsky (1986: 180) says, "thought and speech have different genetic roots". "Masters of subjects" are *analytical* thinkers, concerned with details, lines of demarcations, and proper definitions; the "puzzlers" are *synthetic* thinkers, operating outside of the pre-established regimes of representations and prior to available vocabularies. The master of subjects are admired for their ability to in great clarity and in accurate and precise vocabularies account for things in detail, but it is the puzzlers that "thinks the new", that are capable of apprehending what is not yet expressed and to point at the connections and associations previously neglected or little attended to. Hayek (1978) uses Alfred North Whitehead as an example of a "puzzler" and Bertrand Russell as an example of a "master of subjects". While Hayek does not state any preference for either types of kind, William James (1978) has been explicitly critical of the analytical type of thinking, making claims of rationality while still ignoring data and imposing lines of demarcation between entities or processes. James is critical of system thinkers because they tend to, in his view, overlook irregularities to support their models: "The ignoring of data is, in fact, the easiest and most popular mode of obtaining unity in one's thought" (James, 1978: 36). Furthermore, James is critical of the "passion for distinguishing" that is characteristic of this analytical tradition of thinking: "It is the impulse to be *acquainted* with the parts rather than to comprehend the whole. Loyalty to clearness and integrity of perception, dislike of blurred outlines, of vague identifications, are its characteristics" (James, 1978: 37–38). In addition to James's two fallacies, Whitehead (1978: 157) speaks of the "subjectivist principle" in the analytical tradition of thinking: "The subjectivist principle is, that the datum in the act of experience can be adequately analyzed purely in terms of universals". The subjectivist principle is thus sharing with what James (1978) calls the "passion for distinguishing" the ignorance of the idiosyncratic, the specific, the details, that which cannot be "sorted out" properly (Bowker and Star, 1999; Roth, 2005; Silvers and Stein, 2003); it is a form of thinking along strictly rationalist categories. While there are domains where the puzzlers are praised for their ability to think in synthetic terms (for instance, in the discipline of philosophy, although primarily in the continental and not in the Anglo-American analytical tradition), it is primarily the masters of subjects that have been privileged in most scientific disciplines.

Implications for organization theory

In organization theory and management studies, the analytical tradition and its emphasis on details, distinctions, and linear relationships has been favoured. Researchers writing in the puzzler tradition (for instance proponents of a sociological perspective on knowledge and innovation as a social practice embedded in a broad variety of human capabilities and resources) have attained substantially less recognition, especially in the U.S. where the fear of treating organization theory as a quasi-science appears to remain a strong sentiment. The point is not that analytical thinking should be reduced or eliminated but that synthetic thinking (that of the puzzlers) is to date relatively underdeveloped. Chia (1996a), drawing on Whitehead, is here talking about the need for "complexify-ing" our thinking and to open up for alternative perspectives: "While the traditional scientific mentality emphasizes the *simplification* of the com-plex multiplicity of our experience into manageable 'principles,' 'axioms,' etc., literature and the arts have persistently emphasized the task of *com-plexifying* our thinking processes and hence sensitizing us to the subtle nuances of contemporary modern life" (Chia, 1996a: 411). In the know-ledge management and innovation management literature, analytical approaches abound. The consequence is that science-based innovation is often envisaged in strictly functionalist and instrumental terms and that the systemic and what R. Cooper (2005) calls relational aspects of scientific practice are comparatively little attended to and theorized. The assemblage model of science-based innovation advocated here is a synthetic model; it points at the connections, relations, and the hetero-geneous components of the assemblage. Complexifying knowledge man-agement and innovation management thinking would help us overcome, speaking with Whitehead (1920: 141), the false idea that nature is a "mere aggregate of independent entities, each capable of isolation". To further advance knowledge management theory, functionalist and instrumental models of how knowledge is constituted, deployed, and circulated within and between organizations need to get critically examined. Tsoukas (2005) is talking about a "closed-world epistemology" and an "open-world episte-mology" in knowledge management theory. To move to the open-world epistemology and to recognize fluidity, flux, and indeterminacy is to take a step in the direction of a more synthetic form of thinking that is poten-tially rewarding for knowledge management theory.

Implications for managerial practice

The pharmaceutical industry has been harshly criticized for being unable of providing new drugs (Angell, 2004) and evidence show that more resources are consumed to produce less in the industry (Styhre and Sundgren, 2005). Angell's (2004) review of the pharmaceutical industry points at some of the challenges for this science-based industry *par excellence*: it primarily produces so-called "me-too drugs", replicas of financially successful drugs; the drugs actually that are innovative are in many cases funded by public money; it invests more resources in marketing and administration than on R&D; it entertains the largest lobby in Washington—"in 2002 it employed 675 lobbyists ... at a cost of $91 million" (Angell, 2004: 198)—to protect its position and interests. Angell (2004: 73) concludes: "Big pharma likes to refer to itself as a research-based industry, but it is hardly that. It could at best be described as an idea-licencing, pharmaceutical formulating and manufacturing, clinical testing, patenting, and marketing industry". No matter if Angell's account of the pharmaceutical industry is a fair one, or if it is primarily reflecting conditions in the American market, not as price-regulated as the European market—the pharmaceutical industry is facing significant challenges in terms of providing new innovative drugs in an environment where the willingness to pay for the drugs is diminishing. The recent tendency has been to develop management systems and procedures, e.g., project management models that enable clarity and overview of the operations but that also in many cases eliminate or undermine opportunities for analytical thinking (Hodgson and Cicmil, 2006). Using the vocabulary developed above, the new regime of new drug development is more favourable to the master of subjects type of thinker while the puzzlers tend to become alienated in an environment where their ability to see connections and associations is downgraded. Like some of the researchers in AstraZeneca claimed, the company and the industry need to be able to balance structural concerns and analytical and explorative objectives. Science-based innovation is not only a matter of structuring and order operations but it also needs to allow for reflection and analysis. The principal managerial implication is then to strike a balance between the masters of subjects and the puzzlers in an organization. Science-based innovation needs to be capable of exploiting both skills.

Summary and conclusion

This book has attempted at formulating some theoretical perspectives on how to conceive and regard what has been referred to as *science-based innovation*, that is, innovation work embedded in idiosyncratic ideologies, practices, and forms of instituted mechanisms for regulation and control constituting a scientific discipline. The concern has been that managerial interests, on the one hand, are not of necessity in full harmony with scientific and professional concerns, objectives, and desired outcomes. In addition, to date, the management literature has been only modestly interested in scientific communities of practice. Rather than being examined as a specific group of experts, researchers and scientists have been lumped together with a variety of "knowledge workers", "professionals", and other kinds of experts and specialists. The problem is that there are substantial differences between managing a group of laboratory researchers and a team of architects or salesmen. The different groups may have numerous shared interests and may make use of similar mechanisms for control, selection, and rewards in their work, but they are nevertheless different in terms of the laboratory researchers' reliance on scientifically based practices, routines, standard operating procedures. An architect or a salesman may choose to overturn an established practice or may challenge a "truth" in the industry. So the scientists may of course do as well, but the verification or falsification of such an act has to be conducted by a number of communities and has to be reviewed and evaluated by the principal gate-keepers and experts of the field. While other creative work is based on the ability to cater new ideas and produce what is novel and exciting, scientific work always needs to be based on an agreement of what is legitimate and illegitimate.

The purpose of this book is then to discuss science-based innovation as a field of research in organization theory and management studies. More specifically, it seeks to conceive of science-based innovation as a specific form of knowledge work evolving as a social practice and mobilizing a variety of heterogeneous resources, skills and capabilities. Rather than assuming that science-based innovation is produced *en bloc*, the attempt has been to follow the ethnographic accounts of scientific work presented in the science and technology studies literature and to emphasize an empirical orientation of the research. In terms of more detailed discussion, the three chapters in the empirical part of the book have addressed the following topics or theoretical domains:

- In Chapter 5, the notions of play and risk-taking have been discussed as a cognitive model for how laboratory researchers regard their day-to-day work and how they motivate themselves in an environment where they know there may be the risk of not participating to progress the launching of new drug products. Play is a term that captures both the need for formal training, skilfulness and expertise and the influence of chance and luck in laboratory work. Hence, the notion of play comprises both "rational" and instrumental facets of laboratory work and the "irrational" or unpredictable nature of any scientific undertaking.

- In Chapter 6, laboratory work is examined as a social practice that is embedded in emotionality and strong affects and consequently it is demanding careful leadership support and guidance. Contrary to scientific ideologies praising positivist virtues such as objectivity and a detached relation vis-à-vis the object of study, the chapter discusses laboratory work as what is in fact putting substantial emotional pressure on the laboratory researchers. Therefore, contrary to much of the literature on professional groups and experts, this case study suggests that professional work is not self-organizing or that professionals defy any attempts at leading the joint activities; laboratory researchers are not opposed to leadership but they expect leaders to make sense out of ambiguous situations and unclear or badly stated objectives.

- In Chapter 7, the notion of management control is examined. In the literature on management control in knowledge-intensive firms, a range of concepts that captures the day-to-day control of the co-workers have been suggested. The case study suggests—very much in line with previous research—that laboratory workers are controlled through a combination of socio-ideological and technocratic forms of control. However, in many cases, it is complicated to separate what is "socio-ideological forms of control" and what is "technocratic forms of control" because these two categories are never wholly separated from one another but are rather corresponding categories. The technocratic forms of control may influence and affect the culture of a firm or organization and, correspondingly, the socio-ideological forms of control can determine how technocratic control is established. In the focal firm, the use of forms of control embedded in what was referred to as "selection and mathematization", in this case a "performance indicator" in medicinal chemistry, draws on the laboratory researchers' enacted scientific ideologies wherein "facts" are written in mathematical characters.

In summary, the book aims at bridging the literature on knowledge management and innovation management, and the literature on science and technology studies and the literature on epistemology. No knowledge management theory or theory of innovation management can forsake the importance of scientific knowledge production in the analysis. Moreover, rather than conceiving of laboratory work as a black box or some "scientific machinery" detached from politics, emotions, social practice, ideologies, beliefs, and a number of other factors derived from the human condition, researchers need to enter the world of scientists in organizations and examine how they conceive of their day-to-day work and what resources, skills, assets and various tricks-of-the-trade they make use of in their undertakings.

Appendix: Glossary

Bioinformatics: Scientific discipline and an organizational function. A subfield of informatics including *computational biology*. The terms bio-informatics and computational biology are often used interchangeably. However bioinformatics more properly refers to the creation and advancement of algorithms, computational and statistical techniques, and theory to solve formal and practical problems inspired from the management and analysis of biological data. Computational biology, on the other hand, refers to hypothesis-driven investigation of a specific biological problem using computers, carried out with experimental or simulated data, with the primary goal of discovery and the advancement of biological knowledge. A common thread in projects in bioinformatics and computational biology is the use of mathematical tools to extract useful information from data produced by high-throughput biological techniques such as genome sequencing. *(Science 2020*: 72)

DMPK & BAC (Drug-Metabolism & Pharmaco-Kinetics & Bioanalytical-Chemistry): Common organizational function in new drug development. The department, and its multidisciplines, support Discovery project phases by investigating biologically active compounds and studying of their metabolism (i.e., absorption, distribution, metabolism, excretion properties). The goal is to provide support to pharmacology and medicinal chemistry functions in target and hit evaluation and to minimize attrition during the Development Phases. Another goal is to support bioscience disciplines in obtaining plasma concentrations of compounds of interest. The department is also responsible for documenting CDs and providing biological sample analysis to support pre-clinical studies and through all clinical phases of drug development. The department consists of about 100 staff and includes core competencies in analytical chemistry, pharmacokinetics, together with physical & computational chemistry.

Genomics: The study of an organism's entire genome. Investigation of single genes, their functions and roles is very common in today's medical and biological research, and cannot be said to be genomics but rather the most typical feature of molecular biology. Genome information can be combined with other biological information to provide answers on how a biological organism responds to a particular pharmaceutical treatment. Genomics was first developed in the 1980s but gained momentum in the 1990s when the Human Genome Project (1995–2001) was initiated. Major tools and methods related to genomics include bioinformatics, genetic analysis, and measurement of gene expression.

Good Clinical Practice (GCP) & Good Laboratory Practice (GLP): Generally refers to a system of management controls for laboratories and research organizations to ensure the consistency and reliability of results. GLP applies to non-clinical studies conducted for the assessment of the safety of chemicals to man, animals and the environment. GCP applies to clinical studies provided by International Conference on Harmonisation (ICH), an international body that defines standards, which governments can transpose into regulations for clinical trials involving human subjects.

High-throughput screening: High-throughput screening (often abbreviated HTS) is a label for a number of methods and techniques employed in laboratory studies examining how a biological entity reacts to the exposure to various chemical compounds. HTS enables the effective testing of hundreds of chemical compounds in a short time. HTS is based on the use of robotics and specialized laboratory equipment.

Integrative Pharmacology: Pharmacology is a biological-based discipline, which studies the pharmacological changes in whole systems (i.e., animals)—hence the term *integrative* pharmacology—by chemical substances, especially the actions of drugs, substances used to treat disease. Integrative pharmacology is focusing on increasing the functional understanding of compounds and to target mechanisms of action in animal disease models. Although other methods (*in vitro*, molecular biological, and *in silico*) have provided critical details about the mechanisms of action from compounds in various disease states, studies in the whole animal are a cornerstone of drug discovery. The actual department in the case study at AstraZeneca, comprised of about 140 employees.

In vivo testing: *In vivo* testing is testing of a chemical compound on laboratory animals. Etymologically, "in vivo" comes from "vivisection", the "cutting up" of a living animal, i.e., the dissection of the animal. Today, *in vivo* refers to any experiment on a living animal. *In vivo* testing is controversial and is therefore heavily regulated and debated and involves a series of ethical considerations. In new drug development, *in vivo* studies include metabolic tests, how drugs are absorbed, metabolized, and excreted by the body when being distributed differently (e.g., orally, intravenously), toxicology tests, tests to specify the maximum tolerable dose, and efficacy tests where an appropriate illness is induced and treated by the selected experimental drug.

In vitro testing: *In vitro* (Latin, meaning "in the glass", i.e., within the test tube) testing is a number of experimental techniques conducted outside the biological organisms. In new drug development, the discipline of molecular pharmacology develops and employs a number of *in vitro* techniques to predict the outcome from the interaction between the biological entity (e.g., cell or organism) and the chemical compound.

In silico testing: *In silico* is an expression meaning "performed on computer or via computer simulation". The expression was coined to paraphrase *in vivo* and *in vitro* testing. In new drug development, *in silico* testing involves the simulation of biological entities to explore how the chemical compound is interacting with the biological entity. Another widely used term is *virtual screening*, denoting the use of computer-mediated automatic identification of promising molecules.

Pharmacogenomics: A set of technoscientific theories, models and practices aimed at the development of personal drugs through the analysis of individual patients' genomes. (*Bioscience 2015*: 125)

Pharmacogenetics: The study of how people respond differently to drugs due to their genetic makeup, in terms of both how well the drug will work and what side effects the person might suffer. (*Bioscience 2015*: 125)

Protein: A large molecule made up of one or more building blocks of amino acids (molecules containing both amine and carboxyl functional groups). Proteins are the principal constituents of living cells and serve as enzymes, structural elements and antibodies. (*Science 2020*: 81)

Proteomics: Proteomics is the large-scale study of proteins, particularly their structures and function. Although proteomics is modelled on genomics and is often regarded as the next step in biotechnology, proteomics is much more complicated than genomics. While the genome is a stable entity, the proteome differs from cell to cell and is constantly changing through the biochemical interaction with the genome and the environment.

Molecular Pharmacology: The role of molecular pharmacology, in contrast to integrative pharmacology, is focused on *in-vitro* approaches (e.g., from molecules to cells, tissue, to organs) for studying effects of drugs at their respective molecular targets. The actual department in the case study at AstraZeneca, comprised of about 200 staff working on a broad range of interrelated sciences such as genomics, biochemistry, cell biology, target validation, cellular physiology, immunology and bioinformatics. One important goal of the department is to explore and invent new concepts and experimental models in order to identify and validate new targets within different disease areas.

Science-based innovation: Science-based innovation includes all innovation work activities that draw on scientific, and primarily laboratory, practices, routines, and institutions. Science-based innovations are employed in a range of industries such as chemical industry, pharmaceutical industry, biotechnology industry, and constitute smaller and specialized departments and divisions in technology-based firms (e.g., in electronic and telecom companies). To fully understand science-based innovation one must examine how the dominant scientific disciplines are organized and regulated.

Scientific ideologies: Originally coined by French philosopher of science Georges Canguilhem, scientific ideology denotes the totality of beliefs, assumptions, and institutions, in short the ideologies guiding, determining, controlling, and integrating a scientific discipline. The scientific ideology is what is called a *strain theory* of ideology (as opposed to *interest theories* of ideology emphasizing "struggles for power"), that is, what Geertz (1973: 205) calls a "remedy", a "patterned reaction to the patterned strains of a social role". Scientific ideologies are particularly concerned with imprinting lines of demarcations between science, quasi-science and non-science, what Gieryn (1983, 1999) names *boundary-work*. Far from being abstract and detached from everyday work, scientific ideologies constitute an "infrastructure" of all scientific work (see also Greenberg, 1999); it is constitutive of scientific activities.

Synthesis Chemistry or Medical Chemistry: Medicinal chemistry is a chemistry-based discipline concerned with the invention, discovery, design, identification and preparation of biologically active compounds, the interpretation of their mode of action at the molecular level and the construction of structure-activity relationships. The actual department in the case study at AstraZeneca, comprised of about 190 employees. The department has core competencies in organic chemistry, medicinal chemistry, together with parallel synthesis and computational chemistry, analytical chemistry, separation sciences as well as extensive support functions.

Systems biology: Systems biology is a multi-disciplinary field seeking to integrate different levels of information to understand how biological systems function. Systems biology investigates the relationships and the interactions between various parts of a biological system (e.g., metabolic pathways, cells, organs). Much of the current systems biology is concerned with the modelling of such systems to generate understandable and testable models of whole biological systems, especially cells. (see *Science 2020*: 82)

Notes

1 Although it makes sense from an analytical perspective (see e.g., Coriat, Orsi and Weinstein, 2003: 233) to distinguish between science and technology, in practice such a separation is problematic. Instead, following the science and technology studies tradition, the term *technoscience*, merging the two terms and underlining the central role of technology in contemporary scientific work and the scientific embedding of technology, is used in this book.

2 The pharmaceutical industry is perhaps the most typical example of an industry relying on science-based innovation. The pharmaceutical industry has demonstrated an annual growth rate of 11.1 percent from 1970 until 2002 (Gassman and Reepmeyer, 2005: 237) and has an estimated future annual growth of about 8 percent (Clarke *et al.*, 2003: 167). The industry was worth more than US$400 billion in sales in 2002 (Gassman and Reepmeyer, 2005: 237), whereof $100 billion in the USA only. The consumption of drugs doubled in the US between 1990 and 2000 (Clarke *et al.*, 2003: 167). The pharmaceutical industry is therefore an adequate industry for studying innovation work and the management of scientific procedures. It is capital intensive, has long new product development times, involves complex intra and extra organizational arrangement and management practices, and is heavily monitored by authorities. In addition, the R&D productivity in terms of the "number of launched new chemical entities (NCEs) is very low for most of the major companies" (Gassman and Reepmeyer, 2005: 236), thereby being a great concerns for pharmaceutical companies.

3 Bakan (2005) offers some figures supporting Busfield's (2006) thesis: "[T]he 80 percent of the world's population that lives in developing countries represents only 20 percent of the global market for drugs. (The entire African continent represents only 1.3 percent of the world market). Conversely, the 20 percent of the world's population who live in North America, Europe, and Japan constitute 80 percent of the world market. Predictably, of the 1,400 new drugs developed between 1975 and 1999, only 13 were designed to treat prevent tropical diseases and 3 to treat tuberculosis. In the year 2000, no drugs were being developed to treat tuberculosis, compared to 8 for impotence or erectile dysfunctions and 7 for baldness. Developing drugs to deal with personality disorders in family pets seems to have higher priority than controlling diseases that kill millions of human beings each year" (Bakan, 2005: 49). For an extensive critique of the pharmaceutical industry, see Marcia Angell's (2004) *The truth about drug companies*, written by a former editor-in-chief of the prestigious *The New England Journal of Medicine*.

4 It is noteworthy that Dougherty and Heller (1994) here represents an opposing view, claiming that innovations are in fact by definition conflicting with predominant beliefs and institutions: "They [innovations] either violate prevailing practice, inside or outside of the firm, or require ways of thinking and acting that are 'undoable', or 'unthinkable', albeit in intractable opaque

ways. The activities of product innovation, therefore, are illegitimate".
(Dougherty & Heller, 1994: 202)
5 From Robert Boyle until the early twentieth century, an element was defined
   as a pure substance that cannot be decomposed into any simpler substance.
6 It is here appropriate to quote Nietzsche's (1967: 267, §4819 original formulation: "In so far as the word 'knowledge' has any meaning, the word is
   knowable; but it is *interpretable* otherwise, it has no meaning behind it, but
   countless meanings—'perspectivism'".
7 *Monitoring* is defined as "gathering information about work activities and
   external conditions affecting work, checking the progress and quality of the
   work, evaluating the performance of individuals and the organizational unit,
   analysing trends, and forecasting external events". *Clarifying Roles and
   Objectives* include: "Assigning tasks, providing direction in how to do the
   work, and communicating a clear understanding of job responsibilities, task
   objectives, deadlines, and performance expectations". Finally, *Consulting*
   denotes "checking with people before making changes that affect them,
   encouraging suggestions for improvement, inviting participants in decision
   making, and incorporating the ideas and suggestions of others in decisions".
   (Amabile *et al.*, 2004: 13)
8 There are similarities here between what Rheinberger calls *conjunctures*
   and what Karl Popper referred to as *conjectures*. The concept of conjecture has
   slightly different meanings in different scientific domains. In his philosophy
   of science, Popper pioneered the use of the term conjecture to denote a
   proposition which is presumed to be real, true, or genuine, mostly based on
   inconclusive grounds, in contrast to the positivist and verficationist concept
   of hypothesis (underlying to theory, axiom, principle) which is a testable
   statement based on accepted grounds. In mathematics, a conjecture is a
   mathematical statement that appears likely to be true, but has not (yet) been
   formally proven to be true under the rules of mathematics. Once a conjecture is formally proven true it is elevated to the status of theorem and may
   be used afterwards without risk in the construction of other formal mathematical proofs.
9 One may make a connection between Vygotsky's clinical psychology and
   Henri Bergson's philosophy. For Bergson, memory and perception are in close
   proximity but contrary to common belief, it is not the perception that
   mobilizes the memory but the memory engendering perception. In Deleuze
   (1988: 63) formulation: "We do not move from the present to the past, from
   perception to recollection, but from the past to the present, from recollection to perception" (see also Bergson, 1988). Similarly to Vygotsky, Bergson
   emphasizes the heterogeneity of the human cognitive, perceptual, and tactile
   capacities.

Bibliography

Abraham, John & Reed, Tim (2002) Progress, innovation and regulatory science in drug development: The politics of international standard-setting, *Social Studies of Science*, 32(3): 337–369.

Acker, Joan (2006) *Class questions. Feminist answers*, Lanham: Rowman & Littlefield.

Ackroyd, Stephen (1996) Organization contra organizations: Professionals and organizational change in the United Kingdom, *Organization Studies*, 17(4): 599–621.

Adorno, Theodor W. (1974) *Minima moralia*, London: Verso.

Agamben, Giorgio (1998) *Homo Sacer: Sovereign power and bare life*, trans. by Daniel Heller-Roazen, Stanford: Stanford University Press.

Akrich, Madeleine, Callon, Michel & Latour, Bruno (2002a) The key success in innovation part I: the art of interessement, *International Journal of Innovation Management*, 6(2): 187–206.

Akrich, Madeleine, Callon, Michel & Latour, Bruno (2002b) The key success in innovation part II: the art of choosing good spokespersons, *International Journal of Innovation Management*, 6(2): 206–225.

Alexander, Amir R. (2002) *The voyages of discovery and the transformation of mathematical practice*, Stanford: Stanford University Press.

Alimo-Metcalfe, Beverly & Alban-Melcalfe, John (2005) Leadership: Time for a new direction?, *Leadership*, 1(1): 51–71.

Alvesson, Mats (1992) Leadership as social integrative action: A study of a computer consultancy company, *Organizational Studies*, 13(2): 185–209.

Alvesson, Mats (1996) *Communication, Power, and Organization*, Berlin: De Gruyter.

Alvesson, Mats (2000) Social identity and the problem of loyalty in knowledge-intensive companies, *Journal of Management Studies*, 37(8): 1101–1123.

Alvesson, Mats (2001) Knowledge work: Ambiguity, image and identity, *Human Relations*, 54(7): 863–886.

Alvesson, Mats (2004) *Knowledge work and knowledge-intensive firms*, Oxford & New York: Oxford University Press.

Alvesson, Mats & Svenningsson, Stefan (2003) Good visions, bad micro-management and ugly ambiguity: Contradiction of (non)-leadership in a knowledge intensive organization, *Organization Studies*, 24(6): 961–988.

Alvesson, Mats & Willmott, Hugh (2002) Identity regulation as organizational control: Producing the appropriate individual, *Journal of Management Studies*, 39(5): 619–644.

Amabile, Teresa M., Schatzel, Elizabeth A., Moneta, Giovanni B. & Kramer, Steve J. (2004) Leader behaviours and the work environment for creativity. Perceived leader support, *Leadership Quarterly*, 15: 5–32.

Amann, K. & Knorr Cetina, K. (1988) The fixation of (visual) evidence, in Lynch, Michael & Woolgar, Steve (eds) (1990) *Representation in scientific practice*, Cambridge & London: The MIT Press, pp. 85–121.

Anderson, Joseph V. (1994) Creativity and play: A systematic approach to managing innovation, *Business Horizons*, 37(2): 80–85.

Anderson, Warwick (2002) Introduction: Postcolonial technoscience, *Social Studies of Science*, 32(5–6): 643–658.

Angell, Marcia (2004) *The truth about the drug companies: How they deceive us and what to do about it*, New York: Random House.

Argyres, Nicholas S. & Silverman, Brian S. (2004) R&D, organization structure, and the development of corporate technological knowledge, *Strategic Management Journal*, 25: 929–958.

Austin, John L. (1962) *How to do things with words*, Oxford: Oxford University Press.

Bachelard, Gaston (1934/1984) *The New Scientific Spirit*, Boston: Beacon Press.

Badiou, Alain (2004) *Theoretical writings*, translated and edited by Ray Brassier & Alberto Toscano, London & New York: Continuum.

Bakan, Joel (2005) *The corporation: The pathological pursuit of profit and power*, London: Constable.

Bakhtin, Michail (1968) *Rabelais and his world*, Bloomington: Indiana University Press.

Balkundi, Prasad & Kilduff, Martin (2005) The ties that lead: A social network approach to leadership, *Leadership Quarterly*, 16: 941–961.

Ball, Kristie & Carter, Chris (2002) The charismatic gaze: Everyday leadership practices of the "new" manager, *Management Decision*, 40(6): 552–565.

Barker, James R. (1993) Tightening the iron cage: Concertive control in self-managing teams, *Administrative Science Quarterly*, 38: 408–437.

Barker, Richard A. (2001) The nature of leadership, *Human Relations*, 54(4): 469–494.

Barley, Stephen R. (1986) Technology as an occasion of structuring: Evidence from observations of CT scanners and the social order of radiology departments, *Administrative Science Quarterly*, 31: 78–108.

Barley, Stephen R. (1990) The alignment of technology and structure through roles and networks, *Administrative Science Quarterly*, 35: 61–103.

Barley, Stephen R. & Kunda, Gideon (1992) Design and devotion: Surges of rational and normative ideologies of control in managerial discourse, *Administrative Science Quarterly*, 37: 363–399.

Barley, Stephen R. & Kunda, Gideon (2006) Contracting: A new form of professional practice, *Academy of Management Perspectives*, 20(1): 45–66.

Barley, Stephen R. & Tolbert, Pamela (1997) Institutionalization and structuration. Studying the links between action and institution, *Organization Studies*, 18(1): 93–117.

Barnes, Barry, Bloor, David & Henry, John (1996) *Scientific knowledge: A sociological analysis*, London: Athlone.

Barney, Jay (1991) "Firm resources and sustained competitive advantage", *Journal of Management*, 17: 99–120.

Barry, Andrew (2005) Pharmaceutical matters: The invention of informed materials, *Theory, Culture & Society*, 22(1): 51–69.

Basadur, Min (2004) Leading others to think innovatively together. Creative leadership, *Leadership Quarterly*, 15: 103–121.

Bateson, Gregory (1972) *Steps to an ecology of mind*, Chicago: Chicago University Press.

Baudrillard, Jean (1998) When Bataille attacked the metaphysical principles of economy, in Bottig, Fred & Wilson, Scott (eds) (1998) *Bataille: A critical reader*, Oxford: Blackwell.

Bauman, Zygmunt (2000) *Liquid modernity*, Cambridge & Malden: Polity Press.

Becker, Howard S., Geer, Blanchie, Highes, Everett C. & Strauss, Anselm L. (1961) *Boys in white: Student culture in medical school*, Chicago: The University of Chicago Press.

Bell, Daniel (1973) *The coming post-industrial society*, New York: Basic Books.

Bendix, Reinhart (1956) *Work and authority in industry*, New York: Wiley.

Benjamin, Walter (1999) *The arcades project*, trans. by Howard Eiland & Kevin McLaughlin, Cambridge: The Belknap Press.

Bensaude-Vincent, Bernadette & Stengers, Isabelle ([1993] 1996) *A history of chemistry*, trans. by Deborah van Dam, Cambridge & London: Harvard University Press.

Berglund, Johan & Werr, Andreas (2000) The invincible character of management consulting rhetoric: How one blends incommensurates while keeping them apart, *Organization*, 7(4): 633–655.

Bergson, Henri (1910/1988) *Matter and Memory*, New York: Zone Books.

Bierly, Paul E., Kessler, Eric H. & Christensen, Edward W. (2000) Organizational learning, knowledge and wisdom, *Journal of Organization Change Management*, 13(6): 595–618.

Bijker, Wiebe E. (1995) *Of bicycles, bakelites, and bulbs: Toward a theory of socio-technical change*, Cambridge & London: The MIT Press.

Bioscience 2015 (2003) Report issues by the Bioscience and Innovation Growth Team, UK. (Available on http://www.bioindustry.org/bigtreport/index2.html Accessed March 9, 2007)

Birkinshaw, Julian & Mol, Michael (2006) How management innovations happens, *Sloan Management Review*, 47(4): 81–88.

Blackler, F., Crump, N. & McDonald, S. (1999) Managing experts and competing through innovation: An activity theoretical analysis, *Organization*, 6(1): 5–31.

Blau, Gary E., Pekny, Joseph F., Varma, Vishal A. & Bunch, Paul R. (2004) Managing a portfolio of interdependent new product candidates in the pharmaceutical industry, *Journal of Product Innovation Management*, 21: 227–245.

Blau, Judith R. & McKinley, William (1979) Ideas, complexity and innovation, *Administrative Science Quarterly*, 24: 200–219.

Boisot, Max H. (1998) *Knowledge assets: Securing competitive advantage in the information economy*, Oxford: Oxford University Press.

Boje, David M. (1991) The storytelling organization: a study of story performance in an office supply firm, *Administrative Science Quarterly*, 36: 106–126.

Boje, David M., Gephart, Robert P. & Thatchenkery, Toyo Joseph (eds) (1996) *Postmodern management and organization theory*, London: Sage.

Bolton, Sharon C. (2004) A simple matter of control? NHS hospital nurses and new management, *Journal of Management Studies*, 41(2): 317–333.

Bourdieu, Pierre (1977) *Outline of a theory of practice*, Cambridge: Cambridge University Press.

Bourdieu, Pierre (1990) *The logic of practice*, Cambridge: Polity Press.

Bourdieu, Pierre (2004) *The science of science and reflexivity*, Chicago & London: The University Of Chicago Press.

Bowker, Geof (1995) Manufacturing truth. The development of industrial research, in Serres, Michel (ed.) (1995) *A History of Scientific Thought*, Oxford: Blackwell.

Bowker, Geoffrey C. & Leight Star, Susan (1999) *Sorting things out: Classification and its consequences*, Cambridge & London: The MIT Press.

Braidotti, Rosi (2006) *Transpositions: On nomadic ethics*, Cambridge & Malden: Polity Press.

Brekhus, Wayne (2000) A mundane manifesto, *Journal of Mundane Behavior*, 1(1): 89–105.

Brewis, Joanna & Linstead, Stephen (2000) *Sex, work and sex work*, London and New York: Routledge.

Brown, Reva B. (1997) Emotions in organizations, *Journal of Applied Behavioral Science*, 33(2): 247–263.

Bryman, Alan (1992) *Leadership & charisma in organizations*, London & Newbury: New Delhi: Sage.

Bryman, Alan (1996) Leadership in organizations, in Clegg, S.R., Hardy, C. & Nord, W.R. (eds) (1996) *Handbook of Organization Studies*, London: Sage.

Bud, Robert (1983) *The uses of life: A history of biotechnology*, Cambridge: Cambridge University Press.

Bunce, D. & West, M.A. (1996) Stress management and innovations at work, *Human Relations*, 49(2): 209–232.

Burawoy, Michael (1979) *Manufacturing consent: Changes in the labour process under monopoly capitalism*, Chicago: University of Chicago Press.

Burns, T. & Stalker, G.M. (1961) *The management of innovation*, London: Tavistock Publications.

Burton-Jones, Alan (1999) *Knowledge capitalism: Business, work, and learning in the new economy*, Oxford: Oxford University Press.

Busfield, Joan (2006) Pills, power, people. Sociological understandings of the pharmaceutical industry, *Sociology*, 40(2): 297–314.

Butterfield, H. (1962) *The origins of modern science, 1300–1800*, London: G. Bell and Sons.

Caillois, Roger (1988) Festival, in Hallier, Dennis (ed.) (1988) *The college of sociology (1937–1939)* Minneapolis: Minnesota University Press.

Caillois, Roger (2001) *Man, play and games*, trans. by Meyer Barash, Urbana & Chicago: University of Illinois Press.

Caillois, Roger (1961/2001) *Man and the sacred*, trans. by Meyer Barash, Urbana & Chicago: The University of Illinois Press.

Caillois, Roger (2003) *The edge of surrealism: A Roger Caillois reader*, Claudine Frank (ed.), trans. by Claudine Frank & Camille Naish, Durham & London: Duke University Press.

Calás, Marta & Smircich, Linda (1991) Voicing seduction to silence leadership, *Organization Studies*, 12(4): 567–602.

Canguilhem, Georges (1988) *Ideology and rationality in the history of the life sciences*, Cambridge: MIT Press.

Cantor, Geoffrey (1989) The rhetoric of experiment, in Gooding, David, Pinch, Trevor & Schaffer, Simon (eds) (1989) *The uses of experiments: Studies in the natural sciences*, Cambridge, New York & Melbourne: Cambridge University Press, pp. 159–180.

Cardinal, Laura B. (2001) Technological innovation in the pharmaceutical industry: The use of organizational control in managing research and development, *Organization Science*, 12(1): 19–36.

Carlsson, Sune (1951) *Executive behaviour: A study of the work load and the working methods of managing directors*, Stockholm: Strömbergs.

Carr, Adrian (2001) Understanding emotion and emotionality in a process of change, *Journal of Organization Change Management*, 14(5): 421–434.

Castoriadis, Cornelis (1997) *The Castoriadis reader*, Oxford: Blackwell.

Cavanaugh, J. Michael & Prasad, Pushkala (1994) Drug testing as symbolic managerial action: In response to "A case against workplace drug testing", *Organization Science*, 5(2): 267–271.

Cavendish, R. (1982) *Women on the line*, London: Routledge and Kegan Paul.

Certeau, Michel, de (1984) *Practices of everyday life*, Berkeley: University of California Press.

Cheng, Y.-T. & Van de Ven, A.H. (1996) "Learning the innovation journey: Order out of chaos?", *Organization Science*, 7(6): 593–605.

Chia, Robert (1996a) Teaching paradigm shifting in management education: University business schools and the entrepreneurial imagination, *Journal of Management Studies*, 33(4): 409–428.

Chia, Robert (1996b) The problem of reflexivity in organizational research: Towards a postmodern science of organization, *Organizations*, 3(1): 31–59.

Chia, Robert (1998) "From complexity of science to complex thinking: Organization as simple location", *Organizations*, 5(3): 341–469.

Chia, Robert & Holt, Robin (2006) Strategy as practical coping. A Heideggerian perspective, *Organization Studies*, 27(5): 635–655.

Clarke, Adele E. & Fujimura, Joan H. (1992) What tools? Which jobs? Why right?, in Clarke, Adele E. & Fujimura, Joan H. (eds) (1992) *The right tools for the job. At work in twentieth-century life sciences*, Princeton: Princeton University Press, pp. 3–45.

Clarke, Adele E., Mamo, Laura, Fishman, Jennifer R., Shim, Janet K. & Fosket, Jennifer Ruth (2003) Biomedicalization. Technoscientific transformations of health, illness, and U.S. biomedicine, *American Sociological Review*, 68: 161–194.

Clegg, Stewart & Courpasson, David (2004) Political hybrids: Tocquevillean views of project organizations, *Journal of Management Studies*, 41(4): 525–547.

Clifford, James (1997) *Routes: Travel and translation in the late twentieth century*, Cambridge: Harvard University Press.

Cilliers, Paul (2005) Complexity, deconstruction and relativism, *Theory, Culture & Society*, 22(5): 255–267.

Cole, Stephen (2004) Merton's contribution to the sociology of science, *Social Studies of Science*, 34(6): 829–844.

Collins, H.M. (1990) *Artificial experts. Social knowledge and intelligent machines*, Cambridge & London: The MIT Press.

Collins, Harry & Pinch, Trevor (2005) *Dr. Golem: How to think about medicine*, Chicago & London: The University of Chicago Press.

Collinson, David L. (2002) Managing humour, *Journal of Management Studies*, 39(3): 269–288.

Collinson, Simon & Wilson, David C. (2006) Inertia in Japanese organizations: Knowledge management routines and failure to innovate, *Organization Studies*, 27(9): 1359–1387.

Conger, Jay A. & Kanungo, Rabindra N. (1987) Toward a behavioral theory of charismatic leadership in organizational settings, *Academy of Management Review*, 12(4): 637–647.

Conger, Jay A. (2004) Developing leadership capability: What's inside the black box?, *Academy of Management Executive*, 18(3): 136–139.

Contu, Alessia & Willmott, Hugh (2005) You spin me round: The realist turn in organization and management studies, *Journal of Management Studies*, 42(8): 1845–1662.

Cooper, Cecily D. (2005) Just joking around? Employee humor expression as an ingratiatory behavior, *Academy of Management Review*, 30(4): 765–776.

Cooper, Robert (2005) Relationality, *Organization Science*, 26(11): 1689–1710.

Cooren, François (2004) Textual agency: How texts do things in organizational settings, *Organization*, 11(3): 373–393.

Coriat, Benjamin, Orsi, Fabienne & Weinstein, Oliver (2003) Does biotech reflect a new science-based innovation regime?, *Industry and Innovation*, 10(3): 231–253.

Covaleski, Mark A., Dirsmith, Mark W., Heian, James, B. & Sajay, Samuel (1998) The calculated and the avowed: Techniques of discipline and struggle over identity in Big Six public accounting firms, *Administrative Science Quarterly*, Vol. 43, No. 2, pp. 293–327.

Czarniawska, Barbara (1997) *Narrating the organization: Dramas of institutional identity*, Chicago & London: The University of Chicago Press.

Czikszentmihalyi, Mihaly (1990) *Flow: The psychology of optimal experience*, New York: Harper & Row.

Damanpour, Fariborz (1992) Organization size and innovation, *Organization Studies*, 13(3): 375–402.

Daston, Lorraine (1999) Objectivity and the escape from perspective, in Biagioli, Mario (ed.) (1999) *The science studies reader*, London & New York: Routledge, pp. 110–123.

Davenport, Thomas H. & Prusak, Laurence (1998) *Working knowledge. How organizations manage what they know*, Boston: Harvard Business School Press.

De Geus, Arie (1997) *The living company: Habits of survival in a turbulent business environment*, Boston: Harvard Business School Press.

De Landa, Manuel (1992) Nonorganic life, in Crary, Jonathan & Kwinter, Sanford (eds) (1992) *Incorporations*, New York: Zone Books, pp. 129–167.

Deery, Stephen, Iversen, Roderick & Walsh, Janet (2002) Work relationships in telephone call centers: Understanding emotional exhaustion and employee withdrawal, *Journal of Management Studies*, 39(4): 471–496.

Deleuze, Gilles (1966/1988) *Bergsonism*, New York: Zone Books.

Deleuze, Gilles & Guattari, Félix (1988) *A thousand plateau*, Minneapolis & London: University of Minnesota Press.

Denzin, Norman K. (2003) The cinematic society and the reflexive interview, in Gubrium, Jaber F. & Holstein, James A. (eds) (2003) *Postmodern interviewing*, London: Thousand Oaks & New Delhi: Sage, pp. 141–155.

Dewey, John (1929/1988) *The quest for certainty*, The later works, 1925–1953: Volume 4: 1929, Edited by Jo Ann Boydston, Carbondale & Edwardsville: Southern Illinois University Press.

DiMasi, J.A., Hansen, R.W. & Grabowski, H.G. (2003) The price of innovation: new estimates of drug development costs, *Journal of Health Economics*, 22: 151–185.

Ditillo, Angelo (2004) Dealing with uncertainty in knowledge-intensive firms: The role of management control systems as knowledge integration mechanisms, *Accounting, Organization and Society*, 29: 401–421.

Dodge, Martin & Kitchin, Rob (2005) Code and the transduction of space, *Annals of the American Geographers*, 95(1): 162–180.

Dodgson, Mark (2000) *The management of technological innovation*, Oxford & New York: Oxford University Press.

Dodgson, Mark, Gann David & Salter, Ammon (2005) *Think, play, do: Technology, innovation, and organization*, Oxford & New York: Oxford University Press.

Donaldson, Lex (2001) Reflections on knowledge and knowledge-intensive firms, *Human Relations*, 54(7): 955–963.

Dougherty, D. (1999) Organizing for innovation, in Clegg, S.R., Hardy, C. & Nord, W.R. (eds) (1999) *Managing Organizations*, London: Sage.

Dougherty, Deborah & Hardy, Cynthia (1996) Sustained product innovation in large mature organizations: Overcoming innovation-to-organization problems, *Academy of Management Journal*, 39(5): 1120–1153.

Dougherty, Deborah & Heller, Trudy (1994) The illegitimacy of successful product innovation in established firms, *Organization Science*, 5(2): 200–218.

Dougherty, Deborah and Takacs, C. Helen (2004) Team play: Heedful inter-relating as the boundary for innovation, *Long Range Planning*, 37(6): 569–590.

Douglas, Mary (1966) *Purity and danger: An analysis of concepts of pollution and taboo*, London & Henley: Routledge & Kegan Paul.

Dreher, George F. (2003) Breaking the glass-ceiling: The effects of sex ratios and work-life programs on female leadership at the top, *Human Relations*, 56(5): 541–562.

Drews, Jürgen (2000) Drug discovery: A historical perspective, *Science*, 287: 1960–1964.

Drucker, Peter F. (1955) *The practice of management*, Melbourne, London & Toronto: Heinemann.

Druskat, Vanessa Urch and Pescosolido, Anthony (2002) The content of effective teamwork mental models in self-managing teams: Ownership, learning and heedful interrelating, *Human Relations*, 55(3): 283–314.

Du Gay, Paul (1996) *Consumption and identity at work*, London: Thousand Oaks & New Delhi: Sage.

Duhem, Pierre (1996) *Essays in the history and philosophy of science*, translated and edited by Roger Ariew & Peter Barker, Indianapolis & Cambridge: Hackett Publishing.

Dummett, Michael (1978a) Truth, in *Truth and other enigmas*, London: Duckworth, pp. 1–24.

Dummett, Michael (1978b) Realism, in *Truth and other enigmas*, London: Duckworth, pp. 145–165.

Dupré, John (1993) *The disorder of things: Metaphysical foundations of the disunity of science*, Cambridge & London: Harvard University Press.

Durkheim, Émile (1912/1995) *The elementary form of religious life*, New York: Free Press.

Dyck, Bruno, Starke, Frederick A., Mischke, Gary A. & Mauws, Michael (2005) Learning to build a car: An empirical investigation of organizational learning, *Journal of Management Studies*, 42(2): 387–416.

Eckert, Hanna and Bajorath, Jürgen (2007) Molecular similarity analysis in virtual screening: Foundations, limitations and novel approaches, *Drug Discovery Today*, 12(5–6): 225–233.

Eco, Umberto (1986) *Faith in fakes: Essays*, trans. by William Weaver, London: Secker & Warburg.

Economist (2007) The RNA revolution: Biology's big bang, June 14th.

Edmondson, Amy C. (2003) Speaking up in the operating room: How team leaders promote learning in interdisciplinary action teams, *Journal of Management Studies*, 40(6): 1419–1452.

Eisenhardt, Kathleen N. (1989) Building theories from case study research, *Academy of Management Review*, 14(4): 532–550.

Empson, Laura (2001) Introduction: Knowledge management in professional service firms, *Human Relations*, 54(7): 811–817.

Enberg, Cecilia, Lindkvist, Lars & Tell, Fredrik (2006) Exploring the dynamics of knowledge integration: Acting and interacting in project teams, *Management Learning*, 37(2): 143–165.

Ezrahi, Yaron (2005) Science and the political imagination in contemporary democracies, in Jasanoff, Sheila (ed.) (2005) *States of knowledge: The co-production of science and social order*, London & New York: Routledge, pp. 254–273.

Ezzy, David (2000) A simulacrum of workplace community: Individualism and engineered culture, *Sociology*, 35(3): 631–650.

Farrell, Catherine & Morris, Jonathan (2003) The neo-bureaucratic state: Professionals, managers and professional managers in schools, general practice and social work, *Organization*, 10(1): 129–156.

Feldman, Martha S. (2000) Organization routines as a source of continuous change, *Organization Science*, 11(6): 611–629.

Feldman, Steven P. (1989) The broken wheel: the inseparability of autonomy and control in innovation within organizations, *Journal of Management Studies*, 26(2): 83–102.

Feldman, Stephen P. (2004) The culture of objectivity: Quanitification, uncertainty, and the evaluation of risk at NASA, *Human Relations*, 57(6): 691–718.

Fiedler, Fred E. (1968) *A theory of leadership effectiveness*, New York: McGraw-Hill.

Figueroa, Robert & Harding, Sandra (eds) (2003) *Science and other cultures: Issues in philosophies of sciences and technology*, London & New York: Routledge.

Fineman, Stephen (1996) Emotion and organizing, in Clegg, S.R., Hardy, C. & Nord, W.R. (eds) (1999) *Handbook of Organization Studies*, London: Sage.

Fishman, Charles (2006) The Wal-Mart effects and a decent society: Who knew shopping was so important?, *The Academy of Management Perspectives*, 20(3): 6–25.

Fleck, Ludwik (1979) *Genesis and development of a scientific fact*, Chicago & London: Chicago University Press.

Fleming, Peter & Spicer, André (2003) Working at cynical distance: Implications for power, subjectivity and resistance, *Organization*, 10(1): 157–179.

Florida, Richard (2002) *The rise of the creative class*, New York: Basic Books.

Flynn, Francis J. & Staw, Barry M. (2003) Lend me your wallet: The effect of charismatic leadership on external support or an organization, *Strategic Management Journal*, 25: 309–330.

Foss, Nicolai J. (1996) Knowledge-based approaches to the theory of the firm: Some critical remarks, *Organization Science*, 7(5): 470–476.

Fox, Nick, Ward, Katie & O'Rourke, Alan (2006) A sociology of technology governance for the information age: The case of pharmaceuticals, consumer advertising and the Internet, *Sociology*, 40(2): 315–334.

Fuchs, Stephan (1992) *The professional quest for truth: a social theory of science and knowledge*, Albany: State University of New York Press.

Fujimura, Joan H. (1992) Crafting science: Standardized packages, boundary objects, and "translation", in Pickering, Andrew (ed.) (1992) *Science as practice and culture*, Chicago & London: The University of Chicago Press.

Fujimura, Joan H. (1995) Ecologies of action: Recombining genes, molecularizing cancer, and transforming biology, in Star, Susan Leigh (ed.) (1996) *Ecologies of knowledge: Work and politics in science and technology*, Albany: State University of New York Press.

Fujimura, Joan H. (1996) *Crafting science: A sociohistory of the quest for the genetics of cancer*, Cambridge, Mass.: Harvard University Press.

Fuller, Steve (2002) *Social epistemology*, 2nd edn, Bloomington & Indianapolis: Indiana University Press.

Gabriel, Yannis (1999) Beyond happy families: A critical reevaluation of the control-resistance-identity triangle, *Human Relations*, 52(2): 179–203.

Gabriel, Yannis (2002) *Essai*: On paragrammatic use of organization theory—A provocation, *Organization Studies*, 23(1): 133–151.

Gadamer, Hans-Georg (1960/1975) *Truth and Method*, London: Sheed and Ward.

Galison, Peter (1999) Trading zone: Coordinating action and belief, in Biagioli, Mario (ed.) (1999) *The science studies reader*, London & New York: Routledge, pp. 137–160.

Galunic, D. Charles & Rodan, Simon (1998) Resource recombinations in the firm: Knowledge structures and the potential for schumpeterian innovation, *Strategic Management Journal*, Vol. 19, pp. 1193–1201.

Garfinkel, Harold (1967) *Studies in Ethnomethodology*, Englewood Cliffs: Prentice-Hall.

Garsten, Christina & Grey, Chris (1997) "How to become oneself: Discourses of subjectivity in post-bureaucratic organizations", *Organization*, Vol. 4, No. 2, pp. 211–228.

Garud, Raghu, Jain, Sanjay & Kumaraswamy, Arun (2002) Institutional entrepreneurship in the sponsorship of common technological standards: The case of Sun Microsystems and Java, *Academy of Management Journal*, 45(1): 196–214.

Garud, Raghu & Rappa, Michael A. (1994) A socio-cognitive model of technology evolution: The case of cochlear implants, *Organization Science*, 5(3): 344–362.

Gassmann, Oliver & Reepmeyer, Gerrit (2005) Organizing pharmaceutical innovation. From science-based knowledge creators to drug-oriented knowledge brokers, *Creativity and Innovation Management*, 14(3): 233–245.

Gatens, Moira (1996) *Imaginary bodies: Ethics, power, and corporeality*, London and New York: Routledge.

Geertz, Clifford (1973) *The interpretation of cultures*, New York: Basic Books.

Gemmill, Gary & Oakley, Judith (1992) The meaning of boredom in organizational life, *Group & Organization Management*, 17(4): 358–370.

Genosko, Gary (2003) The bureaucratic beyond: Roger Caillois and the negation of the sacred in Hollywood cinema, *Economy & Society*, 32(1): 74–89.

Gherardi, Silvia (2006) *Organizational knowledge: The texture of workplace learning*, Cambridge & Malden: Blackwell.

Gherardi, Silvia & Nicolini, Davide (2001) The sociological foundations of organizational learning, in Dierkes, Meinolf, Berthon, Ariane, Child, John & Nonaka, Ikujiro (eds) (2001) *Handbook of organizational learning & knowledge*, Oxford: Oxford University Press.

Gieryn, Thomas F. (1983) Boundary-work and the demarcation of science from non-science: Strains and interest in professional ideologies of scientists, *American Sociological Review*, 48(6): 781–795.

Gieryn, Thomas F. (1999) *Cultural boundaries of science: Credibility on the line*, Chicago & London: The University of Chicago Press.

Gilson, Lucy L., Shalley, Christina E. & Ruddy, Thomas M. (2005) Creativity and standardization: Complementary or conflicting drivers of team effectiveness, *Academy of Management Journal*, 48(3): 521–531.

Gioia, Dennis A. & Chittipeddi, K. (1991) Sensemaking and sensegiving in strategic change initiation, *Strategic Management Journal*, 12: 433–448.

Gitelman, Lisa (1999) *Scripts, grooves, and writing machines. Representing technology in the Edison era*, Stanford: Stanford University Press.

Goffman, Erwin (1959) *The presentation of self in everyday life*, New York: Doubleday Anchor.

Goffman, Erwin (1961) *Asylums*, London: Penguin.

Gooding, David, Pinch, Trevor & Schaffer, Simon (eds) (1989) *The uses of experiments: Studies in the natural sciences*, Cambridge, New York & Melbourne: Cambridge University Press.

Goodman, Nelson (1978) *Ways of worldmaking*, Hassocks: The Harvester Press.

Gourlay, Stephen (2006) Conceptualizing knowledge creation: A critique of Nonaka's theory, *Journal of Management Studies*, 43(7): 1415–1436.

Greenberg, Daniel S. (1967/1999) *The politics of pure science*, 2nd edn, Chicago & London: The University of Chicago Press.

Greve, Heirich R. (2003) A behavioral theory of R&D expenditures and innovations: Evidence from shipbuilding, *Academy of Management Journal*, 46(6): 685–702.

Greve, Henrich R. & Taylor, Alva (2000) Innovations as catalysts for organizational change: Shifts in organizational cognition and search, *Administrative Science Quarterly*, 45: 54–80.

Grey, Chris & Garsten, Christina (2001) Trust, control and post-bureaucracy, *Organization Studies*, 22(2): 229–250.

Griesemer, James R. (1992) The role of instruments in the generative analysis of science, in Clarke, Adele E. & Fujimura, Joan H. (eds) (1992) *The right tools for the job. At work in twentieth-century life sciences*, Princeton: Princeton University Press, pp. 47–67.

Grint, Keith (2005) Problems, problems, problems: The social construction of "leadership", *Human Relations*, 58(11): 1467–1494.

Griseri, Paul (2002) *Management knowledge: A critical view*, Houndmills, Basingstoke: Palgrave.

Grugulis, Irena (2002) Nothing serious? Candidates' use of humour in management training, *Human Relations*, 55(4): 387–406.

Gubrium, Jaber F. & Holstein, James A. (eds) (2003) *Postmodern interviewing*, London: Thousand Oaks & New Delhi: Sage.

Gupta, Anil K., Smith, Ken G. & Shalley, Christine E. (2006) The interplay between exploration and exploitation, *Academy of Management Journal*, 49(6): 693–706.

Hacking, Ian (1983) *Representing and intervening*, Cambridge: Cambridge University Press.

Hacking, Ian (1992) The self-vindicating of the laboratory sciences, in Pickering, Andrew (ed.) (1992) *Science as practice and culture*, Chicago & London: The University of Chicago Press.

Hacking, Ian (2002) Inaugural lecture: Chair of philosophy and history of scientific concepts at the Collège de France, 16 January, 2001, *Economy & Society*, 31(1): 1–14.
Hackman, W.D. (1989) Scientific instruments; Models of brass and aids to discovery, in Gooding, David, Pinch, Trevor & Schaffer, Simon (eds) (1989) *The uses of experiments: Studies in the natural sciences*, Cambridge, New York & Melbourne: Cambridge University Press, pp. 31–65.
Hage, Jerald & Hollingsworth, J. Rogers (2000) A strategy for the analysis of idea innovation networks and institutions, *Organization Studies*, 21(5): 971–1004.
Hallyn, Fernand ([1987] 1990) *The poetic structure of the world: Copernicus and Kepler*, New York: Zone Books.
Hara, Takuji (2003) *Innovation in the pharmaceutical industry: The process of drug discovery development*, Cheltenham & Northampton: Edward Elgar.
Haraway, Donna (1997) *Modest = Witness @ Second = Millenium: Female Man © = Meets = Onco Mouse™*, London: Routledge.
Haraway, Donna J. (2000) *How like a leaf: An interview with Thyrza Nichols Goodeve*, New York & London: Routledge.
Harding, Sandra (2003) A world of sciences, in Figueroa, Robert & Harding, Sandra (eds) (2003) *Science and other cultures. Issues in philosophies of sciences and technology*, London & New York: Routledge, pp. 49–69.
Harding, Sandra & Hintikka, Merrill B. (eds) (2003) *Discovering reality: Feminist perspective on epistemology, metaphysics, methodology, and philosophy of science*, 2nd edn Dordrcht, Boston & London: Kluwer.
Hargadon, Andrew B. (1998) Firms as knowledge brokers: Lessons in pursuing continuous innovation, *California Management Review*, Vol. 40, No. 3, pp. 209–227.
Hargadon, Andrew & Sutton, Robert I. (1997) Technology brokering and innovation in a product development firm, *Administrative Science Quarterly*, 42: 716–749.
Hargadon, Andrew B. & Douglas, Yellowlees (2001) When innovations meet institutions: Edison and the design of the electric light, *Administrative Science Quarterly*, 46: 476–501.
Harman, P.M. (1982) *Energy, force, matter: The conceptualization development of nineteenth-century physics*, Cambridge: Cambridge University Press.
Harré, Rom & Parrott, W. Gerrod (eds) (1996) *The emotions: Social, cultural, and biological dimensions*, London: Thousand Oaks & New Delhi: Sage.
Harris, Lloyd C. (2002) The emotional labour of barristers: An exploration of emotional labour by status professionals, *Journal of Management Studies*, 39(4) 553–584.
Harrison, Denis & Laberge, Murielle (2002) Innovation, identities and resistance: The social construction of an innovation network, *Journal of Management Studies*, 39(4): 497–521.
Harvey, Arlene (2001) A dramaturgical analysis of charismatic leader discourse, *Journal of Organizational Change Management*, 14(3): 253–265.
Hatch, Mary Jo (1997) Irony and the social construction of contradiction in the humor of a management team, *Organization Science*, 8(3): 275–288.
Hayek, Friedrich A. (1978) The two types of mind, in *New Studies in Philosophy, Politics, Economics, and the History of Ideas*, London & Henley: Routledge and Kegan Paul.
Hayles, N. Katherine (1999) *How we became posthuman: Virtual bodies in cyberetics, literature, and informatics*, Chicago & London: The University of Chicago Press.

Hedberg, Bo & Holmqvist, Mikael (2001) Learning in imaginary organizations, in Dierkes, Meinolf, Berthon, Ariane, Child, John & Nonaka, Ikujiro (eds) (2001) *Handbook of organizational learning & knowledge*, Oxford: Oxford University Press.

Hedgecoe, Adam & Martin, Paul (2003) The drug don't work: Expectations and the shaping of pharmacogenetics, *Social Studies of Science*, 33(3): 327–364.

Hedgecoe, Adam (2006) Pharmacogenetics as alien science: Alzheimer's disease, core sets and expectations, *Social Studies of Science*, 36(5): 723–752.

Hegarty, Paul (2000) *George Bataille: Core cultural theorist*, London: Thousand Oaks & New Delhi: Sage.

Heidegger, Martin (1971) *On the Way to Language*, San Francisco: Harper.

Heidegger, Martin (1987) *Nietzsche, Vol. III: The will to power as knowledge and as metaphysics*, trans. By Joan Stambaugh, David Farrell Krell & Frank A. Capuzzi, San Francisco: Harper & Row.

Helfat, Constance, Harris, Dawn & Wolfson, Paul J. (2006) The pipeline to the top: Women and men in the top executive ranks of U.S. corporations, *Academy of Management Perspectives*, 20(4): 42–64.

Hellström, Thomas (2004) Innovation as social action, *Organization*, 11(5): 631–649.

Hilgartner, Steven (2000) *Science on the stage: Expert advice as public drama*, Stanford: Stanford University Press.

Hilgartner, Stephen (2005) Mapping systems and moral order: Constituting property in genome laboratories, in Jasanoff, Sheila (ed.) (2005) *States of knowledge: The co-production of science and social order*, London & New York: Routledge, pp. 131–141.

Hill, R.C. & Levenhagen, M. (1995) Metaphors and mental models: Sensemaking and sensegiving in innovative and entrepreneurial activities, *Journal of Management*, 21(6): 1057–1074.

Hill, Stephen, Martin, Roderick & Harris, Martin (2000) Decentralization, integration and the post-bureaucratic organization: The case of R&D, *Journal of Management Studies*, 37(4): 563–585.

Hitt, Michael E., Hoskisson, Robert E., Johnson, Richard A. & Moesel, Douglas D. (1996) The market for corporate control and firm innovation, *Academy of Management Journal*, 39(5): 1084–1119.

Hlavacek, James D. & Thompson, Victor A. (1973) Bureaucracy and new product innovation, *Academy of Management Journal*, 16(3): 361–372.

Hobsbawm, Eric & Ranger, Terence (eds) (1983) *The invention of tradition*, Cambridge & New York: Cambridge University Press.

Hochschild, Arlie R. (1983) *The managed heart*, Berkeley: University of California Press.

Hodgson, Damian & Cicmil, Svetlana (eds) (2006) *Making projects critical*, Basingstoke & New York: Palgrave.

Holmqvist, Mikael (2004) Experiential learning processes of exploration and exploitation within and between organizations: An empirical study of product development, *Organization Science*, 15(1): 70–81.

Holstein, James A. & Gubrium, Jaber F. (eds) (2003) *Inside interviewing. New lenses, new concerns*, London: Thousand Oaks & New Delhi: Sage.

Huizinga, Johan (1949) *Homo Ludens: A study of the play-element in culture*, London: Routledge & Kegan Paul.

Hullman, A. (2000) Generation, transfer and exploitation of new knowledge, in Jungmittag, A. Reger, A., & Reiss, G. (eds) (2000) *Changing innovation in the pharmaceutical industry: Globalization and new ways of drug development*, Berlin: Springer.

Humphrey, Ronald H. (2002) The many faces of emotional leadership, *Leadership Quarterly*, 13: 493–504.

Humphreys, Michael & Brown, Andrew D. (2002) Narratives of organizational identity and identification. A case study of hegemony and resistance, *Organization Studies*, 23(3): 421–447.

Hung, Shih-Chang (2004) Explaining the process of innovation: The dynamic reconciliation of action and structure, *Human Relations*, 57(11): 1479–1497.

Husserl, Edmund (1970) *The crisis of the European sciences and transcendental philosophy*, Evanston: Northwestern University Press.

Huy, Quy Nguyen (1999) Emotional capability, emotional intelligence, and radical change, *Academy of Management Review*, Vol. 24, No. 2, pp. 325–345.

Huy, Quy Nguyen (2002) Emotional balancing of organizational continuity and radical change: The contribution of middle managers, *Administrative Science Quarterly*, 47: 31–69.

Iedema, Rick (2003) *Discourses of post-bureaucractic organization*, Amsterdam & Philadelphia: John Benjamins.

Inkpen, Andrew C. & Tsang, Eric W.K. (2005) Social capital, networks, and knowledge transfer, *Academy of Management Review*, 30(1): 146–165.

Jacques, R. (1996) *Manufacturing the employee*, London: Sage.

James, William (1978) "The sentiment of rationality", in James, William (1978) *Essays in philosophy*, Cambridge & London: Harvard University Press, pp. 32–64.

Jasanoff, Sheila (ed.) (2004) Science and ideology, London & New York: Routledge.

Jasanoff, Sheila (2005) The idiom of co-production, in Jasanoff, Sheila (ed.) (2005) *States of knowledge: The co-production of science and social order*, London & New York: Routledge, pp. 1–12.

Jassawalla, Avan R. & Sashittal, Hemant C. (2002) Cultures that support product innovation processes, *Academy of Management Executive*, 16(3): 42–54.

Jones, Deborah (2000) Knowledge Workers "R" Us: Academics, practitioners, and "specific intellectuals", in Prichard, Craig, Hull, Richard, Chumer, Mike & Willmott, Hugh (eds) (2000) *Managing knowledge: Critical investigations of work and learning*, New York: St. Martin's Press.

Jordan, Kathleen & Lynch, Michael (1992) The sociology of a genetic engineering technique: Ritual and rationality in the performance of the "plasmic prep", in Clarke, Adele E. & Fujimura, Joan H. (eds) (1992) *The right tools for the job. At work in twentieth-century life sciences*, Princeton: Princeton University Press, pp. 77–114.

Jordanova, Ludmilla (1989) *Sexual visions: Images of gender in science and medicine between the eighteenth and twentieth centuries*, London: Harvester Wheatsheaf.

Kalling, Thomas & Styhre, Alexander (2003) *Knowledge sharing in organizations*, Malmö: Liber; Oslo: Abstrakt; Copenhagen: Copenhagen Business School Press.

Kamoche, Ken & Pina e Cunha, Miguel (2001) Minimal structures: From Jazz improvization to product innovation, *Organization Studies*, 22(5): 733–764.

Kanter, Rosabeth Moss (1977) *Men and women of the corporation*, New York: Basic Books.

Kärreman, Dan & Alvesson, Mats (2004) Cages in tandem: Management control, social identity, and identification in a knowledge-intensive firm, *Organization*, 11(1): 149–175.

Katz, D. & Kahn, R.L. (1966) *The social psychology of organizations*, New York: Wiley.

Kay, Lily E. (2000) *Who wrote the book of life? A history of the genetic code*, Stanford & London: Stanford University Press.

Kelemen, Mihaela (2001) Discipline at work: Distal and proximal views, *Studies in Cultures, Organizations and Societies*, 7: 1–23.

Keller, Evelyn Fox (1985) *Reflections on gender and science*, New Haven & London: Yale University Press.

Keller, Evelyn Fox (2000) *The century of the gene*, Cambridge & London: Harvard University Press.

Keller, Evelyn Fox (2002) *Making sense of life: Explaining biological development with models, metaphors, and machines*, Cambridge & London: Harvard University Press.

Keller, Evelyn Fox (2003) Gender and science, in Harding, Sandra & Hintikka, Merrill B. (eds) (2003) *Discovering reality: Feminist perspective on epistemology, metaphysics, methodology, and philosophy of science*, 2nd edn, Dordrcht, Boston & London: Kluwer, pp. 187–205.

Kitchener, Michael (2000) The "bureaucratization" of professional roles: The case of clinical directors in UK hospitals, *Organization*, 7(1): 129–154.

Knorr Cetina, Karin D. (1981) *The manufacture of knowledge: An essay on the constructivist and contextual nature of science*, Oxford: Pergamon Press.

Knorr Cetina, Karin (1992) The couch, the cathedral, and the laboratory: On the relationship between experiment and laboratory in science, in Pickering, Andrew (ed.) (1992) *Science as practice and culture*, Chicago & London: The University of Chicago Press.

Knorr Cetina, Karin (1995) How superorganisms change: Consensus formation and the social ontology of high-energy physics experiments, *Social Studies of Science*, 25: 119–147.

Knorr Cetina, Karin (2001) Objectual knowledge, in Schatzki, Theodore R., Knorr Cetina, Karin & Savigny, Eike von (eds) (2001) *The practice turn in contemporary theory*, London & New York: Routledge.

Korczynski, Marek (2003) Communities of coping: Collective emotional labour in service work, *Organization* 10(1): 55–79.

Kosmala, Katarzyna & Herrbach, Olivier (2006) The ambivalence of professional identity: On cynism and *jouissance* in audit firms, *Human Relations*, 59(10): 1393–1428.

Kotter, John P. (1982) What effective general managers really do?, *Harvard Business Review*, Nov/Dec, 60(6): 156–168.

Koyré, Alexandre (1968/1992) *Metaphysics and measurement*, Reading: Gordon and Breach Science Publishers.

Kramer, Lawrence (2002) *Musical meanings: Toward a critical theory*, Berkeley, Los Angeles & Oxford: University of California Press.

Krieger, Martin H. (1992) *Doing physics: How physicists take hold of the world*, Bloomington & Indianapolis: Indiana University Press.

Ladurie, Le Roy, E. (1982) *Karnevalen i Romans*, Stockholm: Atlantis.

Lakatos, Imre (1970) *Proofs and refutations, the logic of mathematical discovery*, Cambridge: Cambridge University Press.

Lanzara, Giovan Francesco & Patriotta, Gerardo (2001) Technology and the courtroom: An inquiry into knowledge making in organizations, *Journal of Management Studies*, 38(7): 943–971.

Latour, Bruno (1987) *Science in action*, Cambridge: Harvard University Press.

Latour, Bruno (1988) *The pasteurization of France*, trans. by Alan Sheridan & John Law, Cambridge & London: Harvard University Press.

Latour, Bruno (1991) Technology is society made durable, in Law, John (ed.) (1991) *A sociology of monsters: Essays on power, technology and domination*, London & New York: Routledge.

Latour, Bruno (1993) *We have never been modern*, Hemel Hempstead: Harvester Wheatsheaf.

Latour, Bruno (1995) Joliot: History and physics mixed together, in Serres, Michel (ed.) (1995) *A History of Scientific Thought*, Oxford: Blackwell.

Latour, Bruno (1996) *Aramis or the love of technology*, Cambridge: Harvard University Press.

Latour, Bruno (2004) *The politics of nature: How to bring the science into democracy*, Cambridge & London: Harvard University Press.

Law, John (1986) Laboratories and texts, in Callon, Michel, Law, John & Rip, Arie (eds) (1986) *Mapping the dynamics of science and technology*, Houndmills: Macmillan.

Law, John (1994) *Organizing modernity*, Oxford & Cambridge: Blackwell.

Law, John (2004) *After method: Mess in social science research*, London & New York: Routledge.

Legge, Karin (1995) *Human resource management*, London: Macmillan.

Lenoir, Timothy (1997) *Instituting science. The cultural production of scientific disciplines*, Stanford: Stanford University Press.

Lenoir, Timothy (1998) Inscription practices and materialities of communication, in Lenoir, Timothy (ed.) (1999) *Inscribing science: Scientific texts and the materiality of communication*, Stanford: Stanford University Press, pp. 1–19.

Leonard-Barton, Dorothy (1995) *Wellspring of knowledge: Building and sustaining the sources of innovation*, Boston: Harvard Business School Press.

Liebeskind, Julia Porter (1996) Knowledge, strategy and the theory of the firm, *Strategic Management Journal*, 17, Winter Special Issue, pp. 93–107.

Lindkvist, Lars (2005) Knowledge communities and knowledge collectives. A typology of knowledge work in groups, *Journal of Management Studies*, 42(6): 1189–1210.

Lindkvist, Lars, Söderlund, Jonas & Tell, Fredrik (1998) Managing product development projects: On the significance of fountains and deadlines, *Organization Studies*, 19(6): 931–951.

Linstead, Stephen (2002) Organizational kitsch, *Organization*, 9(4): 657–682.

Lively, Kathryn J. (2000) Reciprocal emotion management: Working together to maintain stratification in private law firms, *Work and Occupations*, 27(1): 32–63.

Livingston, Eric (1986) *The ethnomethodological foundations of mathematics*, London, Boston & Henley: Routledge & Kegan Paul.

Llewellyn, Sue (2001) "Two-way windows". Clinicians as medical managers, *Organization Studies*, 22(4): 593–623.

Luhmann, Niklas (1995) *Social systems*, Stanford: Stanford University Press.

Lukács, Georg (1971) *History and class consciousness: Studies in Marxist dialectics*, London: Merlin Press.

Lundberg, Craig C. & Young, Cheri A. (2001) A note on emotions and consultancy, *Journal of Organization Change Management*, 14(6): 530–538.

Lutz, Catherine A. (1996) Engendered emotions: Gender, power and the rhetoric of emotional control in American discourse, in Harré, Rom & Parrott, W. Gerrod (eds) (1996) *The emotions: Social, cultural, and biological dimensions*, London: Thousand Oaks & New Delhi: Sage.

Lynch, Michael & Woolgar, Steve (1988) Introduction: Sociological orientation to representational practice in science, in Lynch, Michael & Woolgar, Steve (eds) (1990) *Representation in scientific practice*, Cambridge & London: The MIT Press, pp. 1–18.

Lynch, Michael (1985) *Art and artifact in laboratory science. A study of shop work and shop talk in a research laboratory*, London: Routledge & Kegan Paul.

Lynch, Michael (1988) The externalized retina: Selection and mathematization in the visual documentation of objects in the life sciences, in Lynch, Michael & Woolgar, Steve (eds) (1990) *Representation in scientific practice*, Cambridge & London: The MIT Press, pp. 153–186.

Lynch, Michael (1993) *Scientific practice and ordinary action*, Cambridge: Cambridge University Press.

Lynch, Michael (2002) Protocols, practices and the reproduction of technique in molecular biology, *British Journal of Sociology*, 53(2): 203–220.

Lyotard, J.-F. (1984) *The postmodern condition: A report on knowledge*, Manchester: Manchester University Press.

Machlup, Fritz (1962) *The production and distribution of knowledge in the United States*, Princeton: Princeton University Press.

Macintyre, Alasdair (1981) *After virtue*, London: Duckworth.

MacKenzie, Donald (1995) *Knowing machines: Essays on technological change*, Cambridge & London: The MIT Press.

MacKenzie, Donald (1999) Slaying the Kraken: The sociohistory of a mathematical proof, *Social Studies of Science*, 29(1): 7–60.

Mandelbaum, Maurice (1964) *Philosophy, science and sense-perception: Historical and cultural studies*, Baltimore: The John Hopkins Press.

Mandelbaum, Maurice (1984) Definiteness and coherence in sense-perception, in *Philosophy, history, and the sciences. Selected critical essays*, Baltimore & London: John Hopkins University Press, pp. 23–35.

Mannheim, Karl (1936) *Ideology and utopia*, London: Kegan Paul.

Maravelias, Christian (2003) Post-bureaucracy: Control through profesional freedom, *Journal of Organization Change Management*, 16(5): 547–566.

March, James G. (1991) Exploration and exploitation in organizational learning, *Organization Science*, 2(1): 71–87.

Martin, J., Knopoff, K. & Beckman, C. (1998) An alternative to bureaucratic impersonality and emotional labor: Bounded emotionality at the Body Shop, *Administrative Science Quarterly*, 43: 429–469.

McAuley, John, Duberly, Joanne & Cohen, Laurie (2000) The meaning professionals give to management...and strategy, *Human Relations*, 53(1): 87–116.

McDowell, Linda (1997) *Capital culture: Gender at work in the city*, Oxford & Malden: Blackwell.

McKinlay, Alan (2000) The bearable lightness of control: Organizing reflexivity and the politics of knowledge management, in Prichard, Craig, Hull, Richard,

Chumer, Mike & Willmott, Hugh (eds) (2000) *Managing knowledge: Critical investigations of work and learning*, New York: St. Martin's Press.

Mead, George Herbert (1934) *Mind, self and society*, Chicago: University of Chicago Press.

Merton, Robert K. (1957) The sociology of knowledge, in *Social Theory and Social Structure*, Glencoe: Free Press.

Merton, Robert K. (1973) *The sociology of science: Theoretical and empirical investigations* (ed.) Norman W. Storer, Chicago: The University of Chicago Press.

Meyerson, Debra E. (1998) Feeling stressed and burned out: A feminist reading and re-visioning of stress-based emotions within medicine and organization science, *Organization Science*, 9(1): 103–118.

Michaels, Mike (2000): *Reconnecting culture, technology and nature: From society to heterogeneity*, London & New York: Routledge.

Mills, Charles Wright (1951) *White collars: The American middle class*, Oxford: Oxford University Press.

Mills, Charles Wright (1963) *Power, politics and people: The collected essays of C. Wright Mills*, Oxford: Oxford University Press.

Mintzberg, Henry (1973) *The nature of managerial work*, New York: Harper & Row.

Mintzberg, Henry (1983) *Structure in fives*, Englewood Cliffs: Prentice Hall.

Mir, Raza A., Mir, Ali & Upadhyaya, Punya (2003) Toward a postcolonial reading of organizational control, in Prasad, Anshuman (ed.) (2003) *Postcolonial theory and organizational analysis: A critical engagement*, Houndsmills & New York: Palgrave, pp. 47–74.

Mir, Raza & Watson, Andrew (2001) Critical realism and constructivism in strategy research, *Strategic Management Journal*, 22: 1169–1173.

Mol, Annemarie (2002) *The body multiple: ontology in medical practice*, Durham: Duke University Press.

Mueller, Frank, Harvey, Charles & Howorth, Chris (2003) The contestation of archetypes: Negotiating scripts in a UK hospital trust board, *Journal of Management Studies*, 40(8): 1971–1995.

Mumby, Dennis K. & Putnam, Linda L. (1992) The politics of emotion: A feminist reading of bounded emotionality, *Academy of Management Review*, Vol. 17, No. 3, pp. 465–486.

Mumford, Lewis (1934) *Technics and civilization*, San Diego, New York & London: Harcourt Brace Jovanovich.

Mumford, Michael D., Scott, Ginamarie M., Gaddis, Blaine & Strange, Jill M. (2002) Leading creative people. Orchestrating expertise and relationships, *Leadership Quarterly*, 13: 705–750.

Mutch, Alisdair (1999) Critical realism, managers, and information, *British Journal of Management*, 10: 323–333.

Nagel, Thomas (1986) *The view from nowhere*, Oxford and New York: Oxford University Press.

Nahapiet, Janine & Ghosal, Sumantra (1998) Social capital, intellectual capital, and the organizational advantage, *Academy of Management Review*, 23(2): 242–266.

Nelson, Richard R. & Winter, Sidney G. (1982) *An evolutionary theory of the economic change*, Belknap: Cambridge.

Newell, Sue, Robertson, Maxine, Scarbrough, Harry & Swan, Jacky (2002) *Managing knowledge work*, Basingstoke: Palgrave.

Newton, Tim (1998) "Theoretizing subjectivity on organizations: The failure of Foucaultian studies," *Organization Studies*, Vol. 19, No. 3, pp. 415–447.

Nietzsche, Friedrich (1967) *The will to power*, New York: Vintage Books.

Nightingale, Paul (1998) A cognitive model of innovation, *Research Policy*, 27: 698–709.

Nobel, R. & Birkinshaw, J. (1998) Innovation in multinational corporations: Control and communication patterns in international R&D operations, *Strategic Management Journal*, 19: 479–496.

Nohria, Nitin & Gulati, Ranjay (1996) Is slack good for innovation?, *Academy of Management Journal*, 39(5): 1245–1264.

Nonaka, I. (1994) "A dynamic theory of organizational knowledge creation", *Organizational Science*, 5(1): 14–37.

Nonaka, Ikujiro, von Krogh, Georg & Voelpel, Sven (2006) Organizational knowledge creation theory. Evolutionary paths and future advances, *Organization Studies*, 27(8): 1179–1208.

Norris, Christopher (2000) *Quantum theory and the flight from realism*, London & New York: Routledge.

Oakeshott, Michael (1991) The voice of poetry in the conversation of mankind, in Oakeshott, Michael (1991) *Rationalism in politics and other essays*, Indianapolis: Liberty Press, pp. 488–541.

Oliver, Amalya L. & Montgomery, Kathleen (2000) Creating a hybrid organizational form from parental blueprints: The emergence and evolution of knowledge firms, *Human Relations*, 53(1): 33–56.

Orlikowski, Wanda J. (1992) The duality of technology: Rethinking the concept of technology in organizations, *Organization Science*, 3(3): 398–427.

Orlikowski, Wanda J. (2000) Using technology and constituting structures: A practice lens for studying technology in organizations, *Organization Science*, 11(4): 404–428.

Orlikowski, Wanda J. (2002) Knowing in practice. Enacting a collective capability in distributed organizing, *Organization Science*, 13(3): 249–273.

Orr, Julian E. (1996) *Talking about machines: An ethnography of a modern job*, Ithaca and London: Cornell University Press.

Oseen, Collette (1997) Luce Irigaray, sexual difference and theorizing leaders and leadership, *Gender, Work and Organization*, 4(3): 170–184.

O'Shea, Anthony (2002) The (R)evolution of new product innovation, *Organization*, 9(1): 113–125.

Owen-Smith, Jason (2001) Managing laboratory work through scepticism: Processes of evaluation and control, *American Sociological Review*, 66: 427–452.

Owen-Smith, Jason & Powell, Walter W. (2004) Knowledge networks as channels and conduits: The effects of spillovers in the Boston Biotechnology community, *Organization Science*, 15(1): 5–21.

Parker, Martin (2000) *Organization, culture and identity: Unity and division at work*, London: Thousand Oaks & New Delhi: Sage.

Parsons, Talcott (1951/1991) *The social system*, London & New York: Routledge.

Patriotta, Gerardo (2003) *Organization knowledge in the making: How firms create, use, and institutionalize knowledge*, Oxford & New York: Oxford University Press.

Patton, Paul (2001) Notes for a glossary, in Genosko, Gary (ed.) (2001) *Deleuze and Guattari: Critical assessment of leading philosophers*, London & New York: Routledge.

Pearce, Fred (2003) Introduction: The Collège de sociologie and French social thought, *Economy & Society*, 32(1): 1–6.

Penrose, Edith T. (1959) *The theory of the growth of the firm*, Oxford: Blackwell.

Pentland, Brian T. & Rueter, Henry H. (1994) Organization routines as grammars of action, *Administrative Science Quarterly*, 39(3): 484–510.

Perrow, Charles (1986) *Complex organizations: A critical perspective*, New York: McGraw-Hill.

Pickering, Andrew (1995) *The mangle of practice: Time, agency, and science*, Chicago & London: The University of Chicago Press.

Pirola-Merlo, Andrew, Härtel, Charmine, Mann, Leon & Hirst, Giles (2002) How leaders influence the impact of effective events on team climate and performance in R&D teams, *Leadership Quarterly*, 13: 561–581.

Poland, Blake F. (2003) Transcription quality, in Holstein, James A. & Gubrium, Jaber F. (eds) (2003) *Inside interviewing. New lenses, new concerns*, London: Thousand Oaks & New Delhi: Sage, pp. 267–287.

Popper, Karl R. (1959) *The logic of scientific discovery*, London: Hutchinson.

Popper, Karl R. (1963) *Conjectures and refutations: The growth of scientific knowledge*, London & Henley: Routledge and Kegan Paul.

Porter, Theodore M. (1995) *Trust in numbers: The pursuit of objectivity in science and public life*, Princeton: Princeton University Press.

Powell, Walter W. (1998) Learning from collaboration: Knowledge and networks in the biotechnology and pharmaceutical industries, *California Management Review*, Vol. 40, No. 3, pp. 228–240.

Powell, Walter W., Koput, Kenneth W. & Smith-Doerr, Laurel (1996) Inter-organizational collaboration and the locus of innovation: Networks of learning in biotechnology, *Administrative Science Quarterly*, 41: 116–145.

Power, Michael (2004) Counting, control and calculation: Reflection on measuring and management, *Human Relations*, 57(6): 765–783.

Pye, Annie (2005) Leadership and organizing. Sensemaking in action, *Leadership*, 1(1): 31–50.

Quinn, Ryan W. (2005) Flow in knowledge work: High performance experience in the design of national security technology, *Administrative Science Quarterly*, 50: 610–641.

Rabinow, Paul (1992) Artificiality and enlightenment: From sociobiology to biosociality, Crary, Jonathan & Kwinter, Sanford (eds) (1992) *Incorporations*. New York: Zone Books, pp. 234–251.

Rabinow, Paul (1996) *Making PCR: A story of biotechnology*, Chicago & London: The University of Chicago Press.

Rabinow, Paul (1999) *French DNA. Trouble in purgatory*, Chicago & London: The University of Chicago Press.

Rabinow, Paul (2003) *Anthropos today: Reflections on modern equipment*, Princeton & Oxford: Princeton University Press.

Rabinow, Paul & Dan-Cohen, Talia (2005) *A machine to make a future: Biotech chronicles*, Princeton: Princeton University Press.

Raelin, Joseph A. (1985) *The clash of cultures: Managers and professionals*, Boston: Harvard Business School Press.

Ramirez, Paulina & Tylecote, Andrew (2004) Hybrid corporate governance and its effects innovation. A case study of AsraZeneca, *Technology Analysis & Strategic Management*, 16(1): 97–119.

Reed, Michael I. (2001) Organization, trust and control: A realist analysis, *Organization Studies*, 22(2): 201–228.

Reed, Michael (2005) Reflections on the realist turn in organization and management studies, *Journal of Management Studies*, 42(8): 1621–1644.

Reichenbach, Hans (1938) *Experience and prediction*, Chicago: Chicago University Press.

Rheinberger, Hans-Jörg (1997) *Toward a history of epistemic things: Synthesizing proteins in the test tube*, Stanford: Stanford University Press.

Rheinberger, Hans-Jörg (1998) Experimental systems, graphematic spaces, in Lenoir, Timothy (ed.) (1999) *Inscribing science: Scientific texts and the materiality of communication*, Stanford: Stanford University Press, pp. 285–303.

Rheinberger, Hans-Jörg (2003) "Discourses of circumstances": A note on the author in science, in Biagliolo, Mario & Galison, Peter (eds) (2003) *Scientific authorship: Credit and intellectual property in science*, London & New York: Routledge, pp. 309–324.

Richman, Michèle (2003) Myth, power and the sacred. Anti-utilitarianism in the Collège de sociologie 1937–9, *Economy & Society*, 32(1): 29–47.

Roberts, John (2005) The power of the "imaginary" in disciplinary processes, *Organization*, 12(5): 619–642.

Robertson, Maxine & Swan, Jacky (2003) "Control—what control?" Culture and ambiguity within a knowledge intensive firm, *Journal of Management Studies*, 40(4): 831–858.

Robertson, Maxine & Swan, Jacky (2004) Going public: The emergence and effects of soft bureaucracy within a knowledge-intensive firm, *Organization*, 11(1): 123–148.

Romano, Claudio (1990) Identifying factors which influence product innovation: A case study approach, *Journal of Management Studies*, 27(1): 75–95.

Ropo, Arja & Parviainen, Jaana (2001) Leadership and bodily knowledge in expert organizations: Epistemological rethinking, *Scandinavian Journal of Management*, 17: 1–18.

Rorty, Richard (1989) *Contingency, irony, and solidarity*, Cambridge: Cambridge University Press.

Rorty, Richard (1999) *Philosophy and social hope*, Harmondsworth: Penguin.

Rose, Nicholas (1990) *Governing the soul: The shaping of the private self*, London: Routledge.

Rosenblatt, Paul C. (2003) Interviewing at the border of fact and fiction, in Gubrium, Jaber F. & Holstein, James A. (eds) (2003) *Postmodern interviewing*, London: Thousand Oaks & New Delhi: Sage, pp. 225–241.

Rosenthal, Patrice (2004) Management control as an employee resource: The case of front-line service workers, *Journal of Management Studies*, 41(4): 601–622.

Roth, Wolff-Michael (2005) Making classifications (at) work: Ordering practices in science, *Social Studies of Science*, 35(4): 581–621.

Sackmann, Sonja (1992) Cultures and subcultures: An analysis of organizational knowledge, *Administrative Science Quarterly*, 37: 140–161.

Salaman, Graeme & Storey, John (2002) Managers' theories about the process of innovation, *Journal of Management Studies*, 39(2): 147–165.

Sams-Dodd, F. (2005) Optimizing the discovery organization for innovation, *Drug Discovery Today*, 10(15): 1049–1056.

Sanchez, Ron (2001) Managing knowledge and competence: The five learning cycles of the competent organization, in Sanchez, Ron (ed.) (2001) *Knowledge management and organizational competence,* Oxford: Oxford University Press.

Sanders, Teela (2004) Controllable laughter: Managing sex work through humour, *Sociology,* 38(2): 273–291.

Scarbrough, Harry & Swan, Jacky (2003) Discourses of knowledge management and the learning organization: Their production and consumption, in Easterby-Smith, Mark & Lyles, Marjorie A. (2003) *Handbook of organization learning and knowledge management,* Oxford & Malden: Blackwell, pp. 495–512.

Scarbrough, Harry, Robertson, Maxine & Swan, Jacky (2005) Professional media and management fashion: The case of knowledge management, *Scandinavian Journal of Management,* 21: 197–208.

Schaffer, Simon (1989) Glass works: Newton's prisms and the uses of experiments, in Gooding, David, Pinch, Trevor & Schaffer, Simon (eds) (1989) *The uses of experiments: Studies in the natural sciences,* Cambridge, New York & Melbourne: Cambridge University Press, pp. 67–104.

Schaffer, Simon (1996) Making up discovery, in Boden, Margaret A. (ed.) (1996) *Dimensions of creativity,* Cambridge & London: The MIT Press.

Schatzki, Theodore R. (2002) *The site of the social: A philosophical account of the constitution of social life and change,* University Park: The Pennsylvania State University Press.

Schiller, Friedrich (1795/2004) *On the aesthetic education of man,* Mineola: Dover Publications.

Schmidt, Volker H. (2001) Oversocialized epistemology: A critical appraisal of constructivism, *Sociology,* 35(1): 135–157.

Schopenhauer, Arthur (1995) *The world as will and idea,* London: Everyman.

Schroeder, Roger G., Van de Ven, Andrew H., Scudder, Gary D. & Polley, Douglas (2000) The development of innovation ideas, in Van de Ven, Andrew, Angle, Harold L. & Poole, Marshall Scott (eds) (2000) *Research on the management of innovation,* Oxford & New York: Oxford University Press, pp. 107–134.

Schrödinger, Erwin (1954/1996) *Nature and the Greek & science and humanism,* Cambridge: Cambridge University Press.

Schultz, Majken, Hatch, Mary Jo & Larsen, Mogens Holten (eds) (2000) *The expressive organization: Linking identity, reputation, and the corporate brand,* Oxford: Oxford University Press.

Schulze, Anja & Hoegl, Martin (2006) Knowledge creation in new product development projects, *Journal of Management,* 32(2): 210–236.

Schultze, Ulrike (2000) A confessional account of an ethnography about knowledge work, *MIS Quarterly,* 24(1): 3–41.

Schumpeter, Joseph A. (1934) *The theory of economic development,* Boston: Harvard University Press.

Schumpeter, Joseph A. (1939) *Business cycles,* Vol. 1, New York: McGraw-Hill.

Schweizer, Lars (2005) Organizational integration of acquired biotechnology companies into pharmaceutical companies: The need for a hybrid approach, *Academy of Management Journal,* 48(6): 1051–1074.

Science 2020 (2006) Microsoft Research, Cambridge, UK. (Available on http://research.microsoft.com/towards2020science/ Accessed March 9, 2007)

Scott, Susanne G. & Bruce, Reginald A. (1994) Determinants of innovative behavior: A path model of individual innovation in the workplace, *Academy of Management Journal*, 37(3): 580–607.

Selznick, P. (1957) *Leadership in Administration*, Berkeley, Los Angeles and London: University of California Press.

Serres, Michel (1995) *Genesis*, Ann Arbor: University of Michigan Press.

Sewell, Graham (2005) Nice work? Rethinking managerial control in an era of knowledge work, *Organization*, 12(5): 685–704.

Shalley, Christina E. & Gilson, Lucy L. (2004) What leaders need to know: A review of social and contextual factors that can foster or hinder creativity, *Leadership Quarterly*, 15: 33–53.

Shapin, Steven (1994) *A social history of truth: Civility and science in seventeenth-century England*, Chicago & London: The Chicago of University Press.

Shapin, Steven & Schaffer, Simon (1985) *Leviathan and the airpump*, Princeton: Princeton University Press.

Sharma, Anurag (1999) Central dilemmas of managing innovation in large firms, *California Management Review*, 41(3): 146–164.

Sheremata, Willow A. (2000) Centrifugal and centripetal forces in radical new product development under time pressure, *Academy of Management Review*, 25(2) 389–408.

Silvers, Anita & Stein, Michael Ashley (2003) Essentially empirical: The role of biological and legal classifications in effectively prohibiting genetic discrimination, in Figueroa, Robert & Harding, Sandra (eds) (2003) *Science and other cultures. Issues in philosophies of sciences and technology*, London & New York: Routledge, pp. 129–153.

Simmel, George (1971) The metropolis and mental life, *in On individuality and social forms, selected writings*, Levine, D.A. (ed.) Chicago: The University Press of Chicago, pp. 324–339.

Singer, Linda (1992) Feminism and postmodernism, in Butler, J. & Scott, J.W. (eds) (1992) *Feminists theorize the political*, London & New York: Routledge, pp. 464–475.

Slappendel, Carol (1996) Perspectives on innovation in organizations, *Organization Studies*, 17(1): 107–129.

Sole, Deborah & Edmondson, Amy (2002) Situated knowledge and learning in dispersed teams, *British Journal of Management*, 13: S17–S34.

Sommerlund, Julie (2006) Classifying microorganisms: The multiplicity of classifications and research practices in molecular microbial ecology, *Social Studies of Science*, 36(6): 909–928.

Sowa, Yoshihiro (2006) Present state and advances in personalized medicine: Importance of the development of information service systems for the public, *Quarterly Review*, No. 18, National Institute of Science and Technology Policy, Japan (Available on www.nistep.go.jp/achiev/ftx/eng/stfc/stt018e/qr18pdf/STTqr1801.pdf Accessed March 9, 2007)

Spender, J.-C. (1996) Making knowledge the basis of a dynamic theory of the firm, *Strategic Management Journal*, Vol. 17, Winter Special issue, pp. 45–62.

Spender, J.-C. (1998) "Pluralist epistemology and the knowledge-based theory of the firm", *Organization*, 5(2) 233–256.

Spender, J.-C. & Grant, Robert M. (1996) Knowledge and the firm: Overview, *Strategic Management Journal*, 17 (Winter Special Issue) 5–9.

Spencer, Jennifer W. (2003) Firms' knowledge-sharing strategies in the global innovation system: Empirical evidence from the flat panel display industry, *Strategic Management Journal*, 24: 217–233.

Stallybrass, Peter & White, Allan (1986) *The politics and poetics of transgression*, Ithaca: Cornell University Press.

Star, Susan Leigh & Griesemer, James R. (1989) Institutional ecology, "translations" and boundary objects: Amateurs and professionals in Berkeley's Museum of Vertebrate Zoology, 1907–39, *Social Studies of Science*, 19(3): 387–420.

Starbuck, William H. (1992) Learning by knowledge-intensive firms, *Journal of Management Studies*, 29(6): 713–740.

Starbuck, William H. (2004) Why I stopped trying to understand the real world, *Organization Studies*, 25(7): 1233–1254.

Stengers, Isabelle (1997) *Power and invention: Situating science*, Minneapolis & London: Minnesota University Press.

Sternberg, Robert J. (2003) WICS: A model of leadership in organizations, *Academy of Management Learning & Education*, 2(4): 386–401.

Steyrer, Johannes (1998) Charisma and the archetypes of leadership, *Organization Studies*, 19(5): 807–828.

Strauss, A.L. & Corbin, J. (1998) *Basics of qualitative research*, 2nd edn, London: Thousand Oaks & New Delhi: Sage.

Sturdy, Andrew (1998) "Customer care in customer society: Smiling and sometimes mean it", *Organizations*, 5(1): 27–53.

Sturdy, Andrew (2003) Knowing the unknowable? A discussion of methodological and theoretical issues in emotional research and organizational studies, *Organization* 10(1): 81–105.

Styhre, Alexander (2003) *Understanding knowledge management: Critical and postmodern perspectives*, Malmö: Liber; Oslo: Abstrakt; Copenhagen: Copenhagen Business School Press.

Styhre, Alexander & Sundgren, Mats (2005) *Managing organization creativity: Critique and practices*, Basingstoke & New York: Palgrave.

Subramaniam, Mohan & Venkatraman, N. (2001) Determinants of transnational new product development capability: Testing the influence of transferring and deploying new knowledge, *Strategic Management Journal*, 22: 359–378.

Subramaniam, Mohan & Youndt, Mark A. (2005) The influence of intellectual capital on the types of innovative capabilities, *Academy of Management Journal*, 48(3): 450–463.

Suddaby, Roy & Greenwood, Royston (2001) Colonizing knowledge: Commodification as a dynamic of jurisdictional expansion in professional service firms, *Human Relations*, 54(7): 933–953.

Sundgren, Mats & Styhre, Alexander (2006) Leadership as de-paradoxification: Leading new drug development work at three pharmaceutical companies, *Leadership*, 2(1): 31–52.

Sutton, Robert I. (1991) Maintaining norms about expressed emotions: The case of bill collectors, *Administrative Science Quarterly*, 36: 245–268.

Tam Yeauk-Miu May, Korczynski, Marek & Frenkel, Stephen J. (2002) Organizational and occupational commitment: Knowledge workers in large corporations, *Journal of Management Studies*, 39(6): 775–801.

Tannenbaum, Arnold S. (1968) *Control in organizations*, New York: McGraw-Hill.

Tasić, Vladimir (2001) *Mathematics and the roots of postmodern thought*, Oxford & New York: Oxford University Press.

Teece, David J. (2000) *Managing intellectual capital: Organizational, strategic and policy dimensions*, Oxford & New York: Oxford University Press.

Teece, D.J., Pisano, G. & Shuen, A. (1997) "Dynamic capabilities and strategic management", *Strategic Management Journal*, Vol. 18, No. 7, pp. 509–533.

Tell, Fredrik (2004) What do organizations know? Dynamics of justification context in R&D activities, *Organization*, 11(4): 443–471.

Tengblad, Stefan (2002) Time and space in managerial work, *Scandinavian Journal of Management*, 18: 543–565.

Terrion, Jenepher Lennox & Ashforth, Blake E. (2002) From "I" to "we": the role of putdown humor and identity in the development of a temporary group, *Human Relations*, 55(1): 55–88.

Theodosius, Catherine (2006) Recovering emotions from emotion management, *Sociology*, 40(5): 893–910.

Thomke, Stefan (2001) Enlightened experimentation: The new imperative for innovation, *Harvard Business Review*, 79(2): 66–75.

Thrift, Nigel (2005) *Knowing capitalism*, London: Thousand Oaks & New Delhi: Sage.

Tiles, Mary (1991) *Mathematics and the image of reason*, London & New York: Routledge.

Tomlinson, Gary (1993) *Music in the renaissance magic: Towards historiography of others*, Chicago & London: The University of Chicago Press.

Traweek, Sharon (1988) *Beamtimes and lifetimes: The world of high energy physicists*, Cambridge & London: Harvard University Press.

Tsang, Eric W.K. & Kwan, Kai-Man (1999) Replication and theory development in organizational science: A critical realist perspective, *Academy of Management Review*, 24(4): 759–780.

Tsoukas, Haridimos (1996) The firm as distributed knowledge system: A constructionist approach, *Strategic Management Journal*, 17 (Winter special issue): 11–25.

Tsoukas, Haridimos (2005) *Complex knowledge: Studies in organizational epistemology*, Oxford & New York: Oxford University Press.

Tsoukas, Haridimos & Hatch, Mary Jo (2001) Complex thinking, complex practice: The case for a narrative approach to organizational complexity, *Human Relations*, 54(8): 979–1013.

Tsoukas, Haridimos & Mylonopoloulos, Nikos (2004) Introduction: Knowledge construction and creation in organizations, *British Journal of Management*, 15: S1–S8.

Tsoukas, Haridimos & Vladimirou, Efi (2001) What is organizational knowledge?, *Journal of Management Studies*, 38(7): 973–993.

Turner, Karynne L. & Makhija, Mona V. (2006) The role of organizational controls in managing knowledge, *Academy of Management Review*, 31(1): 197–217.

Turner, Steven R. (2001) On telling regulatory tales: rBST comes to Canada, *Social Studies of Science*, 31(4): 475–506.

Tushman, Michael L. & Nelson, Richard R. (1990) Introduction: Technology, organizations, and innovation, *Administrative Science Quarterly*, 35: 1–8.

Urry, John (2000) *Sociology beyond societies: Mobilities for the twenty-first century*, London & New York: Routledge.

Van de Ven, Andrew (1986) Central problems in the management of innovation, *Management Science*, 32(5): 590–607.

Van de Ven, Andrew, Angle, Harold L. & Poole, Marshall Scott (eds) (2000) *Research on the management of innovation*, Oxford & New York: Oxford University Press.

Van de Ven, Andrew H. & Poole, Marshall Scott (2000) Methods for studying innovation processes, in Van de Ven, Andrew, Angle, Harold L. & Poole, Marshall Scott (eds) (2000) *Research on the management of innovation*, Oxford & New York: Oxford University Press, pp. 31–54.

Vattimo, G. (1992) *The end of modernity*, Cambridge: Polity Press.

Vince, Russ (2002) Power and emotions in organizational learning, *Human Relations*, 54(10): 1325–1351.

Virilio, Paul (1994) *The vision machine*, Bloomington and Indianapolis: Indiana University Press.

Von Hippel, Eric (1998) Economics of product development by users: The impact of "sticky" local information, *Management Science*, 44(5): 629–644.

Von Krogh, Georg, Ichijo, Kazuo & Nonaka, Ikujiro (2000) *Enabling knowledge creation*, Oxford: Oxford University Press.

Vygotsky, Lev (1978) *Mind in society: The development of higher psychological processes* (eds) Michael Cole, Vera John-Steiner, Sylvia Scribner & Ellen Souberman, Cambridge & London: Harvard University Press.

Vygotsky, Lev (1986) Thought and language, trans. by Alex Kozulin, Cambridge & London: The MIT Press.

Wajcman, Judy & Martin, Bill (2002) Narratives of identity in modern management. The corrosion of gender difference?, *Sociology*, 36(4): 985–1002.

Walters, W. Patrick, Stahl, Matthew T. & Murcko, Mark A. (1998) Virtual screening – An overview, *Drug Discovery Today*, 3: 160–178.

Weber, Max (1948) Science as a vocation, in *From Max Weber: Essays in sociology* (eds) H.H. Gerth & C. Wright Mills, London: Routledge and Kegan Paul, pp. 129–156.

Weber, M. (1992) *The Protestant ethic and the spirit of capitalism*, London & New York: Routledge.

Weierter, Stuart J.M. (2001) The organization of charisma: Promoting, creating, and idealizing self, *Organization Studies*, 22(1): 91–115.

Weick, Karl E. & Roberts, Karlene H. (1993) Collective mind in organizations: Heedful interrelating on flight decks, *Administrative Science Quarterly*, 38: 357–381.

Wellington, Christine A. & Bryson, John R. (2001) At face value? Image consultancy, emotional labour and professional work, *Sociology*, 35(4): 933–946.

Werr, Andreas, & Stjernberg, Torbjörn (2003) Exploring management consulting firms as knowledge systems, *Organization Studies*, 24(6): 881–908.

Westwood, Robert & Rhodes, Carl (eds) (2007) *Humour, work and organization*, London & New York: Routledge.

Whitehead, A.N. (1920) *The concept of nature*, Cambridge: Cambridge University Press.

Whitehead, A.N. (1967) *Adventures of ideas*, New York: Free Press.

Whitehead, A.N. (1978) *Process and reality*, New York: Free Press.

Whitley, Richard (2000) The institutional structuring of innovation strategies: Business systems, firm types, and patterns of technical change in different market economies, *Organization Studies*, 21(5): 855–886.

Whyte, W.H. (1956) *The organization man*, New York: Simon and Schuster.

Willem, Annick & Scarbough, Harry (2006) Social capital and political bias in knowledge sharing: An exploratory study, *Human Relations*, 59(10): 1343–1370.

Willmott, H. (1993) Strength is ignorance; Slavery is freedom: Managing culture in modern organizations, *Journal of Management Studies*, 30(4): 515–553.

Willmott, Hugh (2005) Theorizing contemporary control: Some post-structuralist responses to some critical realist questions, *Organization*, 12(5): 747–780.

Winnicott, D.W. (1971) *Playing and reality*, London: Tavistock.

Wittgenstein, L. (1922) *Tractatus Logico-Philosophicus*, London: Routledge and Kegan Paul.

Wolfe, Richard A. (1994) Organization innovation: Review, critique and suggested research directions, *Journal of Management Studies*, 31(3): 405–431.

Wood, Martin (2005) The fallacy of misplaced leadership, *Journal of Management Studies*, 42(6): 1101–1121.

Wray-Bliss, Edward (2002) Abstract ethics, embodied ethics: The strange marriage of Foucault and positivism in labour process theory, *Organization*, 9(1): 5–39.

Wylie, Alison (2003) Why standpoint matter, in Figueroa, Robert & Harding, Sandra (eds) (2003) *Science and other cultures. Issues in philosophies of sciences and technology*, London & New York: Routledge, pp. 26–48.

Yammarino, Francis J., Dionne, Shelley D., Uk Chun, Jea & Dansereau, Fred (2005) Leadership and level of analysis: A state-of-the-science review, *Leadership Quarterly*, 16: 879–919.

Yanow, Dvora (2004) Translating local knowledge at organizational peripheries, *British Journal of Management*, 15: S9–S25.

Yearley, Steven (2005) *Making sense of science: Understanding the social study of science*, London: Thousand Oaks & New Delhi: Sage.

Yin, R.K. (1994) *Case study research. Design and methods*, London: Sage.

Yli-Renka, Helena, Autio, Erkko & Sapienza, Harry J. (2001) Social capital, knowledge acquisition, and knowledge exploitation in young technology-based firms, *Strategic Management Journal*, 22: 587–613.

Yu, H. and Adedoyin, A. (2003) ADME–Tox in drug discovery: Integration of experimental and computational technologies, *Drug Discovery Today*, 8(18): 852–861.

Zivin, J.A. (2000) Understanding clinical trials, *Scientific American*, April: 49–55.

Index

Abraham, J.   103, 105, 108
Acker, J.   174
Ackroyd, S.   197
Actants   10, 32
Actualization   8, 36, 56
Adedoyin, A.   102
Adorno, T.W.   16
Agamben, G.   135
Agôn   116, 140–142, 148–149
Akrich, M.   46–47, 241
Alban-Metcalfe, J.   171–172
Alchemy   62
Alea   140–142, 149
Alexander, A.R.   57–58
Alimo-Metcalfe, B.   171–172
Alvesson, M.   6, 34, 172, 175, 194,
   196–198, 210–211, 213
Amabile, T., et al.   177, 179, 240
Amann, K.   85
Anderson, J.V.   101, 132, 134
Anti-realism   116, 130
Architecture firms   49
Aristotelian physics   56
Armitage, J.   8
Articulation   32, 34, 35
Actor-Network Theory   10, 53, 55
Angell, M.   131, 229–230
Angle, H.L.   45
Aperspectival objectivity   121–122
Argyres, N.S.   43
Ashforth, B.E.   145
Assemblage   16, 35, 48, 52, 64, 80,
   120–121, 199, 211–213, 222–223,
   225, 229
AstraZeneca   xi, 3, 94, 110, 125, 143,
   151–152, 176, 180, 184, 187–188,
   203–206, 211, 214–219, 230, 235,
   237
Augé, M.   8
Austin, J.   83
Aventis   107
Axiomatic knowledge   28

Bacon, F.   61
Bachelard, G.   75, 119, 212
Badiou, A.   85, 201
Bakan, J.   239
Bakhtin, M.   138
Balkundi, P.   171–172
Ball, K.   169
Bajorath, J.   106
Barker, J.   173–174, 195
Barley, S.R.   4, 9, 32
Barnard, C.   173
Barney, J.   38
Barry, A.   103–104
Basadur, M.   177
Bateson, G.   52, 163
Bataille, G.   134–137
Baudrillard, J.   137
Bauman, Z.   8
Beck, U.   8
Becker, H., et al.   212
Beckman, C.   162
Bell, D.   24–25
Bendix, R.   161
Benjamin, W.   140
Bensaude-Vincent, B.   63, 105
Berglund, J.   39
Bergson, H.   36, 74, 240
Bierly, P., et al.   26–27
Birkinshaw, J.   43
Biomedicalization   4–5
Biosociality   4
Blackler, F.   37, 43
Blanchot, M.   134
Blau, G.E., et al.   106–107
Blau, J.P.   49–50
Bohr, N.   83
Boisot, M.   25, 39
Boje, D.M.   10, 193
Bolton, S.C.   198
Boundary-work   98–100
Bourdieu, P.   7, 11, 64, 67, 201–202,
   221

Bijker, W.   47
Bloor, D.   66
Blockbuster drugs   107
Bounded emotionality   162
Bowker, G.   15, 27, 228
Boyle, R.   14, 60, 89, 221, 240
Braidotti, R.   80
Brekhus, W.   14
Brewis, J.   162
Bricolage   81, 222
Bristol-Myers Squibb   107
Brown, A.D.   196
Brown, R.B.   162
Bruce, R.A.   43
Bryman, A.   101, 167–170, 175
Bryson, J.R.   163
Bud, R.   63–64
Bunce, D.   42
Busfield, J.   4, 131, 239
Burawoy, M.   164
Bureaucratic control   195–196
Burton-Jones, A.   116
Burns, T.   40
Butterfield, H.   56–57, 62

Caillois, R.   134–135, 137–143, 149, 156
Calás, M.   173
Calculative control   197
Callon, M.   46–47
Candidate drug (CD)   102, 104, 143, 181, 217
Canguilhem, G.   55, 237
Cantor, G.   89
Carlsson, S.   165–166
Carter, C.   169
Castoriadis, C.   32
Capitalism   8, 116, 192
Cardinal, L.B.   43, 178
Carr, A.   163
Cavanaugh, K.M.   194
Cavendish, R.   164
Certeau, de, M.   11, 14
Charismatic leadership   168–170
Chemical intuition   105–106
Cheng, Y.-T.   43
Chia, R.   x, 12
Chittipeddi, K.   198
Clarke, A.E., *et al.*   4–5, 72, 239

Clegg, S.   196–197
Clifford, J.   8
Clinical trial simulation   2
Cole, S.   96
Collège de Sociologie   134–135, 139–140
Collins, H.   81, 84, 220
Collinson, D.A.   163
Collinson, S.   49
Combe, G.   98
Conceptual strata   80, 91
Contu, A.   118
Concertive control   195
Conger, J.A.   170
Corbin, J.   127
Coriat, B., *et al.*   239
Cooren, F.   10
Combinatorial chemistry   1, 106
Complexity theory   54
Concretization   77, 78
Cooper, R.   9
Courpasson, D.   196–197
Covaleski, M.A., *et al.*   196
Crick, F.   96
Critical realism   117–118
Crump, D.   37
Czarniawska, B.   10
Csikszentmihalyi, M.   133

Damanpour, F.   43–44, 50
Dan-Cohen, T.   126
Daston, L.   122–126
Davenport, T.H.   38–39
Deep acting   165
Deery, S.   163
De Geus, A.   133
De Landa, M.   56
Denzin, N.   125
Descartes, R.   56, 59–61
Dictionary knowledge   28
Dieudonné, J.   201
DiMasi, J.A.   102
Directory knowledge   28
Dodge, M.   32
Dodgson, M.   43, 132, 134
Donaldson, L.   196
Double-bind situation   163
Dougherty, D.   163
Douglas, M.   164

Douglas, Y.   43, 46
Dreher, G.F.   173
Drews, J.   1, 106
Drucker, P.   26, 43
Druskat, V.U.   178
Duberly, J.   176, 198
Du Gay, P.   195
Duhem, P.   27, 83, 85
Duhem thesis   27, 70
Dummett, M.   116
Dupré, J.   124
Durkheim, É.   134–136
Dyck, B., *et al.*   31
Dynamic capability   39

Eco, U.   138
Eckert, H.   106
Economist, The   1
Edison, Thomas Alva   46
Edmondson, A.C.   1, 178
Emic category   36, 38
Empson, L.   28–29
Enactment   123, 179
Enberg, C.   32
Epistemic things   68–70, 74, 120,
    199–200, 225
Etic category   32, 36, 38
Epistopics   65
Exceptionalism   100–101
Expert knowledge   28–29, 35,
    43
Experimental systems   68–69
Ezrahi, Y.   3–4
Ezzy, D.   196

Farrell, C.   197
Feldman, M.   9
Feldman, S.   43, 116, 121
Festival   137–139
Fact-making   66, 72, 74, 224
Fiedler, F.   165, 167
Figueroa, R.   100–101
Final vocabulary   52
Fineman, S.   162
Fishman, C.   2
Fleck, L.   54, 86
Fleming, P.   190
Florida, R.   197
Flynn, F.J.   169

Food and Drug Administration (FDA),
    USA   115, 131, 203
Foss, N.J.   38
Foucault, M.   16
Fourier, J.   96
Frenkel, S.J.   37
Fujimura, J.   65–66, 70–71, 76–77,
    79, 82
Fuller, S.   66
Fuchs, S.   66, 80–81
Fox, N.   108

Gabriel, Y.   194, 198
Garsten, C.   194
Gadamer, H.-G.   94
Galileo, G.   56–57
Galison, P.   124
Galunic, D.C.   43
Gann, D.   43, 132, 134
Garfinkel, H.   164
Garud, R.   81
Gassman, O.   105, 107, 109, 239
Gatens, M.   159
Gemmill, G.   172
Gephart, R.P.   193
Genomics   1, 2, 108–109, 187,
    234–235, 237
Genetics   69, 102, 108, 205
Genosko, G.   135
Gherardi, S.   32
Ghosal, S.   28, 47
Giddens, A.   8
Gieryn, T.   98, 237
Gilson, L.L.   176–177
Gioia, D.   198
Gitelman, L.   46
GlaxoSmithKline   107
Goffman, E.   9, 35
Gooding, D.   74
Goodman, N.   66
Gourlay, S.   24
Grabowski, H.G.   102
Grammars of action   9
Grant, R.   ix, 23
Graphematic space   73
Greenberg, D.S.   101
Greenwood, R.   39
Greve, H.R.   43
Grey, C.   196

Griesemer, J.   78
Grint, K.   165
Griseri, P.   165, 193
Grugulis, I.   163
Gubrium, J.   125
Gulati, R.   43, 50
Gupta, A.K.   48

Hackman, W.D.   61, 74–75
Harding, S.   100–101, 117
Hacking, I.   61, 72, 78, 83
Hallyn, F.   59
Hage, J.   43
Hansen, R.W.   102
Hara, T.   102, 104, 112
Haraway, D.   61
Hardy, C.   43–44
Hargadon, A.B.   43, 46
Harman, P.M.   62
Harré, R.   164
Harris, L.C.   163
Harris, M.   196
Harrison, D.   43–44, 47
Harvey, A.   198
Hatch, M.J.   163, 196
Hawthorne studies   162
Hayek, F. von   17, 225–226
Hayles, N.K.   80
Hedberg, B.   30
Hedgecoe, A.   108–109
Heedful interrelating   132, 178, 179
Hegarty, P.   137
Helfat, C.   173
Hellström, T.   44
Heidegger, M.   27, 160
Heller, T.   41, 239
Herrbach, O.   190
High energy physicists   87
High-throughput screening (HTS)   2,
   106, 235
Hilgartner, S.   76, 90–91
Hill, R.C.   198
Hill, S.   196
Hintikka, M.B.   101
Hitt, M., *et al.*   51
Hlavacek, J.D.   50
Hobsbawm, E.   171
Hochschild, A.   159, 162
Hoegl, M.   31

Holley, R.   96
Holstein, J.A.   125
Holt, R.   12
Hollingsworth, J.R.   43
Holmqvist, M.   30
Howorth, C.   198
Huizinga, J.   140
Hullman, A.   113
Humphrey, R.H.   176
Humphreys, M.   196
Hume, D.   14
Hung, S.-C.   45
Husserl, E.   200, 203
Huy, Q.N.   163

ICH Conference   108, 235
Iedema, R.   195
Ichijo, K.   194
Ilinx   140–141
Illusio   67–68
Imagination   59, 61, 227
Inkpen, A.C.   28
Inscription   72, 83
Institution   11–12, 60, 98, 138
Institutionalization   32, 34–36, 64,
   167
Interaction order   9
Interviewing   xi, 125–126
In silico testing   109, 199, 236
Investigation of a New Drug (IND)
   113
Iversen, R.   163

Jacob, F.   89, 96
Jacques, R.   193
Jain, S.   81
James, W.   35, 228
Jasanoff, S.   64–65, 76
Jassawalla, A.R.   42
Jones. D.   43
Jordan, K.   79
Jordanova, L.   101

Kahn, R.L.   165
Kaiser Willhelm I of Germany   171
Kamoche, K.   43
Kanter, R.M.   163
Kärreman, D.   34, 194, 198, 213
Katz, D.   165

Kalling, T.   176
Kanungo, R.N.   169–170
Kay, L.E.   96
Keller, E.F.   74, 101, 124
Kepler, J.   58, 60
Kelemen, M.   195, 210
Khorana, H.G.   96
Kitchin, R.   32
Kilduff, M.   171–172
Kitchener, M.   176
Kojève, A.   172
Koyré, A.   56, 58–60
Knopoff, K.   162
Knorr Cetina, K.   48, 75, 77, 85, 89,
   160, 199
Knowledge commodification   39
Knowledge-how   24
Knowledge-that   24
Knowledge in the making   35–36
Knowledge-intensive firms (KIFs)   6,
   19, 193, 219, 225, 232
Koput, K.W.   43, 46
Korczynski, M.   37
Kosmala, K.   190
Kotter, J.P.   166
Kramer, L.   122
Krieger, M.H.   84
Kumaraswamy, A.   81
Kunda, G.   4, 195
Kwan, K.-M.   116

Laboratory ethnographies   4
Laboratory work   ix, 13, 80, 134,
   150, 182, 208, 232–233
Laberge, M.   43–44
Lacan, J.   65
Ladurie, Le Roy, E.   138
Lakatos, I.   119, 201
Lanzara, G.F.   34, 222
Laplace, de, P.S.   62
Larsen, M.H.   196
Latour, B.   46–47, 53, 72, 74
Lavoisier, A.L.   63
Law, J.   65, 120, 122–123, 219
Leadership (Trait approach, Style
   approach, Contingency
   approach, New leadership
   approach)   167–168
Leibniz, G.W.   62, 202

Leiris, M.   134–135
Legge, K.   18
Lenoir, T.   64, 72
Leonard-Barton, D.   43
Levenhagen, M.   198
Llewellyn, S.   176
Lindkvist, L.   32
Linstead, S.   137, 162
Lively, K.J.   163
Local knowledge   28–29
Liebeskind, J.   25
Lincoln, A.   171
Lindblom, C.   127
Livingston, E.   200–201
Luhmann, N.   8
Lundberg, C.C.   163
Lukács, G.   172
Lutz, C.A.   159–160
Lynch, M.   13, 64–65, 79–80, 84,
   86–87
Lyotard, J.-F.   2, 53

Machlup, F.   23
MacKenzie, D.   75, 200
Makhija, M.W.   198
Maravelias, C.   195
Master of subjects   228, 230
Mathematization   64, 84–85,
   199–200, 202, 211–213, 232
McDonald, S.   37, 43
Macintyre, A.   11–12
Mach, E.   58
Machinic performances   80
Mandelbaum, M.   58, 117
Mannheim, K.   23
March, J.M.   42
Martin, B.   196
Martin, J.   162
Martin, P.   108–109
Martin, R.   196
Marum, van, M.   75
Marx, K.   197
Matthaei, J.H.   96
Matthew effect   95–97
McAuley, J.   176, 198
McDowell, L.   174
McKinlay, A.   196
McKinley, W.   49–50
Mauss, M.   134–135

Mayo, E. 162
Meaning 11–12, 33, 59, 125, 136, 156, 195, 222, 240
Medical imaging 1
Medical informatics 1
"Me-too" drugs 131
Mendeleev, D. 63
Merck 115
Merton, R. 17, 23, 64, 66, 95, 97
Meyerson, D. 162
Michaels, M. 32
Microbes 71–72
Mills, C.W. 161
Mimicry 140–141
Minnesota Innovation Research Program 45
Mintzberg, H. 190
Mir, A. 223
Mir, R. 118–119, 223
Mise en equation 85
Modest witnessing 14, 55, 60, 190, 217, 221
Mol, A.M. 99–100, 107, 123
Monod, J. 96
Montgomery, K. 6
Mueller, F. 198
Mumby, D. 162
Mumford, L. 155
Mumford, M.D., *et al.* 176
Murcko, M.A. 106
Morris, J. 197
Mutch, A. 118
Mylonopoloulos, N. 33

Nagel, T. 121
Nahapiet, J. 32, 47
Narratives 10, 13, 65–66, 86–87, 90–91
National Academy of the Sciences (USA) 90
National Health Services (NHS) (UK) 198
National Research Council (USA) 90
Natura naturans 76
Natura naturata 76
Nelson, R.R. 9, 43
New Chemical Entity (NCE) 102, 105
New leadership genre 167, 169, 172

Newell, S., *et al.* 26
Newton, I. 60, 202
Newton, T. 196
Nicolini, D. 32
Nietzsche, F. 8, 120
Nightingale, P. 2, 105
Nirenberg, M.W. 96
Nobel, R. 43
Nobel Prize 96
Nohria, N. 43, 50
Nonaka, I. 30, 194
Normative control 195, 197
Novartis 107

Oakley, J. 172
Oakeshott, M. 66
Objectivity 37, 65, 95, 121–123, 202–203
Oliver, A.L. 6
Oncogene research 70, 77–80, 82, 98
OncoMouse 80
Open-world ontology 9
Orlikowski, W.J. 32
Orr, J. 10
O'Shea, A. 42
Owen-Smith, J. 4, 88, 192

Parker, M. 176, 196
Parviainen, J. 171
Pasteur, L. v, 71–72
Patriotta, G. 34–36, 222
Parrott, W.G. 164
Parsons, T. 8
Pearce, F. 136
Penrose, E. 5
Pentland, B.T. 9
Performativity 2, 16, 28
Péron, E. 171
Perrow, C. 88, 195
Personalized medicine 109
Perspectivism 240
Pescosolido, A. 178
Pfizer 105, 107, 152
Pinch, T. 74, 81
Pharmacogenomics 1, 108–109, 236
Phrenology 98
Pickering, A. 80–81, 199
Pina e Cunha, M. 43

Pirola-Merlo, A., *et al.* 178
Pisano, G. 39
Plato 26, 85, 201
Poincaré, H. 201
Poland, B.F. 126
Poole, M.S. 45
Popper, K.R. 156–157, 240
Porter, T.M. 202–203
Post-bureaucratic control 195
Posthuman space 80
Post-industrial society 24, 164
Powell, W.W. 43, 46, 196
Power, M. 194
Premise-based control 88
Professional Service Firms 39
Professional control 197
Prasad, P. 194
Proteomics 1, 108, 155, 187, 236
Proto-oncogene theory 70
Prusak, L. 38–39
Putnam, L.L. 162
Puzzlers 225–228, 230
Pye, A. 172–173

Quinn, R.W. 133–134
Quanta 200, 203, 211

Rabinow, P. 13, 53, 92–93, 126
Raelin, J.A. 197
Ramirez, P. 2
Ranger, T. 171
Rappa, M.A. 81
Realism 64, 73, 116–118, 120
Reed, M.I. 118
Reed, T. 103
Reepmeyer, G. 105, 107–109
Reichenbach, H. 52, 66
Reification 44, 114, 172
Relationality 9, 224
Relativism panic 117
Recipe knowledge 28
Reputational control 197
Rheinberger, H.-J. 68–69, 71–74, 76,
    86, 89, 123, 199, 223–224
Rhodes, C. 163
Richman, M. 136
Rodan, S. 43
Rorty, R. 52, 66
Robertson, M. 23, 196

Ropo, A. 171
Romano, C. 43
Rose, N. 195
Rosenblatt, P.C. 125
Rosenthal, P. 198, 212
Roth, W.M. 27, 228
Ruddy, T.M. 198
Rueter, H.M. 9

Sackmann, S. 28
Sacred, the 134–139, 142–143
Salaman, G. 43
Salter, A. 43, 132, 134
Sanchez, R. 25–26
Sanders, T. 163–164
Sams-Dodd, F. 110
Sashittal, H.C. 42
Scarbrough, H. 23, 28, 114
Schmidt, V.H. 117
Schrödinger, E. 61
Schultz, M. 196
Scientific instruments 74
Scott, S.G. 43
Scripts 9–10, 13, 131
SECI model 30–31
Second modernity 8
Schatzki, T.R. 12
Schroeder, R., *et al.* 45
Shuen, A. 39
Schopenhauer, A. 53
Schultze, U. 36–38, 219
Science 2020 report 2
Science and technology studies ix,
    115, 232, 239
Science-in-the-making 81
Schumpeter, J. 40
Schweizer, L. 107
Selye, H. 95
Selznick, P. 81, 167
Sensationalist principle 67
Sense-experiences 61
Serres, M. 74, 80
Shalley, C.E. 48, 176–177, 198
Silverman, B.S. 43
Silvers, A. 228
Singer, L. 134
Situational knowledge 31
Shapin, S. 14, 60–61, 89
Sharma, A. 49

274   *Index*

Schaffer, S.   14, 65, 74, 79, 92
Sheremata, W.A.   48
Schiller, F.   135
Simmel, G.   165
Slappendel, C.   40–42
Smith, K.G.   48
Smith-Doerr, L.   43, 192
Smircich, L.   173
Sommerlund, J.   99
Sole, D.   31
Social action   44
Social capital   3, 27, 47
Socio-ideological control   196, 211–212
Sociology of knowledge   23
Sowa, Y.   109
Söderlund, J.   48
Spencer, J.W.   43
Spender, J.-C.   ix, 23, 33
Spicer, A.   190
Staw, B.M.   169
Stahl, G.E.   63
Stahl, M.T.   106
Stalker, G.M.   40
Starbuck, W.H.   33–34, 67, 196, 221
Star, S.L.   27, 199, 243
Stein, M.A.   228
Stengers, I.   63, 67, 89, 105, 222
Steyrer, J.   169
Stjernberg, T.   35, 39
Storey, J.   43
Strategic apex   190
Subramaniam, M.   28, 42, 47
Suddaby, R.   39
Sutton, R.I.   43, 163
Swan, J.   23, 114, 196
Strauss, A.L.   127
Sturdy, A.   162
Styhre, A.   165, 230
Sundgren, M.   176
Surface acting   162, 165
Svenningsson, S.   172

Takacs, C.H.   43, 132, 178
Tam, Y.-M.   37
Tannenbaum, A.S.   193, 197
Tasić, V.   201
Taxonomy   17

Taylor, A.   43
Teece, D.J.   39
Tell, F.   28, 32
Technoscience   53, 80, 91, 239
Technocratic control   196, 212–213, 232
Tengblad, S.   166
Terrion, J.L.   163
Textual agency   10
Thénard, L.-J.   63
Thomke, S.   43
Tomlinson, G.   63
Thatchenkery, T.J.   193
Theodosius, C.   163–164
Thompson, V.A.   50
Thought collective   54
Thought experiments   55, 58–59
Thought style   54
Thrift, N.   8, 192
Tiles, M.   200–201
Tolbert, P.   9
Traweek, S.   87
Transformational leadership   168–172, 184
Turner, K.L.   198
Turner, R.S.   87
Triumphalism   100–101
Trust-based control   195
Tsang, E.W.K.   28, 116
Tushman, M.L.   43
Tsoukas, H.   8–10, 31, 33, 225
Tylecote, A.   2–3
Tyndall, J.   101

Unobtrusive control   88, 195
Upadhyaya, P.   193
Urry, J.   8

Van de Ven, A.H.   42–45
Vattimo, G.   8
Venkatraman, N.   42
Vince, R.   163
Virilio, P.   116
Virtuality   8
Virtual chemistry space   106
Vladimirou, E.   31
von Hippel, E.   42
Von Krogh, G.   30, 194
Vygotsky, L.   226–228

Wahl, J.   135
Wajcman, J.   196
Wal-Mart   248
Walsh, J.   163
Walters, W.P.   106
Ward, K.   108
Watson, A.   118–119
Weber, M.   13, 53, 67, 170
Weick, K.E.   178
Weierter, S.J.M.   169
Wellington, C.A.   163
Werr, A.   35, 39
West, M.A.   42
Westwood, R.   163
Whitehead, A.N.   61, 67, 173–174, 228–229
Wöhler, F.   63
Winter, S.   9
Willem, A.   28
Willmott, H.   118–120, 196
Wittgenstein, L.   226

Whyte, W.H.   161
Wilson, D.   49
Winnicott, D.W.   133, 140
Wisdom   viii, 26, 58
Wolfe, R.A.   40–41
Wolfson, P.J.   173
Wood, M.   173–174
Woolgar, S.   13
Wray-Bliss, E.   196
Wylie, A.   119

Yammarino, F.J., *et al.*   169–171
Yearley, S.   95
Yanow, D.   28–29
Yli-Renka, H., *et al.*   28
Youndt, M.A.   28, 47
Young, C.A.   163
Yu, H.   102

Zivin, A.   113
Zymotechnology   63